PENGUI  KU-714-643

# CONFESSIONS OF AN ENGLISH OPIUM-EATER

## BY THOMAS DE QUINCEY

THOMAS DE QUINCEY (1785–1859). Essayist and critic, made famous by his extraordinary and imaginative memoir *Confessions of an English Opium-Eater*.

Thomas de Quincey was born at Manchester in 1785, the second son of a linen merchant. He was educated in Bath, Winkfield and Manchester Grammar School, but he ran away from the last establishment to wander homeless in Wales and London, experiences which he later recounted in his *Confessions*. He went to Worcester College, Oxford, where in 1804 he first indulged in opium. After becoming acquainted with Wordsworth and Coleridge, he settled briefly at Grasmere in the Lake District. By 1812 he had become an opium addict. In 1817 he married Margaret Simpson, a farmer's daughter, and they had eight children. He made his name in 1822 with the publication of *Confessions of an English Opium-Eater*. He wrote many stories, articles and reviews, and most of his subsequent published work was journalistic, appearing in magazines such as *Blackwood's*. His most notable pieces include 'Suspiria de Profundis' (1845) and 'The English Mail Coach' (1849), which analysed the importance of childhood sufferings revealed through dreams – twenty-five years before Freud was even born. Two of his articles, revealing De Quincey at his most brilliant, are 'On the Knocking on the Gate in *Macbeth*' and 'On Murder Considered as One of the Fine Arts' and his black humour and vivid, evocative language influenced many writers, from Baudelaire to Edgar Allan Poe. Thomas de Quincey died at Edinburgh in 1859.

*Confessions of an English Opium-Eater* is De Quincey's fascinating study of his personal experiences when addicted to opium. A surrealist and ground-breaking work, it is a disturbing depiction of the ruination of a genius's mind through overuse of drugs, and is as relevant in today's society as on its first appearance in 1822.

# CONFESSIONS OF AN ENGLISH OPIUM-EATER

## THOMAS DE QUINCEY

PENGUIN BOOKS

PENGUIN BOOKS

Published by the Penguin Group
Penguin Books Ltd, 27 Wrights Lane, London w8 5TZ, England
Penguin Putnam Inc., 375 Hudson Street, New York, New York 10014, USA
Penguin Books Australia Ltd, Ringwood, Victoria, Australia
Penguin Books Canada Ltd, 10 Alcorn Avenue, Toronto, Ontario, Canada M4V 3B2
Penguin Books (NZ) Ltd, Private Bag 102902, NSMC, Auckland, New Zealand

Penguin Books Ltd, Registered Offices: Harmondsworth, Middlesex, England

First published 1821-2
Published in Penguin Popular Classics 1997
3 5 7 9 10 8 6 4 2

Printed in England by Cox & Wyman Ltd, Reading, Berkshire

# CONFESSIONS OF AN ENGLISH OPIUM-EATER

# ORIGINAL PREFACE IN THE YEAR
## 1821

I HERE present you, courteous reader, with the record of
a remarkable period of my life; and according to my
application of it, I trust that it will prove, not merely an
interesting record, but, in a considerable degree, instruc-
tive. In *that* hope it is that I have drawn it up; and
*that* must be my apology for breaking through those
restraints of delicate reserve, which, for the most part,
intercept the public exposure of our own errors and
infirmities.

Guilt and misery shrink, by a natural instinct, from
public notice: they court privacy and solitude; and,
even in the choice of a grave, will sometimes voluntarily
sequester themselves from the general population of the
churchyard, as if declining to claim fellowship with the
great family of man; thus, in a symbolic language universally understood, seeking (in the affecting language
of Wordsworth)

> ' Humbly to express
> A penitential loneliness.'

It is well, upon the whole, and for the interest of us all,
that it should be so; nor would I willingly, in my own
person, manifest a disregard of such salutary feelings.
But, on the one hand, as my self-accusation does not
amount to a confession of guilt, so, on the other, it is
possible that, if it did, the benefit resulting to others,
from the record of an experience purchased at so heavy
a price of suffering and of self-conquest, might com-
pensate, by a vast overbalance, any violence done to the
feelings I have noticed, and justify a breach of the general
rule. Infirmity and misery do not, of necessity, imply
guilt. They approach, or recede from, the shades of that
dark alliance, in proportion to the probable motives and
prospects of the offender, and to the palliations, known or
secret, of the offence; in proportion as the temptations

to it were potent from the first, and the resistance to it, in act or in effort, was earnest to the last. For my own part, without breach of truth or modesty, I may affirm that my life has been, on the whole, the life of a philosopher : from my birth, I was made an intellectual creature ; and intellectual in the highest sense my pursuits and pleasures have been, even from my schoolboy days. If opium-eating be a sensual pleasure, and if I am bound to confess that I have indulged in it to an excess not yet *recorded* of any other man, it is no less true that I have struggled against this fascination with a fervent zeal, and have at length accomplished what I never yet heard attributed to any other man, have untwisted, almost to its final links, the chain which fettered me. Such a self-conquest may reasonably be set off in counterbalance to any kind or degree of self-indulgence. Not to insist that, in my case, the self-conquest was unquestionable, but the self-indulgence open to doubts of casuistry, according as that name shall be extended to acts aiming at the bare relief of pain, or shall be restricted to such as aim at the excitement of superfluous pleasure.

Guilt, therefore, I do not acknowledge ; and, if I did, it is possible that I might still resolve on the present act of confession, in consideration of the service which I may thereby render to the whole class of opium-eaters. But who are they? Reader, I am bound to say, a very numerous class indeed. Of this I became convinced, some years ago, by computing at that time the number of those in one small class of English society (the class of men distinguished for talent and notoriety) who were known to me, directly or indirectly, as opium-eaters; such, for instance, as the eloquent and benevolent William Wilberforce; the late Dean of Carlisle, Dr. Isaac Milner;[1] the first Lord Erskine; Mr. ——,[2] the

---

[1] '*Isaac Milner*' :—He was *nominally* known to the public as Dean of Carlisle, being colloquially always called *Dean* Milner ; but virtually he was best known in his own circle as the head of Queens' College, Cambridge, where he usually resided. In common with his brother, Joseph of Hull, he was substantially a Wesleyan Methodist ; and in that

[2] See note, pages 3 and 4.

philosopher; a late under-secretary of State (viz., Mr. Addington, brother to the first Lord Sidmouth, who described to me the sensation which first drove him to

character, as regarded principles and the general direction of his sympathies, he pursued his deceased brother's History of the Christian Church down to the era of Luther. In these days, he would perhaps not be styled a Methodist, but simply a Low-Churchman. By whatever title described, it is meantime remarkable that a man confessedly so conscientious as Dean Milner could have reconciled to his moral views the holding of Church preferment so important as this deanery in combination with the headship of an important college. One or other must have been consciously neglected. Such a record, meantime, powerfully illustrates the advances made by the Church during the last generation in practical homage to self-denying religious scruples. A very lax man would not in these days allow himself to do that which thirty years ago a severe Church-Methodist (regarded by many even as a fanatic) persisted in doing, without feeling himself called on for apology. If I have not misapprehended its tenor, this case serves most vividly to illustrate the higher standard of moral responsibility which prevails in this current generation. We do injustice daily to our own age; which, by many a sign, palpable and secret, I feel to be more emphatically than any since the period of Queen Elizabeth and Charles I., an intellectual, a moving, and a self-conflicting age: and inevitably, where the intellect has been preternaturally awakened, the moral sensibility must soon be commensurately stirred. The very distinctions, psychologic or metaphysical, by which, as its hinges and articulations, our modern thinking moves, proclaim the subtler character of the questions which now occupy our thoughts. Not as pedantic only, but as suspiciously unintelligible such distinctions would, one hundred and thirty years ago, have been viewed as indictable; and perhaps (in company with Mandeville's 'Political Economy') would have been seriously presented as a nuisance to the Middlesex Quarter-Sessions. Recurring, however, to Dean Milner, and the recollections of his distinguished talents amongst the contemporary circles of the first generation in this nineteenth century, I wish to mention that these talents are most feebly measured by any of his occasional writings, all drawn from him apparently by mere pressure of casual convenience. In conversation it was that he asserted *adequately* his pre-eminent place. Wordsworth, who met him often at the late Lord Lonsdale's table, spoke of him uniformly as the chief potentate colloquially of his own generation, and as the man beyond all others (Burke being departed) who did not live upon his recollections, but met the demands of every question that engaged his sympathy by spontaneous and elastic movements of novel and original thought. As an opium-eater, Dean Milner was understood to be a strenuous wrestler with the physical necessity that coerced him into this habit. From several quarters I have heard that his daily *ration* was 34 grains (or about 850 drops of laudanum), divided into four portions, and administered to him at regular intervals of six hours by a confidential valet.

² Who is Mr. Dash, the philosopher? Really I have forgot. Not through any fault of my own, but on the motion of some absurd coward having a voice potential at the press, all the names were struck out

the use of opium in the very same words as the Dean of Carlisle,—viz., 'that he felt as though rats were gnawing at the coats of his stomach'); Samuel Taylor Coleridge, and many others, hardly less celebrated. Now, if one class, comparatively so limited, could furnish so many scores of cases (and those within the instant reach of one sudden and brief inquiry), it was a natural inference that the entire population of England would furnish a number that, on first starting in such an inquiry, would have seemed incredible. The soundness of this inference, however, I doubted, until some facts became known to me, which satisfied me that it was not incorrect. I will mention two. First, three respectable London druggists, in widely remote quarters of London, from whom I happened to be purchasing small quantities of opium, assured me that the number of *amateur* opium-eaters (as I may term them) was at this time immense; and that the difficulty of distinguishing these persons, to whom habit had rendered opium necessary, from such as were purchasing it with a view to suicide, occasioned them daily trouble and disputes. This evidence respected London only. But, secondly (which will possibly surprise the reader more), some years ago, on passing through Manchester, I was informed by several cotton manufacturers, that their work-people were rapidly getting into the practice of opium-eating; so much so, that on a Saturday afternoon the counters of the druggists were strewed with pills of one, two, or three grains, in preparation for the known demand of the evening. The

behind my back in the first edition of the book, thirty-five years ago. I was not consulted; and did not discover the absurd blanks until months afterwards, when I was taunted with them very reasonably by a caustic reviewer. Nothing could have a more ludicrous effect than this appeal to shadows—to my Lord Dash, to Dean Dash, and to Mr. Secretary Dash. Very naturally it thus happened to Mr. Philosopher Dash that his burning light, alas! was extinguished irrecoverably in the general *mêlée*. Meantime, there was no excuse whatever for this absurd interference such as might have been alleged in any personality capable of causing pain to any one person concerned. All the cases, except, perhaps, that of Wilberforce (about which I have at this moment some slight lingering doubts), were matters of notoriety to large circles of friends. It is due to Mr. John Taylor, the accomplished publisher of the work, that I should acquit *him* of any share in this absurdity.

immediate occasion of this practice was the lowness of wages, which at that time would not allow them to indulge in ale or spirits; and, wages rising, it may be thought that this practice would cease: but, as I do not readily believe that any man, having once tasted the divine luxuries of opium, will afterwards descend to the gross and mortal enjoyments of alcohol, I take it for granted

> 'That those eat now who never ate before;
> And those who always ate, now eat the more.

Indeed, the fascinating powers of opium are admitted even by those medical writers who are its greatest enemies: thus, for instance, Awsiter, apothecary to Greenwich Hospital, in his *Essay on the Effects of Opium* (published in the year 1763), when attempting to explain why Mead had not been sufficiently explicit on the properties, counter-agents, etc., of this drug, expresses himself in the following mysterious terms (perfectly intelligible, however, to those who are in the secret): —'Perhaps he thought the subject of too delicate a nature to be made common; and, as many people might then indiscriminately use it, it would take from that necessary fear and caution which should prevent their experiencing the extensive power of this drug; *for there are many properties in it, if universally known, that would habituate the use, and make it more in request with us than the Turks themselves;* the result of which knowledge,' he adds, 'must prove a general misfortune.' In the necessity of this conclusion I do not at all concur; but upon that point I shall have occasion to speak more freely in the body of the work itself. And at this point I shall say no more than that opium, as the one sole *catholic* anodyne which hitherto has been revealed to man; secondly, as the one sole anodyne which in a vast majority of cases is *irresistible;* thirdly, as by many degrees the most potent of all known counter-agents to nervous irritation, and to the formidable curse of *tædium vitæ;* fourthly, as by possibility, under an argument undeniably plausible, alleged by myself, the sole known agent — not for curing *when* formed, but for

intercepting whilst likely to be formed — the great
English scourge of pulmonary consumption ;—I say
that opium, as wearing these, or *any* of these, four
beneficent characteristics—I say that any agent whatever
making good such pretensions, no matter what its name,
is entitled haughtily to refuse the ordinary classification
and treatment which opium receives in books. I say
that opium, or any agent of equal power, is entitled to
assume that it was revealed to man for some higher
object than that it should furnish a target for moral
denunciations, ignorant where they are not hypocritical,
childish where not dishonest ; that it should be set up
as a theatrical scarecrow for superstitious terrors, of
which the *result* is oftentimes to defraud human suffering
of its readiest alleviation, and of which the *purpose* is,
' Ut pueris placeant et declamatio fiant.' [1]

In one sense, and remotely, all medicines and modes
of medical treatment offer themselves as anodynes—that
is, so far as they promise ultimately to relieve the
suffering connected with physical maladies or infirmities.
But we do not, in the special and ordinary sense,
designate as 'anodynes' those remedies which obtain
the relief from pain only as a secondary and distant
effect following out from the *cure* of the ailment ; but
those only we call anodynes which obtain this relief and
pursue it as the *primary* and *immediate* object. If, by
giving tonics to a child suffering periodic pains in the
stomach, we were ultimately to banish those pains, this
would not warrant us in calling such tonics by the name
of anodynes ; for the neutralisation of the pains would
be a circuitous process of nature, and might probably
require weeks for its evolution. But a true anodyne
(as, for instance, half-a-dozen drops of laudanum, or a
dessert-spoonful of some warm carminative mixed with
brandy) will often banish the misery suffered by a child
in five or six minutes. Amongst the most potent of
anodynes, we may rank hemlock, henbane, chloroform,

---

[1] That they may win the applause of schoolboys, and furnish matter
for a prize essay.

and opium. But unquestionably the three first have a most narrow field of action, by comparison with opium. This, beyond all other agents made known to man, is the mightiest for its command, and for the extent of its command, over pain ; and so much mightier than any other, that I should think, in a Pagan land, supposing it to have been adequately made known [1] through experimental acquaintance with its revolutionary magic, opium would have had altars and priests consecrated to its benign and tutelary powers. But this is not my own object in the present little work. Very many people have thoroughly misconstrued this object ; and therefore I beg to say here, in closing my Original Preface, a little remodelled, that what I contemplated in these Confessions was to emblazon the power of opium—not over bodily disease and pain, but over the grander and more shadowy world of dreams.

[1] *'Adequately made known'* : — Precisely this, however, was impossible. No feature of ancient Pagan life has more entirely escaped notice than the extreme rarity, costliness, and circuitous accessibility of the more powerful drugs, especially of mineral drugs ; and of drugs requiring elaborate preparation, or requiring much manufacturing skill. When the process of obtaining any manufactured drug was slow and intricate it could most rarely be called for. And rarely called for, why should it be produced ? By looking into the history and times of Herod the Great, as reported by Josephus, the reader will gain some notion of the mystery and the suspicion surrounding all attempts at importing such drugs as could be applied to murderous purposes, consequently of the delay, the difficulty, and the peril in forming any familiar acquaintance with opium.

# PREFACE TO THE COLLECTED EDITION

WHEN it had been settled that, in the general series of these republications, the *Confessions of an English Opium-Eater* should occupy the Fifth Volume, I resolved to avail myself most carefully of the opening thus made for a revision of the entire work. By accident, a considerable part of the Confessions (all, in short, except the Dreams) had originally been written hastily; and, from various causes, had never received any strict revision, or, *virtually*, so much as an ordinary verbal correction. But a great deal more was wanted than this. The main narrative should naturally have moved through a succession of secondary incidents; and with leisure for recalling these, it might have been greatly inspirited. Wanting all opportunity for such advantages, this narrative had been needlessly impoverished. And thus it had happened, that not so properly correction and retrenchment were called for, as integration of what had been left imperfect, or amplification of what, from the first, had been insufficiently expanded.

With these views, it would not have been difficult (though toilsome) to re-cast the little work in a better mould; and the result might, in all reason, count upon the approbation at least of its own former readers. Compared with its own former self, the book must certainly tend, by its very principle of change, whatever should be the *execution* of that change, to become better: and in my own opinion, after all drawbacks and allowances for the faulty exemplification of a good principle, it *is* better. This should be a matter of mere logical or inferential necessity; since, in pure addition to everything previously approved, there would now be a clear surplus of extra matter—all that might be good in the old work, and a great deal beside that was new. Meantime this improvement has been won at a price of labour and suffering that, if they could be truly stated, would seem incredible. A nervous malady, of very peculiar character, which has attacked me intermittingly for the last eleven years, came on in May last, almost concurrently with the commencement of this revision ; and so obstinately has this malady pursued its noiseless, and what I may call subterraneous, siege, since none of the symptoms are externally manifested, that, although pretty nearly dedicating myself to this one solitary labour, and not intermitting or relaxing it for a single day, I have yet spent, within a very few days, six calendar months upon the re-cast of this one small volume.

The consequences have been distressing to all concerned. The press has groaned under the chronic visitation ; the compositors shudder at the sight of my handwriting, though not objectionable on the score of legibility ; and I have much reason to fear that, on days when the pressure of my complaint has been heaviest, I may have so far given way to it, as to have suffered greatly in clearness of critical vision. Sometimes I may have overlooked blunders, mis-statements, or repetitions, implicit or even express. But more often I may have failed to appreciate the true effects from faulty management of style and its colourings. Sometimes, for instance, a heavy or too intricate arrangement of sentences may have defeated the tendency of what, under its natural presentation, would have been affecting ; or it is possible enough that, by unseasonable levity at other times, I may have repelled the sympathy of my readers—all or some. Endless are the openings for such kinds of mistake—that is, of mistakes not fully seen *as* such. But even in a case of unequivocal mistake, seen and acknowledged, yet when it is open to remedy only through a sudden and energetic act, then or never, the press being for twenty minutes, suppose, free to receive an alteration, but beyond that time closed and sealed inexorably : such being supposed the circumstances, the humane reader will allow for the infirmity which even wilfully and consciously surrenders itself to the error, acquiescing in it deliberately, rather than face the cruel exertion of correcting it most elaborately at a moment of sickening misery, and with the prevision that the main correction must draw after it half-a-dozen others for the sake of decent consistency. I am not speaking under any present consciousness of such a case existing against myself : I believe there *is* none such. But I choose to suppose an extreme case of even conscious error, in order that venial cases of oversight may, under shelter of such an *outside* license, find toleration from a liberal critic. To fight up against the wearying siege of an abiding sickness, imposes a fiery combat. I attempt no description of this combat, knowing the unintelligibility and the repulsiveness of all attempts to communicate the Incommunicable. But the generous reader will not, for that forbearance on my part, the less readily show his indulgence, if a case should (unexpectedly to myself) arise for claiming it.

I have thus made the reader acquainted with one out of two cross currents that tended to thwart my efforts for improving this little work. There was, meantime, another, less open to remedy from my own uttermost efforts. All along I had relied upon a crowning grace, which I had reserved for the final pages of this volume, in a succession of some twenty or twenty-five dreams and noon-day visions, which had arisen under the latter stages of opium influence. These have disappeared : some under circumstances which allow me a reasonable prospect of recovering them ; some unaccountably ; and some dishonourably. Five or six, I believe, were burned in a sudden conflagration which arose from the spark of a candle falling unobserved amongst a very large pile of papers in a bedroom, when I was alone and reading. Falling not *on*, but *amongst* and *within* the papers, the fire would soon have been ahead of conflict ; and, by communicating with the slight woodwork and draperies of a bed, it would have immediately enveloped the laths of a ceiling overhead, and thus the house, far from fire-engines, would have been burned down in half-an-hour. My attention was first drawn by a sudden light upon my book : and the whole difference between a total destruction of the premises and a trivial loss (from books charred) of five guineas, was due to a large Spanish cloak. This, thrown over, and then drawn down tightly, by the aid of one sole person, somewhat agitated, but retaining her presence of mind, effectually extinguished the fire. Amongst the papers burned partially, but not so burned as to be absolutely irretrievable, was the 'Daughter of Lebanon'; and this I have printed, and have intentionally placed it at the end, as appropriately closing a record in which the case of poor Ann the Outcast formed not only the most memorable and the most suggestively pathetic incident, but also *that* which, more than any other, coloured— or (more truly I should say) shaped, moulded and remoulded, composed and decomposed—the great body of opium dreams. The search after the lost features of Ann, which I spoke of as pursued in the crowds of London, was in a more proper sense pursued through many a year in dreams. The general idea of a search and a chase reproduced itself in many shapes. The person, the rank, the age, the scenical position, all varied themselves for ever; but the same leading traits more or less faintly remained of a lost Pariah woman, and of some shadowy malice which withdrew her, or attempted to withdraw her, from restoration and from hope. Such is the explanation which I offer why that particular addition, which some of my friends had been authorised to look for, has not in the main been given, nor for the present *could* be given; and, secondly, why that part which *is* given has been placed in the conspicuous situation (as a closing passage) which it now occupies.

*November*, 1856.

# CONFESSIONS OF

# AN ENGLISH OPIUM-EATER

I HAVE often been asked—how it was, and through what series of steps, that I became an opium-eater. Was it gradually, tentatively, mistrustingly, as one goes down a shelving beach into a deepening sea, and with a knowledge from the first of the dangers lying on that path; half-courting those dangers, in fact, whilst seeming to defy them? Or was it, secondly, in pure ignorance of such dangers, under the misleadings of mercenary fraud? since oftentimes lozenges, for the relief of pulmonary affections, found their efficacy upon the opium which they contain, upon this, and this only, though clamorously disavowing so suspicious an alliance: and under such treacherous disguises multitudes are seduced into a dependency which they had not foreseen upon a drug which they had not known; not known even by name or by sight: and thus the case is not rare—that the chain of abject slavery is first detected when it has inextricably wound itself about the constitutional system. Thirdly, and lastly, was it ( *Yes*, by passionate anticipation, I answer, before the question is finished)—was it on a sudden, overmastering impulse derived from bodily anguish? Loudly I repeat, *Yes;* loudly and indignantly—as in answer to a wilful calumny. Simply as an anodyne it was, under the mere coercion of pain the severest, that I first resorted to opium; and precisely that same torment it is, or some variety of that torment, which drives most people to make acquaintance with that same insidious remedy. Such was the fact; such by accident. Meantime, without blame it might have been otherwise. If in early days I had fully understood the subtle powers lodged in this mighty drug (when judiciously regulated), (1) to tranquillise all irritations of the nervous system; (2) to stimulate the capacities of enjoyment; and (3) under any call for extraordinary exertion (such as all men meet at times), to sustain through twenty-four consecutive hours the else drooping animal energies—most certainly, knowing or suspecting all this, I should have inaugurated my opium career in the character of one seeking *extra* power and enjoyment, rather than of one shrinking from *extra* torment. And why not? If *that* argued any fault, is it not a fault that most of us commit every day with regard to alcohol? Are we entitled to use *that* only as a medicine? Is wine unlawful, except as an anodyne? I hope not: else I shall be obliged to counterfeit and to plead some anomalous *tic* in my little finger; and thus gradually, as in any Ovidian metamorphosis, I, that am at present a truth-loving man, shall change by daily inches into a dissembler. No: the whole race of man proclaim it lawful to drink wine without pleading a medical certificate as a qualification. That same license extends itself therefore to the use of opium; what a man may lawfully seek in wine surely he may lawfully find in opium; and much more so in those many cases (of which mine happens to be one) where opium deranges the animal economy less by a great deal than an equivalent quantity of alcohol. Coleridge, therefore, was doubly in error when he allowed himself to aim most unfriendly blows at my supposed voluptuousness in the use of opium; in error as to a principle, and in error as to a fact. A letter of his, which I will hope that he did not design to have published, but which, however, *has* been published, points the attention of his correspondent to a broad distinction separating my case as an opium-eater from his own: he, it seems, had fallen excusably (because unavoidably) into this habit of eating opium—as the one sole therapeutic resource available against his particular malady; but I, wretch that I am, being so notoriously charmed by fairies against pain, must have resorted to opium in the abominable character of an adventurous voluptuary, angling in all streams for variety of pleasures. Coleridge is wrong to the whole extent of what was possible; wrong in his fact, wrong in his doctrine; in his little fact, and his big doctrine. I did not do the thing which he charges upon me; and if I *had* done it, this would not convict me as a citizen of Sybaris or Daphne. There never was a distinction more groundless and visionary than that which it has pleased him to draw between my motives and his own; nor could Coleridge have possibly owed this mis-statement to any false information; since no man surely, on a question of my own private experience, could have pretended to be better informed than myself. Or, if there really is such a person, perhaps he will not think it too much trouble to re-write these Confessions from first to last, correcting their innumerable faults; and, as it happens that some parts of the unpublished sections for the present are missing, would he kindly restore them—brightening the colours that may have faded, rekindling the inspiration that may have drooped; filling up all those chasms which else are likely to remain as permanent disfigurations of my little work? Meantime the reader, who takes any interest in such a question, will find that I myself (upon such a theme not simply the best, but surely the sole authority) have, without a shadow of variation, always given a different account of the matter. Most truly I have told the reader, that not any search after pleasure, but mere extremity of pain from rheumatic toothache—this and nothing else it was that first drove me into the use of opium. Coleridge's bodily affliction was simple rheumatism. Mine, which intermittingly raged for ten years, was rheumatism in the face combined with toothache. This I had inherited from my father; or inherited (I should rather say) from my own desperate ignorance; since a trifling dose of colocynth, or of any similar medicine, taken three times a week, would more certainly than opium have delivered me from that terrific curse.¹ In this ignorance, however, which misled me into making war upon toothache when ripened and manifesting itself in effects of pain, rather than upon its germs and gathering causes, I did but follow the rest of the world. To intercept the evil whilst yet in elementary stages of formation, was the true policy; whereas I in my blindness sought only for some mitigation to the evil when already formed, and past all reach of interception. In this stage of the suffering, formed and perfect, I was thrown passively upon chance advice, and therefore, by a natural consequence, upon opium— that being the one sole anodyne that is almost notoriously such, and which in that great function is universally appreciated.

Coleridge, therefore, and myself, as regards our baptismal initiation into the use of that mighty drug, occupy the very same position. We are embarked in the selfsame boat; nor is it within the compass even of angelic hair-splitting, to show that the dark shadow thrown by our several trespasses in this field, mine and his, had by so much as a pin's point any assignable difference. Trespass against trespass (if any trespass there were)— shadow against shadow (if any shadow were really thrown

---

¹ '*That terrific curse*':—Two things blunt the general sense of horror, which would else connect itself with toothache—viz., first, its enormous diffusion; hardly a household in Europe being clear of it, each in turn having some one chamber intermittingly echoing the groans extorted by this cruel torture. There—viz., in its ubiquity— lies one cause of its slight valuation. A second cause is found in its immunity from danger. This latter ground of undervaluation is noticed in a saying ascribed (but on what authority I know not) to Sir Philip Sidney—viz., that supposing toothache liable in ever so small a proportion of its cases to a fatal issue, it would be generally ranked as the most dreadful amongst human maladies; whereas the certainty that it will in no extremity lead to death, and the knowledge that in the very midst of its storms sudden changes may be looked for, bringing long halcyon calms, have an unfair effect in lowering the appreciation of this malady considered as a trial of fortitude and patience. No stronger expression of its intensity and scorching fierceness can be imagined than this fact—that, within my private knowledge, two persons, who had suffered alike under toothache and cancer, have pronounced the former to be, on the scale of torture, by many degrees the worse. In both, there are *at times* what surgeons call 'lancinating' pangs—keen, glancing, arrowy radiations of anguish; and upon these the basis of comparison was rested—paroxysm against paroxysm —with the result that I have stated.

by this trespass over the snowy disk of pure ascetic
morality), in any case, that act in either of us would
read into the same meaning, would count up as a debt
into the same value, would measure as a delinquency
into the same burden of responsibility. And vainly,
indeed, does Coleridge attempt to differentiate two cases
which ran into absolute identity, differing only as rheumatism differs from toothache. Amongst the admirers
of Coleridge, I at all times stood in the foremost rank;
and the more was my astonishment at being summoned
so often to witness his carelessness in the management
of controversial questions, and his demoniac inaccuracy
in the statement of facts. The more also was my sense
of Coleridge's wanton injustice in relation to myself
individually. Coleridge's gross mis-statement of facts,
in regard to our several opium experiences, had its
origin, sometimes in flighty reading, sometimes in partial
and incoherent reading, sometimes in subsequent forget-
fulness; and any one of these lax habits (it will occur
to the reader) is a venial infirmity. Certainly it is; but
surely *not* venial, when it is allowed to operate dis-
advantageously upon the character for self-control of a
brother, who had never spoken of *him* but in the spirit
of enthusiastic admiration; of that admiration which his
exquisite works so amply challenge. Imagine the case
that I really *had* done something wrong, still it would
have been ungenerous—me it would have saddened,
I confess, to see Coleridge rushing forward with a public
denunciation of my fault:—'Know all men by these
presents, that I, S. T. C., *a noticeable man with large
grey eyes*,[1] am a licensed opium-eater, whereas this other
man is a buccaneer, a pirate, a flibustier,[2] and can have

---

[1] See Wordsworth's exquisite picture of S. T. C. and himself as
occasional denizens in the *Castle of Indolence*.

[2] This word—in common use, and so spelled as I spell it, amongst
the grand old French and English buccaneers contemporary with our
own admirable Dampier, at the close of the seventeenth century—has
recently been revived in the journals of the United States, with a view
to the special case of Cuba, but (for what reason I know not) is now
written always as *filli*busters. Meantime, written in whatsoever way,
it is understood to be a Franco-Spanish corruption of the English word
*freebooter*.

none but a forged licence in his disreputable pocket.
In the name of Virtue, arrest him!' But the truth is,
that inaccuracy as to facts and citations from books was
in Coleridge a mere necessity of nature. Not three
days ago, in reading a short comment of the late Archdeacon Hare (*Guesses at Truth*) upon a bold speculation
of Coleridge's (utterly baseless) with respect to the
machinery of Etonian Latin verses, I found my old
feelings upon this subject refreshed by an instance that
is irresistibly comic, since everything that Coleridge
had relied upon as a citation from a book in support
of his own hypothesis, turns out to be a pure fabrication
of his own dreams; though, doubtless (which indeed it
is that constitutes the characteristic interest of the case),
without a suspicion on his part of his own furious
romancing. The archdeacon's good-natured smile upon
that Etonian case naturally reminded me of the case
now before us, with regard to the history of our separate
careers as opium-eaters. Upon which case I need say
no more, as by this time the reader is aware that
Coleridge's entire statement upon that subject is perfect
moonshine, and, like the sculptured imagery of the
pendulous lamp in *Christabel*,

'All carvèd from the carver's brain.'

This case, therefore, might now be counted on as disposed of; and what sport it could yield might reasonably
be thought exhausted. Meantime, on consideration,
another and much deeper oversight of Coleridge's becomes apparent; and as this connects itself with an
aspect of the case that furnishes the foundation to the
whole of these ensuing Confessions, it cannot altogether
be neglected. Any attentive reader, after a few moments'
reflection, will perceive that, whatever may have been the
casual *occasion* of mine or Coleridge's opium-eating, this
could not have been the permanent *ground* of opium-
eating; because neither rheumatism nor toothache is
any *abiding* affection of the system. Both are intermitting maladies, and not at all capable of accounting

for a *permanent* habit of opium-eating. Some months are requisite to found *that*. Making allowance for constitutional differences, I should say that *in less than* 120 *days* no habit of opium-eating could be formed strong enough to call for any extraordinary self-conquest in renouncing it, and even suddenly renouncing it. On Saturday you are an opium-eater, on Sunday no longer such. What then was it, after all, that made Coleridge a slave to opium, and a slave that could not break his chain? He fancies, in his headlong carelessness, that he has accounted for this habit and this slavery; and in the meantime he has accounted for nothing at all about which any question has arisen. Rheumatism, he says, drove him to opium. Very well; but with proper medical treatment the rheumatism would soon have ceased; or even, without medical treatment, under the ordinary oscillations of natural causes. And when the pain ceased, then the opium should have ceased. Why did it not? Because Coleridge had come to taste the genial pleasure of opium; and thus the very impeachment, which he fancied himself in some mysterious way to have evaded, recoils upon him in undiminished force. The rheumatic attack would have retired before the habit could have had time to form itself. Or suppose that I underrate the strength of the possible habit—this tells equally in *my* favour; and Coleridge was not entitled to forget in *my* case a plea remembered in his own. It is really memorable in the annals of human self-deceptions, that Coleridge could have held such language in the face of such facts. I, boasting not at all of my self-conquests, and owning no moral argument against the free use of opium, nevertheless on mere *prudential* motives break through the vassalage more than once, and by efforts which I have recorded as modes of transcendent suffering. Coleridge, professing to believe (without reason assigned) that opium-eating is criminal, and in some mysterious sense more criminal than wine-drinking or porter-drinking, having, therefore, the strongest *moral* motive for abstaining from it, yet suffers himself to fall into a captivity to this same wicked opium, deadlier than was ever heard of, and under no coercion whatever that he has anywhere explained to us. A slave he was to this potent drug not less abject than Caliban to Prospero—his detested and yet despotic master. Like Caliban, he frets his very heart-strings against the rivets of his chain. Still, at intervals through the gloomy vigils of his prison, you hear muttered growls of impotent mutineering swelling upon the breeze:

> ' Irasque leonum
> Vincla recusantum '——

recusantum, it is true, still refusing yet still accepting, protesting for ever against the fierce, overmastering curb-chain, yet for ever submitting to receive it into the mouth. It is notorious that in Bristol (to *that* I can speak myself, but probably in many other places) he went so far as to hire men—porters, hackney-coachmen, and others—to oppose by force his entrance into any druggist's shop. But, as the authority for stopping him was derived simply from himself, naturally these poor men found themselves in a metaphysical fix, not provided for even by Thomas Aquinas or by the prince of Jesuitical casuists. And in this excruciating dilemma would occur such scenes as the following:—

' Oh, sir,' would plead the suppliant porter—suppliant, yet semi-imperative (for equally if he *did*, and if he did *not*, show fight, the poor man's daily 5s. seemed endangered)—'really you must not; consider, sir, your wife and——'

*Transcendental Philosopher.*—'Wife! what wife? I have no wife.'[1]

*Porter.*—'But, really now, you must not, sir. Didn't you say no longer ago than yesterday——'

*Transcend. Philos.*—'Pooh, pooh! yesterday is a long time ago. Are you aware, my man, that people are known to have dropped down dead for timely want of opium?'

*Porter.*—'Ay, but you tell't me not to hearken——'

*Transcend. Philos.*—'Oh, nonsense. An emergency,

[1] Vide *Othello*.

a shocking emergency, has arisen—quite unlooked for. No matter what I told you in times long past. That which I *now* tell you, is—that, if you don't remove that arm of yours from the doorway of this most respectable druggist, I shall have a good ground of action against you for assault and battery.'

Am I the man to reproach Coleridge with this vassalage to opium? Heaven forbid! Having groaned myself under that yoke, I pity, and blame him not. But undeniably, such a vassalage must have been created wilfully and consciously by his own craving after genial stimulation; a thing which I do not blame, but Coleridge *did*. For my own part, duly as the torment relaxed in relief of which I had resorted to opium, I laid aside the opium, not under any meritorious effort of self-conquest; nothing of that sort do I pretend to; but simply on a prudential instinct warning me not to trifle with an engine so awful of consolation and support, nor to waste upon a momentary uneasiness what might eventually prove, in the midst of all-shattering hurricanes, the great elixir of resurrection. What was it that did in reality make me an opium-eater? That affection which finally drove me into the *habitual* use of opium, what was it? Pain was it? No, but misery. Casual overcasting of sunshine was it? No, but blank desolation. Gloom was it that might have departed? No, but settled and abiding darkness.

> 'Total eclipse,
> Without all hope of day!'[1]

Yet whence derived? Caused by what? Caused, as I might truly plead, by youthful distresses in London; were it not that these distresses were due, in their ultimate origin, to my own unpardonable folly; and to that folly I trace many ruins. Oh, spirit of merciful interpretation, angel of forgiveness to youth and its aberrations, that hearkenest for ever as if to some sweet choir of far-off female intercessions! will ye, choir that intercede—wilt thou, angel that forgivest—join together,

[1] *Samson Agonistes.*

and charm away that mighty phantom, born amidst the gathering mists of remorse, which strides after me in pursuit from forgotten days—towering for ever into proportions more and more colossal, overhanging and overshadowing my head as if close behind, yet dating its nativity from hours that are fled by more than half-a-century? Oh heavens! that it should be possible for a child not seventeen years old, by a momentary blindness, by listening to a false, false whisper from his own bewildered heart, by one erring step, by a motion this way or that, to change the currents of his destiny, to poison the fountains of his peace, and in the twinkling of an eye to lay the foundations of a life-long repentance! Yet, alas! I must abide by the realities of the case. And one thing is clear, that amidst such bitter self-reproaches as are now extorted from me by the anguish of my recollections, it cannot be with any purpose of weaving plausible excuses, or of evading blame, that I trace the origin of my confirmed opium-eating to a necessity growing out of my early sufferings in the streets of London. Because, though true it is that the re-agency of these London sufferings did in after years *enforce* the use of opium, equally it is true that the sufferings themselves grew out of my own folly. What really calls for excuse, is not the recourse to opium, when opium had become the one sole remedy available for the malady, but those follies which had themselves produced that malady.

I, for my part, after I had become a regular opium-eater, and from mismanagement had fallen into miserable excesses in the use of opium, did nevertheless, four several times, contend successfully against the dominion of this drug; did four several times renounce it; renounced it for long intervals; and finally resumed it upon the warrant of my enlightened and deliberate judgment, as being of two evils by very much the least. In this I acknowledge nothing that calls for excuse. I repeat again and again, that not the application of opium, with its deep tranquillising powers to the mitigation of evils, bequeathed by my London hardships, is what reasonably calls for sorrow, but that extravagance of childish folly which precipitated me into scenes naturally producing such hardships.

These scenes I am now called upon to retrace. Possibly they are sufficiently interesting to merit, even on their own account, some short record; but at present, and at this point, they have become indispensable as a key to the proper understanding of all which follows. For in these incidents of my early life is found the entire substratum, together with the secret and under-lying motive[1] of those pompous dreams and dream-sceneries which were in reality the true objects—first and last—contemplated in these Confessions.

My father died when I was in my seventh year, leaving six children, including myself (viz., four sons and two daughters), to the care of four guardians and of our mother, who was invested with the legal authority of a guardian. This word '*guardian*' kindles a fiery thrill-ing in my nerves; so much was that special power of guardianship, as wielded by one of the four, concerned in the sole capital error of my boyhood. To this error my own folly would hardly have been equal, unless by concurrence with the obstinacy of others. From the bitter remembrance of this error in myself—of this obstinacy in my hostile guardian, suffer me to draw the privilege of making a moment's pause upon this subject of legal guardianship.

There is not (I believe) in human society, under whatever form of civilisation, any trust or delegated duty which has more often been negligently or even perfidiously administered. In the days of classical Greece and Rome, my own private impression, founded on the collation of many incidental notices, is—that this, beyond all other forms of domestic authority, fur-nished to wholesale rapine and peculation their very amplest arena. The relation of father and son, as was that of *patron* and *client*, was generally, in the practice

---

[1] *Motive* :—The word *motive* is here used in the sense attached by artists and connoisseurs to the technical word *motivo*, applied to pictures, or to the separate movements in a musical theme.

of life, cherished with religious fidelity: whereas the solemn duties of the *tutor* (*i.e.* the *guardian*) to his ward, which had their very root and origin in the tenderest adjurations of a dying friend, though subsequently refreshed by the hourly spectacle of helpless orphanage playing round the margins of pitfalls hidden by flowers, spoke but seldom to the sensibilities of a Roman through any language of oracular power. Few indeed, if any, were the obligations, in a proper sense *moral*, which pressed upon the Roman. The main fountains of moral obligation had in Rome, by law or by custom, been thoroughly poisoned. Marriage had corrupted itself through the facility of divorce, and through the consequences of that facility (viz., levity in choosing, and fickleness in adhering to the choice), into so exquisite a traffic of selfishness, that it could not yield so much as a phantom model of sanctity. The relation of husband and wife had, for all moral impressions, perished amongst the Romans. The relation of father and child had all its capacities of holy tenderness crushed out of it under the fierce pressure of penal and vindictive enforcements. The duties of the client to his patron stood upon no basis of simple gratitude or simple fidelity (corresponding to the feudal *fealty*), but upon a basis of prudential terror; terror from positive law, or from social opinion. From the first intermeddling of law with the movement of the higher moral affections, there is an end to freedom in the act —to purity in the motive—to dignity in the personal relation. Accordingly, in the France of the pre-revolutionary period, and in the China of all periods, it has been with baleful effects to the national morals that positive law has come in aid of the paternal rights. And in the Rome of ancient history it may be said that this one original and rudimental wrong done to the holy freedom of human affections, had the effect of extinguishing thenceforward all *conscientious* movement in whatever direction. And thus, amongst a people naturally more highly principled than the Greeks, if you except ebullitions of public spirit and patriotism (too

often of mere ignoble nationality), no class of actions
stood upon any higher basis of motive than (1) legal
ordinance; (2) superstitious fear; or (3) servile compliance with the insolent exactions of popular usage.
Strange, therefore, it would have been if the *tutor* of
obscure orphans, with *extra* temptations and *extra*
facilities for indulging them, should have shown himself more faithful to his trust than the governor of
provinces—prætorian or proconsular. Yet who more
treacherous and rapacious than he? Rarest of men was
the upright governor that accepted no bribes from the
criminal, and extorted no ransoms from the timid. He
nevertheless, as a *public* trustee, was watched by the
jealousy of political competitors, and had by possibility
a solemn audit to face in the senate or in the forum;
perhaps in both. But the tutor, who administered a
private trust on behalf of orphans, might count on the
certainty that no public attention could ever be attracted
to concerns so obscure, and politically so uninteresting.
Reasonably, therefore, and by all analogy, a Roman
must have regarded the ordinary domestic *tutor* as
almost inevitably a secret delinquent using the opportunities and privileges of his office as mere instruments
for working spoliation and ruin upon the inheritance
confided to his care. This deadly and besetting evil of
Pagan days must have deepened a hundredfold the
glooms overhanging the death-beds of parents. Too
often the dying father could not fail to read in his own
lifelong experience, that, whilst seeking special protection for his children, he might himself be introducing
amongst them a separate and imminent danger. Leaving behind him a little household of infants, a little
fleet (as it might be represented) of fairy pinnaces, just
raising their anchors in preparation for crossing the
mighty deeps of life, he made signals for 'convoy.'
Some one or two (at best imperfectly known to him),
amongst those who traversed the same seas, he accepted
in that character; but doubtfully, sorrowfully, fearfully;
and at the very moment when the faces of his children
were disappearing amongst the vapours of death, the

miserable thought would cross his prophetic soul—that too probably this pretended 'convoy,' under the strong temptations of the case, might eventually become pirates; robbers, at the least; and by possibility wilful misleaders to the inexperience of his children.

From this dreadful aggravation of the anguish at any rate besetting the death-beds of parents summoned away from a group of infant children, there has been a mighty deliverance wrought in a course of centuries by the vast diffusion of Christianity. In these days, wheresoever an atmosphere is breathed that has been purified by Christian charities and Christian principles, this household pestilence has been continually dwindling: and in the England of this generation there is no class of peculation which we so seldom hear of: one proof of which is found in the indifference with which most of us regard the absolute security offered to children by the Court of Chancery. My father, therefore, as regarded the quiet of his dying hours, benefited by the felicity of his times and his country. He made the best selection for the future guardianship of his six children that his opportunities allowed; from his circle of intimate friends, he selected the four who stood highest in his estimation for honour and practical wisdom: which done, and relying for the redressing of any harsh tendencies in male guardians upon the discretional power lodged in my mother, thenceforth he rested from his anxieties. Not one of these guardians but justified his choice so far as honour and integrity were concerned. Yet, after all, there is a limit (and sooner reached perhaps in England than in other divisions of Christendom) to the good that can be achieved in such cases by prospective wisdom. For we, in England, more absolutely than can be asserted of any other nation, are not *fainéans*: rich and poor, all of us have something to do. To Italy it is that we must look for a peasantry idle through two-thirds of their time. To Spain it is that we must look for an aristocracy *physically*[1] degraded

---

[1] It is asserted by travellers—English, French, and German alike—that the ducal order in Spain (as that order of the Spanish peerage

under the ignoble training of women and priests; and for princes (such as Ferdinand VII.) that make it the glory of their lives to have embroidered a petticoat. Amongst ourselves of this current generation, whilst those functions of guardianship may be surely counted on which presume conscientious loyalty to the interests of their wards; on the other hand, all which presume continued vigilance and provision from afar are, in simple truth, hardly compatible with our English state of society. The guardians chosen by my father, had they been the wisest and also the most energetic of men, could not in many conceivable emergencies have fulfilled his secret wishes. Of the four men, one was a merchant (not in the narrow sense of Scotland, derived originally from France, where no class of merchant princes has ever existed, but in the large noble sense of England—of Florence—of Venice): consequently, his extensive relations with sea-ports and distant colonies continually drawing off his attention, and even his personal presence, from domestic affairs, made it hopeless that he should even attempt more on behalf of his wards than slightly to watch the administration of their pecuniary interests. A second of our guardians was a rural magistrate, but in a populous district close upon Manchester, which even at that time was belted with a growing body of turbulent aliens—Welsh and Irish. He therefore, overwhelmed by the distractions of his official station, rightly perhaps conceived himself to have fulfilled his engagements as a guardian, if he stood ready to come forward upon any difficulty arising, but else in ordinary cases devolved his functions upon those who enjoyed more leisure. In that category stood, beyond a doubt, a third of our guardians, the Rev. Samuel H., who was at the time of my father's death a curate at some church (I believe) in Manchester or in

---

most carefully withdrawn from what Kentucky would call the *rough-and-tumble* discipline of a popular education) exhibit in their very persons and bodily development undisguised evidences of effeminate habits operating through many generations. It would be satisfactory to know the unexaggerated truth on this point; the truth unbiassed alike by national and by democratic prejudices.

Salford.[1] This gentleman represented a class—large enough at all times by necessity of human nature, but in those days far larger than at present—that class, I mean, who sympathise with no spiritual sense or spiritual capacities in man; who understand by religion simply a respectable code of ethics—leaning for support upon some great mysteries dimly traced in the background, and commemorated in certain great church festivals by the *elder* churches of Christendom; as, *e.g.*, by the English, which does not stand as to age on the Reformation epoch, by the Romish, and by the Greek. He had composed a body of about 330 sermons, which thus, at the rate of two every Sunday, revolved through a cycle of three years; that period being modestly assumed as sufficient for insuring to their eloquence total oblivion. Possibly to a cynic, some shorter cycle might have seemed equal to that effect, since their topics rose but rarely above the level of prudential ethics; and the style, though scholarly, was not impressive. As a preacher, Mr. H. was sincere, but not earnest. He was a good and conscientious man; and he made a high valuation of the pulpit as an organ of civilisation for co-operating with books; but it was impossible for any man, starting from the low ground of themes so unimpassioned and so desultory as the benefits of industry, the danger from bad companions, the importance of setting a good example, or the value of perseverance—to pump up any persistent stream of earnestness either in himself or in his auditors. These auditors, again, were not of a class to desire much earnestness. There were no naughty people among

---

[1] Salford is a large town legally distinguished from Manchester for parliamentary purposes, and divided from it physically by a river, but else virtually, as regards intercourse and reciprocal influence, is a quarter of Manchester; in fact, holding the same relation to Manchester that Southwark does to London; or, if the reader insists upon having a classical illustration of the case, the same relation that in ancient days Argos did to Mycenæ. An invitation to dinner given by the public herald of Argos could be heard to the centre of Mycenæ, and by a gourmand, if the dinner promised to be specially good, in the remoter suburb.

them : most of them were rich, and came to church in carriages : and, as a natural result of their esteem for my reverend guardian, a number of them combined to build a church for him—viz., St. Peter's, at the point of confluence between Moseley Street and the newly projected Oxford Street—then existing only as a sketch in the portfolio of a surveyor. But what connected myself individually with Mr. H. was, that two or three years previously I, together with one of my brothers (five years my senior), had been placed under his care for classical instruction. This was done, I believe, in obedience to a dying injunction of my father, who had a just esteem for Mr. S. H. as an upright man, but apparently too exalted an opinion of his scholarship : for he was but an indifferent Grecian. In whatever way the appointment arose, so it was that this gentleman, previously *tutor* in the Roman sense to all of us, now became to my brother and myself tutor also in the common English sense. From the age of eight, up to eleven and a-half, the character and intellectual attainments of Mr. H. were therefore influentially important to myself in the development of my powers, such as they were. Even his 330 sermons, which rolled overhead with such slender effect upon his general congregation, to me became a real instrument of improvement. One-half of these, indeed, were all that I heard; for, as my father's house (Greenhay) stood at this time in the country, Manchester not having yet overtaken it, the distance obliged us to go in a carriage, and only to the morning service; but every sermon in this morning course was propounded to me as a textual basis upon which I was to raise a mimic duplicate—sometimes a pure miniature abstract—sometimes a rhetorical expansion—but preserving as much as possible of the original language, and also (which puzzled me painfully) preserving the exact succession of the thoughts ; which might be easy where they stood in some dependency upon each other, as, for instance, in the development of an argument, but in arbitrary or chance arrangements was often as trying to my powers as any feat of rope-dancing.

I, therefore, amongst that whole congregation,[1] was the one sole careworn auditor—agitated about that which, over all other heads, flowed away like water over marble slabs—viz., the somewhat torpid sermon of my somewhat torpid guardian. But this annoyance was not wholly lost: and those same $\frac{330}{2}$ sermons, which (lasting only through sixteen minutes each) were approved and forgotten by everybody else, for me became a perfect palæstra of intellectual gymnastics far better suited to my childish weakness than could have been the sermons of Isaac Barrow or Jeremy Taylor. In these last, the gorgeous imagery would have dazzled my feeble vision, and in both the gigantic thinking would have crushed my efforts at apprehension. I drew, in fact, the deepest benefits from this weekly exercise. Perhaps, also, in the end it ripened into a great advantage for me, though long and bitterly I complained of it, that I was not allowed to use a pencil in taking notes: all was to be charged upon the memory. But it is notorious that the memory strengthens as you lay burdens upon it, and becomes trustworthy as you trust it. So that, in my third year of practice, I found

[1] ' *That whole congregation*':—Originally at churches which I do not remember, where, however, in consideration of my tender age, the demands levied upon my memory were much lighter. Two or three years later, when I must have been nearing my tenth year, and when St. Peter's had been finished, occurred the opening, and consequently (as an indispensable pre-condition) the consecration of that edifice by the bishop of the diocese (viz., Chester). I, as a ward of the incumbent, was naturally amongst those specially invited to the festival; and I remember a little incident which exposed broadly the conflict of feelings inherited by the Church of England from the Puritans of the seventeenth century. The architecture of the church was Grecian; and certainly the enrichments, inside or outside, were few enough, neither florid nor obtrusive. But in the centre of the ceiling, for the sake of breaking the monotony of so large a blank white surface, there was moulded, in plaster-of-Paris, a large tablet or shield, charged with a cornucopia of fruits and flowers. And yet, when we were all assembled in the vestry waiting—rector, churchwardens, architect, and trains of dependants—there arose a deep buzz of anxiety, which soon ripened into an articulate expression of fear, that the bishop would think himself bound, like the horrid eikonoclasts of 1645, to issue his decree of utter *averruncation* to the simple decoration overhead. Fearfully did we all tread the little aisles in the procession of the prelate. Earnestly my lord looked upwards; but finally—were it courtesy, or doubtfulness as to his ground, or approbation—he passed on.

my abstracting and condensing powers sensibly enlarged.
My guardian was gradually better satisfied; for unfortunately (and in the beginning it *was* unfortunate)
always one witness could be summoned against me
upon any impeachment of my fidelity—viz., the sermon
itself; since, though lurking amongst the 330, the
wretch was easily forked out. But these appeals grew
fewer; and my guardian, as I have said, was continually
better satisfied. Meantime, might not I be continually
less satisfied with *him* and his 330 sermons? Not at
all: loving and trusting, without doubt or reserve, and
with the deepest principles of veneration rooted in my
nature, I never, upon meeting something more impressive than the average complexion of my guardian's
discourses, for one moment thought of him as worse
or feebler than others, but simply as different; and no
more quarrelled with him for his characteristic languor,
than with a green riband for not being blue. By mere
accident, I one day heard quoted a couplet which
seemed to me sublime. It described a preacher such
as sometimes arises in difficult times, or in fermenting
times, a son of thunder, that looks all enemies in the
face, and volunteers a defiance even when it would have
been easy to evade it. The lines were written by
Richard Baxter—who baffled often with self-created
storms from the first dawn of the Parliamentary War
in 1642, through the period of Cromwell (to whom he
was personally odious), and, finally, through the trying
reigns of the second Charles and of the second James.
As a pulpit orator, he was perhaps the Whitfield of the
seventeenth century—the *Leuconomos* of Cowper. And
thus it is that he describes the impassioned character of
his own preaching—

> ‘ I preach'd, as never sure to preach again;

[Even *that* was telling; but then followed this thunder-*peal*]

> And as a dying man to dying men.’

This couplet, which seemed to me equally for weight
and for splendour like molten gold, laid bare another

aspect of the Catholic church; revealed it as a Church
militant and crusading.

Not even thus, however, did I descry any positive
imperfection in my guardian. He and Baxter had fallen
upon different generations. Baxter's century, from first
to last, was revolutionary. Along the entire course of
that seventeenth century, the great principles of representative government and the rights of conscience[1] were
passing through the anguish of conflict and fiery trial.
Now again in my own day, at the close of the eighteenth
century, it is true that all the elements of social life were
thrown into the crucible—but on behalf of our neighbours, no longer of ourselves. No longer, therefore, was
invoked the heroic pleader, ready for martyrdom, preaching, therefore, 'as never sure to preach again'; and I
no more made it a defect in my guardian that he wanted
energies for combating evils now forgotten, than that
he had not in patriotic fervour leaped into a gulf, like
the fabulous Roman martyr Curtius, or in zeal for
liberty had not mounted a scaffold, like the real English
martyr Algernon Sidney. Every Sunday, duly as it
revolved, brought with it this cruel anxiety. On Saturday night under sad anticipation, on Sunday night under
sadder experimental knowledge, of my trying task, I
slept ill: my pillow was stuffed with thorns; and until
Monday morning's inspection and *armilustrium* had
dismissed me from parade to 'stand at ease,' verily I
felt like a false steward summoned to some killing audit.
Then suppose Monday to be invaded by some horrible
intruder, visitor perhaps from a band of my guardian's
poor relations, that in some undiscovered nook of
Lancashire seemed in fancy to blacken all the fields,
and suddenly at a single note of '*caw, caw,*' rose in
one vast cloud like crows, and settled down for weeks

---

[1] '*The rights of conscience*':—With which it is painful to know
that Baxter did not sympathise. Religious toleration he called 'Soul-
murder.' And, if you reminded him that the want of this toleration
had been his own capital grievance, he replied, 'Ah, but the cases
were very different: I was in the right; whereas the vast majority of
those who will benefit by this newfangled toleration are shockingly in
the wrong.'

at the table of my guardian and his wife, whose noble hospitality would never allow the humblest among them to be saddened by a faint welcome. In such cases, very possibly the whole week did not see the end of my troubles.

On these terms, for upwards of three-and-a-half years—that is, from my eighth to beyond my eleventh birth-day—my guardian and I went on cordially: he never once angry, as indeed he never had any reason for anger; I never once treating my task either as odious (which in the most abominable excess it was), or, on the other hand, as costing but a trivial effort, which practice might have taught me to hurry through with contemptuous ease. To the very last I found no ease at all in this weekly task, which never ceased to be 'a thorn in the flesh': and I believe that my guardian, like many of the grim Pagan divinities, inhaled a flavour of fragrant incense, from the fretting and stinging of anxiety which, as it were some holy vestal fire, he kept alive by this periodic exaction. It gave him pleasure that he could reach me in the very recesses of my dreams, where even a Pariah might look for rest; so that the Sunday, which to man, and even to the brutes within his gates, offered an interval of rest, for me was signalised as a day of martyrdom. Yet in this, after all, it is possible that he did me a service: for my constitutional infirmity of mind ran but too determinately towards the sleep of endless reverie, and of dreamy abstraction from life and its realities.

Whether serviceable or not, however, the connexion between my guardian and myself was now drawing to its close. Some months after my eleventh birth-day, Greenhay[1] was sold, and my mother's establishment—both children and servants—was translated to Bath: only that for a few months I and one brother were still

---

[1] *Greenhay* :—A country-house built by my father; and at the time of its foundation (say in 1791 or 1792) separated from the last outskirts of Manchester by an entire mile; but now, and for many a year, overtaken by the hasty strides of this great city, and long since (I presume) absorbed into its mighty uproar.

left under the care of Mr. Samuel H.; so far, that is, as
regarded our education.   Else, as regarded the luxurious
comforts of a thoroughly English home, we became
the guests, by special invitation, of a young married
couple in Manchester—viz., Mr. and Mrs. K——l.
This incident, though otherwise without results, I look
back upon with feelings inexpressibly profound, as
a jewelly parenthesis of pathetic happiness—such as
emerges but once in any man's life.   Mr. K. was a
young and rising American merchant; by which I
mean, that he was an Englishman who exported to the
United States.   He had married about three years
previously a pretty and amiable young woman—well
educated, and endowed with singular compass of intellect.   But the distinguishing feature in this household was the spirit of love which, under the benign
superintendence of the mistress, diffused itself through
all its members.

The late Dr. Arnold of Rugby, amongst many novel
ideas, which found no welcome even with his friends,
insisted earnestly and often upon this—viz., that a great
danger was threatening our social system in Great Britain,
from the austere separation existing between our educated and our working classes, and that a more con-
ciliatory style of intercourse between these two bisections
of our social body must be established, or else—a
tremendous revolution.   This is not the place to discuss
so large a question; and I shall content myself with
making two remarks.   The first is this—that, although
a change of the sort contemplated by Dr. Arnold might,
if considered as an operative *cause*, point forward to
some advantages, on the other hand, if considered as
an *effect*, it points backward to a less noble constitution
of society by much than we already enjoy.   Those
nations whose upper classes speak paternally and caress-
ingly to the working classes, and to servants in particular. do so because they speak from the lofty stations
of persons having civil rights to those who have none.
Two centuries back, when a military chieftain addressed
his soldiers as '*my children*,' he did so because he was

an irresponsible despot exercising uncontrolled powers of life and death. From the moment when legal rights have been won for the poorest classes, inevitable respect on the part of the higher classes extinguishes for ever the affectionate style which belongs naturally to the state of pupilage or infantine bondage.

That is my first remark: my second is this—that the change advocated by Dr. Arnold, whether promising or not, is practically impossible; or possible, I should say, through one sole channel—viz., that of domestic servitude. There only do the two classes concerned come hourly into contact. On that stage only they meet without intrusion upon each other. There only is an opening for change. And a wise mistress, who possesses tact enough to combine a gracious affability with a self-respect that never slumbers nor permits her to descend into gossip, will secure the attachment of all young and impressible women. Such a mistress was Mrs. K——. She had won the gratitude of her servants from the first, by making the amplest provision for their comfort; their confidence, by listening with patience, and counselling with prudence; and their respect, by refusing to intermeddle with gossiping personalities always tending to slander. To this extent, perhaps, most mistresses might follow her example. But the happiness which reigned in Mrs. K——'s house at this time depended very much upon special causes. All the eight persons had the advantage of youth; and the three young female servants were under the spell of fascination, such as could rarely be counted on, from a spectacle held up hourly before their eyes, that spectacle which of all others is the most touching to womanly sensibilities, and which any one of these servants might hope, without presumption, to realise for herself—the spectacle, I mean, of a happy marriage union between two persons, who lived in harmony so absolute with each other, as to be independent of the world outside. How tender and self-sufficing such an union might be, they saw with their own eyes. The season was then midwinter, which of itself draws closer all household ties. Their own labours, as generally in respectable English services, were finished for the most part by two o'clock; and as the hours of evening drew nearer, when the master's return might be looked for without fail, beautiful was the smile of anticipation upon the gentle features of the mistress: even more beautiful the reflex of that smile, half-unconscious, and half-repressed, upon the features of the sympathising hand-maidens. One child, a little girl of two years old, had then crowned the happiness of the K——s. She naturally lent her person at all times, and apparently in all places at once, to the improvement of the family groups. My brother and myself, who had been trained from infancy to the courteous treatment of servants, filled up a vacancy in the graduated scale of ascending ages, and felt in varying degrees the depths of a peace which we could not adequately understand or appreciate. Bad tempers there were none amongst us; nor any opening for personal jealousies; nor, through the privilege of our common youth, either angry recollections breathing from the past, or fretting anxieties gathering from the future. The spirit of hope and the spirit of peace (so it seemed to me, when looking back upon this profound calm) had, for their own enjoyment, united in a sisterly league to blow a solitary bubble of visionary happiness—and to sequester from the unresting hurricanes of life one solitary household of eight persons within a four months' lull, as if within some Arabian tent on some untrodden wilderness, withdrawn from human intrusion, or even from knowledge, by worlds of mist and vapour.

How deep was that lull! and yet, as in a human atmosphere, how frail! Did the visionary bubble burst at once? Not so: but silently and by measured steps, like a dissolving palace of snow, it collapsed. In the superb expression of Shakspere, minted by himself, and drawn from his own aerial fancy, like a cloud it '*dislimned*'; lost its lineaments by stealthy steps. Already the word '*parting*' (for myself and my brother were under summons for Bath) hoisted the first signal for breaking up. Next, and not very long afterwards, came a mixed signal: alternate words of joy and grief—marriage and death severed the sisterly union amongst the young female servants. Then, thirdly, but many years later, vanished from earth, and from peace the deepest that can support itself on earth, summoned to a far deeper peace, the mistress of the household herself, together with her first-born child. Some years later, perhaps twenty from this time, as I stood sheltering myself from rain in a shop within the most public street of Manchester, the master of the establishment drew my attention to a gentleman on the opposite side of the street—roaming along in a reckless style of movement, and apparently insensible to the notice which he attracted. 'That,' said the master of the shop, 'was once a leading merchant in our town; but he met with great commercial embarrassments. There was no impeachment of his integrity, or (as I believe) of his discretion. But what with these commercial calamities, and deaths in his family, he lost all hope; and you see what sort of consolation it is that he seeks'—meaning to say that his style of walking argued intoxication. I did not think so. There was a settled misery in his eye, but complicated with *that* an expression of nervous distraction, that, if it should increase, would make life an intolerable burden. I never saw him again, and thought with horror of his being called in old age to face the fierce tragedies of life. For many reasons, I recoiled from forcing myself upon his notice: but I had ascertained, some time previously to this casual rencontre, that he and myself were, at that date, all that remained of the once joyous household. At present, and for many a year, I am myself the sole relic from that household sanctuary—sweet, solemn, profound—that concealed, as in some ark floating on solitary seas, eight persons, since called away, all except myself, one after one, to that rest which only could be deeper than ours was then.

When I left the K——s, I left Manchester; and during the next three years I was sent to two very different schools; first, to a public one—viz., the Bath

Grammar School, then and since famous for its excellence—secondly, to a private school in Wiltshire. At the end of the three years, I found myself once again in Manchester. I was then fifteen years old, and a trifle more; and as it had come to the knowledge of Mr. G., a banker in Lincolnshire (whom hitherto I have omitted to notice amongst my guardians, as the one too generally prevented from interfering by his remoteness from the spot, but whom otherwise I should have recorded with honour, as by much the ablest amongst them) that some pecuniary advantages were attached to a residence at the Manchester Grammar School, whilst in other respects that school seemed as eligible as any other, he had counselled my mother to send me thither. In fact, a three years' residence at this school obtained an annual allowance for seven years of nearly (if not quite) £50; which sum, added to my own patrimonial income of £150, would have made up the annual £200 ordinarily considered the proper allowance for an Oxford under-graduate. No objection arising from any quarter, this plan was adopted, and soon afterwards carried into effect.

On a day, therefore, it was in the closing autumn (or rather in the opening winter) of 1800 that my first introduction took place to the Manchester Grammar School. The school-room showed already in its ample proportions some hint of its pretensions as an endowed school, or school of that class which I believe peculiar to England. To this limited extent had the architectural sense of power been timidly and parsimoniously invoked. Beyond that, nothing had been attempted; and the dreary expanse of whitewashed walls, that at so small a cost might have been embellished by plaster-of-Paris friezes and large medallions, illustrating to the eye of the youthful student the most memorable glorifications of literature—these were bare as the walls of a poor-house or a lazaretto; buildings whose functions, as thoroughly sad and gloomy, the mind recoils from drawing into relief by sculpture or painting. But this building was dedicated to purposes that were noble.

The naked walls clamoured for decoration : and how easily might tablets have been moulded—exhibiting (as a first homage to literature) Athens, with the wisdom of Athens, in the person of Pisistratus, concentrating the general energies upon the revisal and recasting of the *Iliad*. Or (second) the Athenian captives in Sicily, within the fifth century B.C., as winning noble mercy for themselves by some

> ' Repeated air
> Of sad Electra's poet.'

Such, and so sudden, had been the oblivion of earthly passions wrought by the contemporary poet of Athens that in a moment the wrath of Sicily, with all its billows, ran down into a heavenly calm ; and he that could plead for his redemption no closer relation to Euripides than the accident of recalling some scatterings from his divine verses, suddenly found his chains dropping to the ground ; and himself, that in the morning had risen a despairing slave in a stone-quarry, translated at once as a favoured brother into a palace of Syracuse. Or, again, how easy to represent (third) 'the great Emathian conqueror,' that in the very opening of his career, whilst visiting Thebes with vengeance, nevertheless relented at the thought of literature, and

> ' Bade spare
> The house of Pindarus, when Temple and tower
> Went to the ground.'

Alexander might have been represented amongst the colonnades of some Persian capital—Ecbatana or Babylon, Susa or Persepolis—in the act of receiving from Greece, as a *nuzzur* more awful than anything within the gift of the ' barbaric East,' a jewelled casket containing the *Iliad* and the *Odyssey ;* creations that already have lived almost as long as the Pyramids.

Puritanically bald and odious therefore, in my eyes, was the hall up which my guardian and myself paced solemnly—though not Miltonically 'riding up to the Soldan's chair,' yet in fact, within a more limited kingdom, advancing to the chair of a more absolute despot.

This potentate was the head-master, or *archididascalus*, of the Manchester Grammar School; and that school was variously distinguished. It was (1) ancient, having in fact been founded by a bishop of Exeter in an early part of the sixteenth century, so as to be now, in 1856, more than 330 years old; (2) it was rich, and was annually growing richer; and (3) it was dignified by a beneficial relation to the magnificent University of Oxford.

The head-master at that time was Mr. Charles Lawson. In former editions of this work, I created him a doctor; my object being to evade too close an approach to the realities of the case, and consequently to personalities, which (though indifferent to myself) would have been in some cases displeasing to others. A doctor, however, Mr. Lawson was not; nor in the account of law a clergyman. Yet most people, governed unconsciously by the associations surrounding their composite idea of a dignified schoolmaster, invested him with the clerical character. And in reality he *had* taken deacon's orders in the Church of England. But not the less he held himself to be a layman, and was addressed as such by all his correspondents of rank, who might be supposed best to understand the technical rules of English etiquette. Etiquette in such cases cannot entirely detach itself from law. Now, in English law, as was shown in Horne Tooke's case, the rule is, *once a clergyman, and always a clergyman.* The sacred character with which ordination clothes a man is indelible. But, on the other hand, who *is* a clergyman? Not he that has taken simply the initial orders of a deacon, so at least I have heard, but he that has taken the second and full orders of a priest. If otherwise, then there was a great mistake current amongst Mr. Lawson's friends in addressing him as an esquire.

Squire or not a squire, however, parson or not a parson—whether sacred or profane—Mr. Lawson was in some degree interesting by his position and his recluse habits. Life was over with him, for its hopes and for its trials. Or at most one trial yet awaited

him, which was—to fight with a painful malady, and
fighting to die. He still had his dying to do: he was
in arrear as to *that*: else all was finished. It struck me
(but, with such limited means for judging, I might easily
be wrong) that his understanding was of a narrow order.
But that did not disturb the interest which surrounded
him now in his old age (probably seventy-five, or more),
nor make any drawback from the desire I had to spell
backwards and re-compose the text of his life. What
had been his fortunes in this world? Had they travelled
upwards or downwards? What triumphs had he enjoyed
in the sweet and solemn cloisters of Oxford? What
mortifications in the harsh world outside? Two only
had survived in the malicious traditions of 'his friends.'
He was a Jacobite (as were so many amongst my dear
Lancastrian compatriots); had drunk the Pretender's
health, and had drunk it in company with that Dr.
Byrom who had graced the *symposium* by the famous
equivocating *impromptu* [1] to the health of that prince.
Mr. Lawson had therefore been obliged to witness the
final prostration of his political party. That was his
earliest mortification. His second, about seven years
later, was, that he had been jilted; and with circumstances (at least so I heard) of cruel scorn. Was it that
*he* had interpreted in a sense too flattering for himself
ambiguous expressions of favour in the lady? or that

---

[1] '*Equivocating impromptu*':—The party had gathered in a
tumultuary way; so that some Capulets had mingled with the Mon-
tagues, one of whom called upon Dr. Byrom to drink *The King, God
bless him! and Confusion to the Pretender!* Upon which the doctor
sang out—

> ' God bless the king, of church and state defender;
> God bless (no harm in *blessing*) the Pretender!
> But who Pretender is, and who the King—
> God bless us all! that's quite another thing.'

Dr. Byrom was otherwise famous than as a Jacobite—viz., as the
author of a very elaborate shorthand, which (according to some who
have examined it) rises even to a philosophic dignity. David Hartley
in particular said of it that, ' if ever a philosophic language (as projected by Bishop Wilkins, by Leibnitz, etc.) should be brought to
bear, in that case Dr. Byrom's work would furnish the proper character
for its notation.'

she in cruel caprice had disowned the hopes which she had authorised. However this might be, half-a-century of soothing and reconciling years had cicatrised the wounds of Mr. Lawson's heart. The lady of 1752, if living in 1800, must be furiously wrinkled. And a strange metaphysical question arises: Whether, when the object of an impassioned love has herself faded into a shadow, the fiery passion itself can still survive as an abstraction, still mourn over its wrongs, still clamour for redress. I have heard of such cases. In Wordsworth's poem of *Ruth* (which was founded, as I happen to know, upon facts), it is recorded as an affecting incident, that, some months after the first frenzy of her disturbed mind had given way to medical treatment, and had lapsed into a gentler form of lunacy, she was dismissed from confinement; and upon finding herself uncontrolled among the pastoral scenes where she played away her childhood, she gradually fell back to the original habits of her life whilst yet undisturbed by sorrow. Something similar had happened to Mr. Lawson; and some time after his first shock, amongst other means for effacing that deep-grooved impression, he had laboured to replace himself, as much as was possible, in the situation of a college student. In this effort he was assisted considerably by the singular arrangement of the house attached to his official station. For an English house it was altogether an oddity, being, in fact, built upon a Roman plan. All the rooms on both storeys had their windows looking down upon a little central court. This court was quadrangular, but so limited in its dimensions, that by a Roman it would have been regarded as the *impluvium*: for Mr. Lawson, however, with a little exertion of fancy, it transmuted itself into a college quadrangle. Here, therefore, were held the daily 'callings-over,' at which every student was obliged to answer upon being named. And thus the unhappy man, renewing continually the fancy that he was still standing in an Oxford quadrangle, perhaps cheated himself into the belief that all had been a dream which concerned the caprices of the lady, and the lady herself a phantom. College usages also, which served to strengthen this fanciful *alibi*—such, for instance, as the having two plates arranged before him at dinner (one for the animal, the other for the vegetable, food)—were reproduced in Millgate. One sole luxury also, somewhat costly, which, like most young men of easy income, he had allowed himself at Oxford, was now retained long after it had become practically useless. This was a hunter for himself, and another for his groom, which he continued to keep, in spite of the increasing war-taxes, many a year after he had almost ceased to ride. Once in three or four months he would have the horses saddled and brought out. Then, with considerable effort, he swung himself into the saddle, moved off at a quiet amble, and, in about fifteen or twenty minutes, might be seen returning from an excursion of two miles, under the imagination that he had laid in a stock of exercise sufficient for another period of a hundred days. Meantime Mr. Lawson had sought his main consolation in the great classics of elder days. His senior *alumni* were always working their way through some great scenic poet that had shaken the stage of Athens; and more than one of his classes, never-ending, still beginning, were daily solacing him with the gaieties of Horace, in his Epistles or in his Satires. The Horatian jests indeed to *him* never grew old. On coming to the *plagosus Orbilius*, or any other sally of pleasantry, he still threw himself back in his arm-chair, as he *had* done through fifty years, with what seemed heart-shaking bursts of sympathetic merriment. Mr. Lawson, indeed, could afford to be sincerely mirthful over the word *plagosus*. There are gloomy tyrants, exulting in the discipline of fear, to whom and to whose pupils this word must call up remembrances too degrading for any but affected mirth. Allusions that are too fearfully personal cease to be subjects of playfulness. Sycophancy only it is that laughs; and the artificial merriment is but the language of shrinking and grovelling deprecation. Different, indeed, was the condition of the Manchester Grammar School. It was honourable both to the masters and the upper

boys, through whom only such a result was possible,
that in that school, during my knowledge of it (viz.,
during the closing year of the eighteenth century, and
the two opening years of the nineteenth), all punish-
ments, that appealed to the sense of bodily pain, had
fallen into disuse; and this at a period long before
any public agitation had begun to stir in that direction. How then was discipline maintained? It was
maintained through the self-discipline of the senior
boys, and through the efficacy of their example, combined with their system of rules. Noble are the impulses of opening manhood, where they are not utterly
ignoble: at that period, I mean, when the poetic sense
begins to blossom, and when boys are first made sensible
of the paradise that lurks in female smiles. Had the
school been entirely a day-school, too probable it is that
the vulgar brawling tendencies of boys left to themselves
would have prevailed. But it happened that the elder
section of the school—those on the brink of manhood,
and by incalculable degrees the more scholar-like section,
all who read, meditated, or began to kindle into the love
of literature—were boarders in Mr. Lawson's house. The
students, therefore, of the house carried an overwhelming
influence into the school. They were bound together
by links of brotherhood; whereas the day-scholars were
disconnected. Over and above this, it happened luckily
that there was no playground, not the smallest, attached
to the school; that is, none was attached to the *upper*
or *grammar* school. But there was also, and resting on
the same liberal endowment, a *lower* school, where the
whole machinery of teaching was applied to the lowest
mechanical accomplishments of reading and writing.
The hall in which this servile business was conducted
ran under the upper school; it was, therefore, I presume, a subterraneous duplicate of the upper hall.
And, since the upper rose only by two or three feet
above the level of the neighbouring streets, the lower
school should naturally have been at a great depth *below*
these streets. In that case it would be a dark crypt, such
as we see under some cathedrals; and it would have

argued a singular want of thoughtfulness in the founder to have laid one part of his establishment under an original curse of darkness. As the access to this plebeian school lay downwards through long flights of steps, I never found surplus energy enough for investigating the problem. But, as the ground broke away precipitously at that point into lower levels, I presume, upon consideration, that the subterranean crypt will be found open on one side to visitations from sun and moon. So that, for this base mechanic school there may, after all, have been a playground. But for ours in the upper air, I repeat, there was none; not so much as would have bleached a lady's pocket-handkerchief; and this one defect carried along with it unforeseen advantages.

Lord Bacon it is who notices the subtle policy which may lurk in the mere external figure of a table. A square table, having an undeniable head and foot, two polar extremities of what is highest and lowest, a perihelion and an aphelion, together with equatorial sides, opens at a glance a large career to ambition ; whilst a circular table sternly represses all such aspiring dreams, and so does a triangular table. Yet, if the triangle should be right-angled, then the Lucifer seated at the right-angle might argue that he *subtended* all the tenants of the hypothenuse ; being, therefore, as much nobler than they as Atlas was nobler than the globe which he carried. It was, by the way, some arrangement of this nature which constituted the original feature of distinction in John o' Groat's house, and not at all (as most people suppose) the high northern latitude of this house. John, it seems, finished the feuds for precedency, not by legislating this way or that, but by cutting away the possibility of such feuds through the assistance of a round table. The same principle must have guided King Arthur amongst his knights, Charlemagne amongst his paladins, and sailors in their effectual distribution of the peril attached to a mutinous remonstrance by the admirable device of a ' round-robin.' Even two little girls, as Harrington remarks in his *Oceana*, have oftentimes hit upon an expedient, through pure mother-wit, more effectual than all the schools of philosophy could have suggested, for insuring the impartial division of an orange; which expedient is that either of the two shall divide, but then that the other shall have the right of choice. You divide and I choose. Such is the formula; and an angel could not devise a more absolute guarantee for the equity of the division than by thus forcing the divider to become the inheritor of any possible disadvantages that he may have succeeded in creating by his own act of division. In all these cases one seemingly trivial precaution opens, in the next stage, into a world of irresistible consequences. And, in our case, an effect not less disproportionate followed out of that one accident, apparently so slight, that we had no playground. We of the seniority, who, by thoughtfulness, and the conscious dignity of dealing largely with literature, were already indisposed to boyish sports, found through the defect of a playground, that our choice and our pride were also our necessity. Even the proudest of us benefited by that coercion; for many would else have sold their privilege of pride for an hour's amusement, and have become, at least, occasional conformists. A day more than usually fine, a trial of skill more than usually irritating to the sense of special superiority, would have seduced most of us in the end into the surrender of our exclusiveness. Indiscriminate familiarity would have followed as an uncontrollable result; since to mingle with others in common acts of business may leave the sense of reserve undisturbed: but all reserve gives way before a common intercourse in pleasure. As it was, what with our confederation through housemembership, what with our reciprocal sympathies in the problems suggested by books, we had become a club of boys (amongst whom might be four or five that were even young men, counting eighteen or nineteen years) altogether as thoughtful and as self-respecting as can often exist even amongst adults. Even the subterraneous school contributed something to our self-esteem. It formed a subordinate section of our own establishment, that kept before our eyes, by force of contrast, the dignity inherent in our own constitution. Its object was to master humble accomplishments that were within the reach of *mechanic* efforts: everything mechanic is limited; whereas we felt that *our* object, even if our name of *grammar* school presented that object in what seemed too limited a shape, was substantially noble, and tended towards the infinite. But in no long time I came to see that, as to the *name*, we were all of us under a mistake. Being asked what a *grammar* school indicates, what it professes to teach, there is scarcely any man who would not reply, 'Teach? why, it teaches grammar, what else?' But this is a mistake: as I have elsewhere explained, *grammatica* in this combination does not mean grammar (though grammar also obeys the movements of a most subtle philosophy), but *literature*. Look into Suetonius. Those 'grammatici' whom he memorialises as an order of men flocking to Rome in the days of the Flavian family, were not *grammarians* at all, but what the French by a comprehensive name style *littérateurs*— that is, they were men who (1) studied literatnre, (2) who taught literature, (3) who practically produced literature. And, upon the whole, *grammatica* is perhaps the least objectionable Latin equivalent for our word *literature*.

Having thus sketched the characteristic points distinguishing the school and the presiding master (for of masters, senior and junior, there were four in this upper school), I return to my own inaugural examination. On this day, memorable to myself, as furnishing the starting-point for so long a series of days, saddened by haughty obstinacy on one side, made effective by folly on the other, no sooner had my guardian retired than Mr. Lawson produced from his desk a volume of the *Spectator*, and instructed me to throw into as good Latin as I could some paper of Steele's—not the whole, but perhaps a third part. No better exercise could have been devised for testing the extent of my skill as a Latinist. And here I ought to make an explanation. In the previous edition of these *Confessions*, writing sometimes too rapidly, and with little precision in cases of little importance, I conveyed an impression which I had not designed with regard to the true nature of my pretensions as a Grecian; and something of the same correction will apply to that narrower accomplishment which was the subject of my present examination. Neither in Greek nor in Latin was my *knowledge* very extensive; my age made *that* impossible; and especially because in those days there were no decent guides through the thorny jungles of the Latin language, far less of the Greek. When I mention that the *Port Royal* Greek Grammar translated by Dr. Nugent was about the best key extant in English to the innumerable perplexities of Greek diction, and that, for the *res metrica*, Morell's valuable *Thesaurus*, having then never been reprinted, was rarely to be seen, the reader will conclude that a schoolboy's *knowledge* of Greek could not be other than slender. Slender indeed was mine. Yet stop? *what* was slender? Simply my *knowledge* of Greek; for that knowledge stretches by tendency to the infinite; but not therefore my *command* of Greek. The *knowledge* of Greek must always hold some gross proportion to the time spent upon it,—probably, therefore, to the age of the student; but the *command* over a language, the power of adapting it plastically to the expression of your own thoughts, is almost exclusively a gift of nature, and has very little connection with time. Take the supreme trinity of Greek scholars that flourished between the English Revolution of 1688 and the beginning of the nineteenth century—which trinity I suppose to be, confessedly, Bentley, Valckenaer, and Porson: such are the men, it will be generally fancied, whose aid should be invoked, in the event of our needing some eloquent Greek inscription on a public monument. I am of a different opinion. The greatest scholars have usually proved to be the poorest composers in either of the classic languages. Sixty years ago, we had, from four separate doctors, four separate Greek versions of Gray's *Elegy*, all unworthy of the national scholarship. Yet one of these doctors was actually Porson's predecessor in the Greek chair at Cambridge. But, as he (Dr. Cooke) was an obscure man, take an undeniable Grecian, of punctilious precision —viz., Richard Dawes, the well-known author of the *Miscellanea Critica*. This man, a very *martinet* in the delicacies of Greek composition—and who *should* have been a Greek scholar of some mark, since often enough he flew at the throat of Richard Bentley—wrote and published a specimen of a Greek *Paradise Lost*, and also two most sycophantic idyls addressed to George II. on the death of his 'august' papa. It is difficult to imagine anything meaner in conception or more childish in expression than these attempts. Now, against *them* I will stake in competition a copy of iambic verses by a boy, who died, I believe, at sixteen—viz., a son of Mr. Pitt's tutor, Tomline, Bishop of Winchester.[1] Universally I contend that the faculty of clothing the thoughts in a Greek dress is a function of natural sensibility, in a great degree disconnected from the extent or the accuracy of the writer's grammatical skill in Greek.

These explanations are too long. The reader will understand, as their sum, that what I needed in such a case was, not so much a critical familiarity with the syntax of the language, or a *copia verborum*, as great agility in reviewing the relations of one idea to another, so as to present modern and unclassical objects under such aspects as might suggest periphrases in substitution for direct names, where names could not be had, and everywhere to colour my translation with as rich a display of idiomatic forms as the circumstances of the case would allow. I succeeded, and beyond my expectation.

---

[1] '*A copy of iambic verses*':—They will be found in the work on the Greek article by Middleton, Bishop of Calcutta, who was the boy's tutor. On this occasion I would wish to observe that verses like Dawes's, meant to mimic Homer or Theocritus, or more generally dactylic hexameters, are perfectly useless as tests of power to think freely in Greek. If such verses are examined, it will be found that the orchestral magnificence of the metre, and the sonorous cadence of each separate line, absolutely *force* upon the thoughts a mere necessity of being discontinuous. From this signal defect only iambic senarii are free; this metre possessing a power of plastic interfusion similar in kind, though inferior in degree, to the English blank verse when Miltonically written.

For once—being the first time that he had been known to do such a thing, but also the very last—Mr. Lawson did absolutely pay me a compliment. And with another compliment more than verbal he crowned his gracious condescensions—viz., with my provisional instalment in his highest class; not the highest at that moment, since there was one other class above us; but this other was on the wing for Oxford within some few weeks; which change being accomplished, we (viz., I and two others) immediately moved up into the supreme place.

Two or three days after this examination—viz., on the Sunday following—I transferred myself to head-quarters at Mr. Lawson's house. About nine o'clock in the evening, I was conducted by a servant up a short flight of stairs, through a series of gloomy and unfurnished little rooms, having small windows but no doors, to the common room (as in Oxford it would technically be called) of the senior boys. Everything had combined to depress me. To leave the society of accomplished women — *that* was already a signal privation. The season besides was rainy, which in itself is a sure source of depression; and the forlorn aspect of the rooms completed my dejection. But the scene changed as the door was thrown open: faces kindling with animation became visible; and from a company of .boys, numbering sixteen or eighteen, scattered about the room, two or three, whose age entitled them to the rank of leaders, came forward to receive me with a courtesy which I had not looked for. The grave kindness and the absolute sincerity of their manner impressed me most favourably. I had lived familiarly with boys gathered from all quarters of the island at the Bath Grammar School: and for some time (when visiting Lord Altamont at Eton) with boys of the highest aristocratic pretensions. At Bath and at Eton, though not equally, there prevailed a tone of higher polish; and in the air, speech, deportment of the majority could be traced at once a premature knowledge of the world. They had indeed the advantage over my new friends in graceful self-possession; but, on the other hand, the best of them suffered by comparison with these Manchester boys in the qualities of visible self-restraint and of self-respect. At Eton high rank was distributed pretty liberally; but in the Manchester school the parents of many boys were artisans, or of that rank; some even had sisters that were menial servants; and those who stood higher by pretensions of birth and gentle blood were, at the most, the sons of rural gentry or of clergymen. And I believe that, with the exception of three or four brothers, belonging to a clergyman's family at York, all were, like myself, natives of Lancashire. At that time my experience was too limited to warrant me in expressing any opinion, one way or the other, upon the relative pretensions—moral and intellectual—of the several provinces in our island. But since then I have seen reason to agree with the late Dr. Cooke Taylor in awarding the pre-eminence, as regards energy, power to face suffering, and other high qualities, to the natives of Lancashire. Even a century back, they were distinguished for the culture of refined tastes. In musical skill and sensibility, no part of Europe, with the exception of a few places in Germany, could pretend to rival them: and, accordingly, even in Handel's days, but for the chorus-singers from Lancashire, his oratorios must have remained a treasure, if not absolutely sealed, at any rate most imperfectly revealed.

One of the young men, noticing my state of dejection, brought out some brandy—a form of alcohol which I, for my part, tasted now for the first time, having previously taken only wine, and never once in quantities to affect my spirits. So much the greater was my astonishment at the rapid change worked in my state of feeling —a change which at once reinstalled me in my natural advantages for conversation. Towards this nothing was wanting but a question of sufficient interest. And a question arose naturally out of a remark addressed by one of the boys to myself, implying that perhaps I had intentionally timed my arrival so as to escape the Sunday evening exercise. No, I replied; not at all; what *was* that exercise? Simply an off-hand translation from the little work of Grotius [1] on the Evidences of Christianity. Did I know the book? No, I did not; all the direct knowledge which I had of Grotius was built upon his metrical translations into Latin of various fragments surviving from the Greek scenical poets, and these translations had struck me as exceedingly beautiful. On the other hand, his work of highest pretension, *De Jure Belli et Pacis*, so signally praised by Lord Bacon, I had not read at all; but I had heard such an account of it from a very thoughtful person as made it probable that Grotius was stronger, and felt himself stronger, on literary than on philosophic ground. Then, with regard to his little work on the Mosaic and Christian revelations, I had heard very disparaging opinions about it; two especially. One amounted to no more than this—that the question was argued with a logic far inferior, in point of cogency, to that of Lardner and Paley Here several boys interposed their loud assent, as regarded Paley in particular. Paley's *Evidences*, at that time just seven years old, had already become a subject of study amongst them. But the other objection impeached not so much the dialectic acuteness as the learning of Grotius—at least, the appropriate learning. According to the anecdote current upon this subject, Dr. Edward Pococke, the great oriental scholar of England in the seventeenth century, when called upon to translate the little work of Grotius into Arabic or Turkish, had replied by pointing to the idle legend of Mahomet's pigeon or dove, as a reciprocal messenger between the prophet and heaven—which legend had been accredited and adopted by Grotius in the blindest spirit of credulity. Such a baseless fable, Pococke alleged, would work a double mischief: not only it would ruin the authority of that particular book in the East, but would damage Christianity for generations, by making known to the followers of the Prophet that their master was undervalued amongst the Franks on the authority of nursery tales, and that these tales were accredited by the leading Frankish scholars.

[1] Entitled *De Veritate Christianæ Religionis*.

A twofold result of evil would follow: not only would our Christian erudition and our Christian scholars be scandalously disparaged; a consequence that in some cases might not be incompatible with a sense amongst Mahometans that the strength of Christianity itself was left unaffected by the errors and blunders of its champions; but, secondly, there would be in this case a strong reaction against Christianity itself. Plausibly enough it would be inferred that a vast religious philosophy could have no powerful battery of arguments in reserve, when it placed its main anti-Mahometan reliance upon so childish a fable: since, allowing even for a blameless assent to this fable amongst nations having no direct intercourse with Mussulmans, still it would argue a shocking frailty in Christianity that its main pleadings rested, not upon any strength of its own, but simply upon a weakness in its antagonist.

At this point, when the cause of Grotius seemed utterly desperate, G—— (a boy whom subsequently I had reason to admire as equally courageous, truthful, and far-seeing) suddenly changed the whole field of view. He offered no defence for the ridiculous fable of the pigeon; which pigeon, on the contrary, he represented as drawing in harness with that Christian goose which at one time was universally believed by Mahometans to lead the vanguard of the earliest Crusaders, and which, in a limited extent, really had been a true historical personage. So far he gave up Grotius as indefensible. But on the main question, and the very extensive question, of his apparent imbecility when collated with Paley, etc., suddenly and in one sentence he revolutionised the whole logic of that comparison. Paley and Lardner, he said, what was it that they sought! *Their* object was avowedly to benefit by any argument, evidence, or presumption whatsoever, no matter whence drawn, so long as it was true or probable, and fitted to sustain the credibility of any element in the Christian creed. Well, was not *that* object common to them and to Grotius? Not at all. Too often had he (the boy G——) secretly noticed the abstinence of Grotius (apparently unaccountable) from certain obvious advantages of argument, not to suspect that, in narrowing his own field of disputation, he had a deliberate purpose, and was moving upon the line of some very different policy. Clear it was to *him* that Grotius, for some reason, declined to receive evidence except from one special and limited class of witnesses Upon this, some of us laughed at such a self-limitation as a wild bravado, recalling that rope-dancing feat of some verse-writers who, through each several stanza in its turn, had gloried in dispensing with some one separate consonant, some vowel, or some diphthong, and thus achieving a triumph such as crowns with laurel that pedestrian athlete who wins a race by hopping on one leg, or wins it under the inhuman condition of confining both legs within a sack. '*No, no*,' impatiently interrupted G——. 'All such fantastic conflicts with self-created difficulties terminate in pure ostentation, and profit nobody. But the self-imposed limitations of Grotius had a special purpose, and realised a value not otherwise attainable.' If Grotius accepts no arguments or presumptions except from Mussulmans, from Infidels, or from those who rank as Neutrals, then has he adapted his book to a separate and peculiar audience. The Neutral man will hearken to authorities notoriously Neutral ; Mussulmans will show deference to the statements of Mussulmans; the Sceptic will bow to the reasonings of Scepticism. All these persons, that would have been repelled on the very threshold from such testimonies as begin in a spirit of hostility to themselves, will listen thoughtfully to suggestions offered in a spirit of conciliation ; much more so if offered by people occupying the same ground at starting as themselves.

At the cost of some disproportion, I have ventured to rehearse this inaugural conversation amongst the leaders of the school. Whether G—— were entirely correct in this application of a secret key to the little work of Grotius, I do not know. I take blame to myself that I do not ; for I also must have been called upon for my quota to the Sunday evening studies on the *De Veritate*, and must therefore have held in my hands the ready means for solving the question.[1]

Meantime, as a solitary act of silent observation in a boy not fifteen, this deciphering idea of G——'s, in direct resistance to the received idea, extorted my admiration; and equally, whether true or false as regarded the immediate fact. That any person, in the very middle storm of chase, when a headlong movement carries all impulses into one current, should in the twinkling of an eye recall himself to the unexpected 'doubles' of the game, wheel as *that* wheels, and sternly resist the instincts of the one preoccupying assumption, argues a sagacity not often heard of in boyhood. Was G—— right? In that case he picked a lock which others had failed to pick. Was he wrong? In that case he sketched the idea and outline of a better work (better, as more original and more special in its service) than any which Grotius has himself accomplished.

Not, however, the particular boy, but the particular school, it was my purpose, in this place, to signalise for praise and gratitude. In after years, when an undergraduate at Oxford, I had an opportunity of reading as it were in a mirror the characteristic pretensions and the average success of many celebrated schools. Such a mirror I found in the ordinary conversation and in the favourite reading of young gownsmen belonging to the many different colleges of Oxford. Generally speaking, each college had a filial connection (strict[2] or not strict) with some one or more of our great public schools. These, fortunately for England, are diffused through all

---

[1] Some excuse, however, for my own want of energy is suggested by the fact that very soon after my matriculation Mr. Lawson substituted for Grotius, as the Sunday evening lecture-book, Dr. Clarke's Commentary on the New Testament. 'Out of sight, out of mind'; and in that way only can I account for my own neglect to clear up the question. Or perhaps, after all, I *did* clear it up, and in a long life-march subsequently may have dropped it by the wayside.

[2] '*Strict or not strict*':—In some colleges the claims of *alumni* from certain schools were absolute; in some, I believe, conditional; in others, again, concurrent with rival claims from favoured schools or favoured counties.

her counties: and, as the main appointments to the
capital offices in such *public* schools are often vested by
law in Oxford or Cambridge, this arrangement guaran-
tees a sound system of teaching; so that any failures in
the result must presumably be due to the individual
student.    Failures, on the whole, I do not suppose that
there were.    Classical attainments that might be styled
even splendid were not then, nor are now, uncommon.
And yet in one great feature many of those schools, even
the very best, when thus tried by their fruits, left a painful memento of failure; or rather not of failure as in relation to any purpose that they steadily recognised, but
of *wilful* and *intentional* disregard, as towards a purpose
alien from any duty of theirs, or any task which they had
ever undertaken—a failure, namely, in relation to *modern*
literature—a neglect to unroll its mighty charts: and
amongst this modern literature a special neglect (such
as seems almost brutal) of our own English literature,
though pleading its patent of precedency in a voice so
trumpet-tongued.    To myself, whose homage ascended
night and day towards the great altars of English Poetry
or Eloquence, it was shocking and revolting to find in
high-minded young countrymen, burning with sensibility
that sought vainly for a corresponding object, deep un-
consciousness of an all-sufficient object—namely, in that
great inheritance of our literature which sometimes
kindled enthusiasm in our public enemies.    How painful to see or to know that vast revelations of grandeur
and beauty are wasting themselves for ever—forests
teeming with gorgeous life, floral wildernesses hidden
inaccessibly; whilst, at the same time, in contraposition
to that evil, behold a corresponding evil—viz., that with
equal prodigality the great capacities of enjoyment are running also to waste, and are everywhere burning out un-
exercised—waste, in short, in the world of things *enjoy-
able*, balanced by an equal waste in the organs and
the machineries of enjoyment!    This picture—would it
not fret the heart of an Englishman?    Some years (say
twenty) after the era of my own entrance at that Oxford
which then furnished me with records so painful of slight

regard to our national literature, behold at the court of
London a French ambassador, a man of genius blazing
(as some people thought) with nationality, but, in fact,
with something inexpressibly nobler and deeper—viz.,
patriotism. For true and unaffected patriotism will show
its love in a noble form by sincerity and truth. But
nationality, as I have always found, is mean; is dishonest; is ungenerous; is incapable of candour; and,
being continually besieged with temptations to falsehood,
too often ends by becoming habitually mendacious.
This Frenchman above all things valued literature : his
own trophies of distinction were all won upon that field :
and yet, when called upon to review the literature of
Europe, he found himself conscientiously coerced into
making his work a mere monument to the glory of one
man, and that man the son of a hostile land. The
name of Milton, in *his* estimate, swallowed up all others.
This Frenchman was Chateaubriand. The personal
splendour which surrounded him gave a corresponding
splendour to his act. And, because he, as an ambassador, was a representative man, this act might be interpreted as a representative act. The tutelary genius of
France in this instance might be regarded as bending
before that of England. But homage so free, homage
so noble, must be interpreted and received in a corresponding spirit of generosity. It was not, like the
testimony of Balaam on behalf of Israel, an unwilling
submission to a hateful truth : it was a concession, in
the spirit of saintly magnanimity, to an interest of human
nature that *as* such, transcended by many degrees all
considerations merely national.

Now, then, with this unlimited devotion to one great
luminary of our literary system emblazoned so conspicuously in the testimony of a Frenchman—that is, of one
trained, and privileged to be a public enemy—contrast
the humiliating spectacle of young Englishmen suffered
(so far as their training is concerned) to ignore the very
existence of this mighty poet. Do I mean, then, that it
would have been advisable to place the *Paradise Lost*,
and the *Paradise Regained*, and the *Samson*, in the

library of schoolboys? By no means. That mode of sensibility which deals with the Miltonic sublimity is rarely developed in boyhood. And these divine works should in prudence be reserved to the period of mature manhood. But then it should be made known that they *are* so reserved, and upon what principle of reverential regard for the poet himself. In the meantime, selections from Milton, from Dryden, from Pope, and many other writers, though not everywhere appreciable by those who have but small experience of life, would not generally transcend the intellect or sensibility of a boy sixteen or seventeen years old. And, beyond all other sections of literature, the two which I am going to mention are fitted (or might be fitted by skilful management) to engage the interest of those who are no longer boys, but have reached the age which is presumable in English university matriculation—viz., the close of the eighteenth year. Search through all languages, from Benares the mystical, and the banks of the Ganges, travelling westwards to the fountains of the Hudson, I deny that any two such *bibliothecæ* for engaging youthful interest could be brought together as these two which follow:—

First, In contradiction to M. Cousin's recent audacious assertion (redeemed from the suspicion of mendacity simply by the extremity of ignorance on which it reposes) that we English have no tolerable writer of prose subsequent to Lord Bacon, it so happens that the seventeenth century, and specially that part of it concerned in this case—viz., the latter seventy years (A.D. 1628–1700) —produced the highest efforts of eloquence (philosophic, but at the same time rhetorical and impassioned, in a degree unknown to the prose literature of France) which our literature possesses, and not a line of it but is posterior to the death of Lord Bacon. Donne, Chillingworth, Sir Thomas Browne, Jeremy Taylor, Milton, South, Barrow, form a *pleïad*, a constellation of seven golden stars, such as no literature can match in their own class. From these seven writers, taken apart from all their contemporaries, I would undertake to build up an entire body of philosophy [1] upon the supreme interests of humanity. One error of M. Cousin's doubtless lay in overlooking the fact that all conceivable problems of philosophy can reproduce themselves under a theological mask : and thus he had absolved himself from reading many English books, as presumably mere professional pleadings of Protestant polemics, which are in fact mines inexhaustible of eloquence and philosophic speculation.

Secondly, A full abstract of the English Drama from about the year 1580 to the period (say 1635) at which it was killed by the frost of the Puritanical spirit seasoning all flesh for the Parliamentary War. No literature, not excepting even that of Athens, has ever presented such a multiform theatre, such a carnival display, mask and anti-mask, of impassioned life—breathing, moving, acting, suffering, laughing.

> 'Quicquid agunt homines—votum, timor, ira, voluptas,
> Gaudia, discursus' ; [2]

—all this, but far more truly and adequately than was or could be effected in that field of composition which the gloomy satirist contemplated,—whatsoever in fact our mediæval ancestors exhibited in their 'Dance of Death,' drunk with tears and laughter,—may here be reviewed, scenically grouped, draped, and gorgeously coloured. What other national drama can pretend to any competition with this? The Athenian has in a great proportion perished ; the Roman was killed prematurely by the bloody realities of the amphitheatre, as candle-light by day-light ; the Spanish, even in the

---

[1] *'Philosophy'* :—At this point it is that the main misconception would arise. Theology, and not philosophy, most people will fancy, is likely to form the staple of these writers. But I have elsewhere maintained that the main bulk of English philosophy has always hidden itself in the English divinity. In Jeremy Taylor, for instance, are exhibited all the *practical* aspects of philosophy ; of philosophy as it bears upon Life, upon Ethics, and upon Transcendent Prudence— *i.e.* briefly upon the Greek *summum bonum.*

[2] 'All that is done by men—movement of prayer, panic, wrath, revels of the voluptuous, festivals of triumph, or gladiatorship of the intellect.' —*Juvenal,* in the prefatory lines which rehearse the prevailing themes of his own Satires gathered in the great harvests of Rome.

hands of Calderon, offers only undeveloped sketchings; and the French, besides other and profounder objections, to which no justice had yet been done, lies under the signal disadvantage of not having reached its meridian until sixty years (or two generations) after the English. In reality, the great period of the English Drama was exactly closing as the French opened:[1] consequently the French lost the prodigious advantage for scenical effects of a romantic and picturesque age. This had vanished when the French theatre culminated; and the natural result was that the fastidiousness of French taste, by this time too powerfully developed, stifled or distorted the free movements of French genius.

I beg the reader's pardon for this disproportioned digression, into which I was hurried by my love for our great national literature, my anxiety to see it amongst educational resources invested with a ministerial agency of far ampler character, but at all events to lodge a protest against that wholesale neglect of our supreme authors which leaves us open to the stinging reproach of 'treading daily with our clouted shoon' (to borrow the words of Comus) upon that which high-minded foreigners regard as the one paramount jewel in our national diadem.

---

[1] It is remarkable that in the period immediately anterior to that of Corneille, a stronger and more *living* nature was struggling for utterance in French tragedy. Guizot has cited from an early drama (I forget whether of Rotrou or of Hardy) one scene most thoroughly impassioned. The situation is that of a prince who has fixed his love upon a girl of low birth. She is faithful and constant: but the courtiers about the prince, for malicious purposes of their own, calumniate her: the prince is deluded by the plausible air of the slanders which they disperse: he believes them; but not with the result (anticipated by the courtiers) of dismissing the girl from his thoughts. On the contrary, he is haunted all the more morbidly by her image; and, in a scene which brings before us one of the vilest amongst these slanderers exerting himself to the uttermost in drawing off the prince's thoughts to alien objects, we find the prince vainly attempting any self-control, vainly striving to attend, till he is overruled by the tenderness of his sorrowing love into finding new occasions for awakening thoughts of the lost girl in the very words chiefly relied on for calling off his feelings from her image. The scene (as Guizot himself remarks) is thoroughly Shaksperian; and I venture to think that this judgment would have been countersigned by Charles Lamb.

That reproach fell heavily, as my own limited experience inclined me to fear, upon most of our great public schools, otherwise so admirably conducted.[1] But from the Manchester Grammar School any such reproach altogether rebounded. My very first conversation with the boys had arisen naturally upon a casual topic, and had shown them to be tolerably familiar with the outline of the Christian polemics in the warfare with Jew, Mahometan, Infidel, and Sceptic. But this was an exceptional case; and naturally it happened that most of us sought for the ordinary subjects of our conversational discussions in literature—viz., in our own native literature. Here it was that I learned to feel a deep respect for my new school-fellows: deep it was, then; and a larger experience has made it deeper. I have since known many literary men; men whose profession was literature; who were understood to have dedicated themselves to literature; and who sometimes had with some one special section or little nook of literature an acquaintance critically minute. But amongst such men I have found but three or four who had a knowledge which came as near to what I should consider a comprehensive knowledge as really existed amongst those boys collectively. What one boy had not, another had; and thus, by continual intercourse, the fragmentary contribution of one being integrated by the fragmentary contributions of others, gradually the attainments of each separate individual became, in some degree, the collective attainments of the whole senior common room. It is true, undoubtedly, that some parts of literature were inaccessible, simply because the books were inaccessible to boys at school—for instance, Froissart in the old translation by Lord Berners, now more than three centuries old; and some parts were, to the young, essentially repulsive. But, measuring the general quali-

[1] It will strike everybody that such works as the *Microcosm*, conducted notoriously by Eton boys, and therefore, in part, by Canning as one of their leaders at that period, must have an admirable effect, since not only it must have made it the interest of each contributor, but must even have made it his necessity, to cultivate some acquaintance with his native literature.

fications by that standard which I have since found to prevail amongst professional *littérateurs*, I felt more respectfully towards the majority of my senior school-fellows than ever I had fancied it possible that I should find occasion to feel towards any boys whatever. My intercourse with those amongst them who had any con-versational talents greatly stimulated my intellect.

This intercourse, however, fell within narrower limits soon after the time of my entrance. I acknowledge, with deep self-reproach, that every possible indulgence was allowed to me which the circumstances of the estab-lishment made possible. I had, for example, a private room allowed, in which I not only studied, but also slept at night. The room being airy and cheerful, I found nothing disagreeable in this double use of it. Naturally, however, this means of retirement tended to sequester me from my companions: for, whilst liking the society of some amongst them, I also had a deadly liking (perhaps a morbid liking) for solitude. To make my present solitude the more fascinating, my mother sent me five guineas *extra*, for the purchase of an admission to the Manchester Library; a library which I should not at present think *very* extensive, but which, however, benefited in its composition, as also in its administration, by the good sense and intelligence of some amongst its original committees. These two luxuries were truly and indeed such: but a third, from which I had anticipated even greater pleasure, turned out a total failure; and for a reason which it may be useful to mention, by way of caution to others. This was a pianoforte, together with the sum required for regular lessons from a music-master. But the first discovery I made was that practice through eight or even ten hours a day was indispens-able towards any great proficiency on this instrument. Another discovery finished my disenchantment: it was this. For the particular purpose which I had in view, it became clear that no mastery of the instrument, not even that of Thalberg, would be available. Too soon I became aware that to the deep voluptuous enjoyment of music absolute *passiveness* in the hearer is indispensable.

Gain what skill you please, nevertheless activity, vigilance, anxiety must always accompany an elaborate effort of musical execution: and so far is that from being reconcilable with the entrancement and lull essential to the true fruition of music, that, even if you should suppose a vast piece of mechanism capable of executing a whole oratorio, but requiring, at intervals, a co-operating impulse from the foot of the auditor, even *that*, even so much as an occasional touch of the foot, would utterly undermine all your pleasure. A single psychological discovery, therefore, caused my musical anticipations to evanesce. Consequently, one of my luxuries burst like a bubble at an early stage. In this state of things, when the instrument had turned out a bubble, it followed naturally that the music-master should find himself to be a bubble. But he was so thoroughly good-natured and agreeable that I could not reconcile myself to such a catastrophe. Meantime, though accommodating within certain limits, this music-master was yet a conscientious man, and a man of honourable pride. On finding, therefore, that I was not seriously making any effort to improve, he shook hands with me one fine day, and took his leave for ever. Unless it were to point a moral and adorn a tale, the piano had then become useless. It was too big to hang upon willows, and willows there were none in that neighbourhood. But it remained for months as a lumbering monument of labour misapplied, of bubbles that had burst, and of musical visions that, under psychological tests, had foundered for ever.

Yes, certainly, this particular luxury—one out of three —had proved a bubble; too surely this had foundered; but not, therefore, the other two. The quiet study, lifted by two storeys above the vapours of earth, and liable to no unseasonable intrusion; the Manchester Library, so judiciously and symmetrically mounted in all its most attractive departments—no class disproportioned to the rest: these were no bubbles; these had not foundered. Oh, wherefore, then, was it—through what inexplicable growth of evil in myself or in others—

that now in the summer of 1802, when peace was brooding over all the land, peace succeeding to a bloody seven years' war, but peace which already gave signs of breaking into a far bloodier war, some dark sympathising movement within my own heart, as if echoing and repeating in mimicry the political menaces of the earth, swept with storm-clouds across that otherwise serene and radiant dawn which should have heralded my approaching entrance into life? *Inexplicable* I have allowed myself to call this fatal error in my life, because such it *must* appear to others; since, even to myself, so often as I fail to realise the case by reproducing a reflex impression in kind, and in degree, of the suffering before which my better angel gave wáy—yes, even to myself this collapse of my resisting energies seems inexplicable. Yet again, in simple truth, now that it becomes possible, through changes worked by time, to tell the *whole* truth (and not, as in former editions, only a part of it), there really was no absolute mystery at all. But this case, in common with many others, exemplifies to my mind the mere impossibility of making full and frank 'Confessions,' whilst many of the persons concerned in the incidents are themselves surviving, or (which is worse still) if themselves dead and buried, are yet vicariously surviving in the persons of near and loving kinsmen. Rather than inflict mortifications upon people so circumstanced, any kind-hearted man will choose to mutilate his narrative; will suppress facts, and will mystify explanations. For instance, at this point in my record, it has become my right, perhaps I might say my duty, to call a particular medical man of the penultimate generation a blockhead; nay, doubtfully, to call him a criminal blockhead. But could I do this without deep compunction, so long as sons and daughters of his were still living, from whom I, when a boy, had received most hospitable attentions? Often, on the very same day which brought home to my suffering convictions the atrocious ignorance of papa, I was benefiting by the courtesies of the daughters, and by the scientific accomplishments of the son. Not the less this man, at that particular moment when a crisis of gloom was gathering over my path, became effectually my evil genius. Not that singly perhaps he could have worked any durable amount of mischief : but he, as a co-operator unconsciously with others, sealed and ratified that sentence of stormy sorrow then hanging over my head. Three separate persons, in fact, made themselves unintentional accomplices in that ruin (a ruin reaching me even at this day by its shadows) which threw me out a homeless vagrant upon the earth before I had accomplished my seventeenth year. Of these three persons, foremost came myself, through my wilful despair and resolute adjuration of all *secondary* hope : since, after all, some mitigation was possible, supposing that perfect relief might *not* be possible. Secondly, came that medical ruffian through whose brutal ignorance it happened that my malady had not been arrested before reaching an advanced stage. Thirdly, came Mr. Lawson, through whose growing infirmities it had arisen that this malady ever reached its very earliest stage. Strange it was, but not the less a fact, that Mr. Lawson was gradually becoming a curse to all who fell under his influence, through pure zealotry of conscientiousness. Being a worse man, he would have carried far deeper blessings into his circle. If he could have reconciled himself to an imperfect discharge of his duties, he would not have betrayed his insufficiency for those duties. But this he would not hear of. He persisted in travelling over the appointed course to the last inch : and the consequences told most painfully upon the comfort of all around him. By the old traditionary usages of the school, going in at seven A.M., we ought to have been dismissed for breakfast and a full hour's repose at nine. This hour of rest was in strict justice a *debt* to the students—liable to no discount either through the caprice or the tardiness of the supreme master. Yet such were the gradual encroachments upon this hour that at length the bells of the collegiate church, —which, by an ancient usage, rang every morning from half-past nine to ten, and through varying modifications of musical key and *rhythmus* that marked the advancing stages of the half-hour,—regularly announced to us, on issuing from the school-room, that the bread and milk which composed our simple breakfast must be despatched at a pace fitter for the fowls of the air than students of Grecian philosophy. But was no compensatory encroachment for our benefit allowed upon the next hour from ten to eleven? Not for so much as the fraction of a second. Inexorably as the bells, by stopping, announced the hour of ten, was Mr. Lawson to be seen ascending the steps of the school; and he that suffered most by this rigorous exaction of duties could not allege that Mr. Lawson suffered less. If he required others to pay, he also paid up to the last farthing. The same derangement took place, with the same refusal to benefit by any indemnification, at what *should* have been the two-hours' pause for dinner. Only for some mysterious reason, resting possibly upon the family arrangements of the day-scholars,—which, if once violated, might have provoked a rebellion of fathers and mothers,—he still adhered faithfully to five o'clock P.M. as the closing hour of the day's labours.

Here then stood arrayed the whole machinery of mischief in good working order; and through six months or more, allowing for one short respite of four weeks, this machinery had been operating with effect. Mr. Lawson, to begin, had (without meaning it, or so much as perceiving it) barred up all avenues from morning to night through which any bodily exercise could be obtained. Two or three chance intervals of five minutes each, and even these not consecutively arranged, composed the whole available fund of leisure out of which any stroll into the country could have been attempted. But in a great city like Manchester the very suburbs had hardly been reached before that little fraction of time was exhausted. Very soon after Mr. Lawson's increasing infirmities had begun to tell severely in the contraction of our spare time, the change showed itself powerfully in my drooping health. Gradually the liver became affected: and connected with that affection arose, what often accompanies such ailments, profound melancholy. In such circumstances, indeed under any the slightest disturbance of my health, I had authority from my guardians to call for medical advice : but I was not left to my own discretion in selecting the adviser. This person was not a physician, who would of course have expected the ordinary fee of a guinea for every visit ; nor a surgeon; but simply an apothecary. In any case of serious illness a physician would have been called in. But a less costly style of advice was reasonably held to be sufficient in any illness which left the patient strength sufficient to walk about. Certainly it ought to have been sufficient here : for no case could possibly be simpler. Three doses of calomel or blue pill, which unhappily I did not then know, would no doubt have re-established me in a week. But far better, as acting always upon me with a magical celerity and a magical certainty, would have been the authoritative prescription (privately notified to Mr. Lawson) of seventy miles' walking in each week. Unhappily my professional adviser was a comatose old gentleman, rich beyond all his needs, careless of his own practice, and standing under that painful necessity (according to the custom then regulating medical practice, which prohibited fees to apothecaries) of seeking his re-muneration in excessive deluges of medicine. Me, however, out of pure idleness, he forbore to plague with any *variety* of medicines. With sublime simplicity he confined himself to one horrid mixture, that must have suggested itself to him when prescribing for a tiger. In ordinary circumstances, and with plenty of exercise, no creature could be healthier than myself. But my organisation was perilously frail. And to fight simultaneously with such a malady and such a medicine seemed really too much. The proverb tells us that three 'flittings' are as bad as a fire. Very possibly. And I should think that, in the same spirit of reasonable equation, three such tiger-drenches must be equal to one apoplectic fit, or even to the tiger himself. Having taken two of them, which struck me as quite enough for one life, I declined to comply with the injunction of the label pasted upon each several phial—viz., *Repetatur haustus*; [1] and, instead of doing any such dangerous thing, called upon Mr. —— (the apothecary), begging to know if his art had not amongst its reputed infinity of resources any less abominable, and less shattering to a delicate system than this. 'None whatever,' he replied. Exceedingly kind he was; insisted on my drinking tea with his really amiable daughters; but continued at intervals to repeat 'None whatever—none whatever'; then, as if rousing himself to an effort, he sang out loudly 'None whatever,' which in this final utterance he toned down syllabically into 'what*ever—ever—ver—er*.' The whole wit of man, it seems, had exhausted itself upon the preparation of that one infernal mixture.

Now then we three—Mr. Lawson, the somnolent apothecary, and myself—had amongst us accomplished a climax of perplexity. Mr. Lawson, by mere dint of conscientiousness, had made health for me impossible. The apothecary had subscribed *his* little contribution, by ratifying and trebling the ruinous effects of this sedentariness. And for myself, as last in the series, it now remained to clench the operation by my own little contribution, all that I really had to offer—viz., absolute despair. Those who have ever suffered from a profound derangement of the liver may happen to know that of human despondencies through all their infinite gamut none is more deadly. Hope died within me. I could not look for medical relief, so deep being my own ignorance, so equally deep being that of my official counsellor. I could not expect that Mr. Lawson would modify his system—his instincts of duty being so strong, his incapacity to face that duty so steadily increasing. ' It comes then to this,' thought I, ' that in myself only there lurks any arrear of help': as always for every man the ultimate reliance should be on himself. But this *self* of mine seemed absolutely bankrupt; bankrupt of counsel or device—of effort in the way of action, or of suggestion in the way of plan. I had for two months been pursuing with one of my guardians

[1] ' Let the draught be repeated.'

what I meant for a negotiation ·upon this subject; the main object being to obtain some considerable abbreviation of my school residence. But *negotiation* was a self-flattering name for such a correspondence, since there never had been from the beginning any the slightest leaning on my guardian's part towards the shadow or pretence of a compromise. What compromise, indeed, was possible where neither party could concede a *part*, however small: the *whole* must be conceded, or nothing: since no *mezzo termine* was conceivable. In reality, when my eyes first glanced upon that disagreeable truth —that no opening offered for *reciprocal* concession, that the concession must all be on one side—naturally it struck me that no guardian could be expected to do *that*. At the same moment it also struck me that my guardian had all along never for a moment been arguing with a view to any *practical* result, but simply in the hope that he might win over my assent to the reasonableness of what, reasonable or not, was settled immovably. These sudden discoveries, flashing upon me simultaneously, were quite sufficient to put a summary close to the correspondence. And I saw also, which strangely had escaped me till this general revelation of disappointments, that any individual guardian—even if he *had* been disposed to concession —was but one after all amongst five. Well: this amongst the general blackness really brought a gleam of comfort. If the whole object on which I had spent so much excellent paper and midnight tallow (I am ashamed to use so vile a word, and yet truth forbids me to say *oil*), if this would have been so nearly worthless when gained, then it became a kind of pleasure to have lost it. All considerations united now in urging me to waste no more of either rhetoric, tallow, or logic, upon my impassive granite block of a guardian. Indeed, I suspected, on reviewing his last communication, that he had just reached the last inch of his patience, or (in nautical diction) had 'paid out' the entire cable by which he swung; so that, if I, acting on the apothecary's precedent of '*repetatur haustus*,' had endeavoured to administer another bolus or draught of expostulation, he would have followed my course as to the tiger-drench, in applying his potential *No* to any such audacious attempt. To my guardian, meantime, I owe this justice—that, over and above the absence on my side of any arguments wearing even a colourable strength (for to him the suffering from biliousness must have been a mere word), he had the following weighty consideration to offer, 'which even this foolish boy' (to himself he would say) 'will think material some three years ahead.' My patrimonial income, at the moment of my father's death, like that of all my brothers (then three), was exactly £150 per annum.[1] Now, according to the current belief, or boldly, one might say, according to the avowed traditional maxim throughout England, such an income was too little for an undergraduate, keeping his four terms annually at Oxford or Cambridge. Too little—by how much? By £50: the adequate income being set down at just £200. Consequently the precise sum by which my income was supposed (falsely supposed, as subsequently my own experience convinced me) to fall short of the income needed for Oxford, was that very sum which the funds of the Manchester Grammar School allocated to every student resident for a period of three years; and allocated not merely through a corresponding period of three years, but of seven years. Strong should have been the reasons that could neutralise such overwhelming pleadings of just and honourable prudence for submitting to the further residence required. O reader, urge not the crying arguments that spoke so tumultuously against me. Too sorrowfully I feel them. Out of thirty-six months' residence required, I had actually completed nineteen—*i.e.* the better half. Still, on the other hand, it is true that my sufferings were almost insupportable; and, but

[1] '*£150 per annum*':—Why in a long minority of more than fourteen years this was not improved, I never could learn. Nobody was open to any suspicion of positive embezzlement: and yet this case must be added to the other cases of passive neglects and negative injuries which so extensively disfigure the representative picture of guardianship all over Christendom.

for the blind unconscious conspiracy of two persons, these sufferings would either (1) never have existed, or (2) would have been instantly relieved. In a great city like Manchester lay, probably, a ship-load of that same mercury which, by one fragment, not so large as an acorn, would have changed the colour of a human life, or would have intercepted the heavy funeral knell —heavy, though it may be partially muffled—of his own fierce self-reproaches.

But now, at last, came over me, from the mere excess of bodily suffering and mental disappointments, a frantic and rapturous re-agency. In the United States the case is well known, and many times has been described by travellers, of that furious instinct which, under a secret call for saline variations of diet, drives all the tribes of buffaloes for thousands of miles to the common centre of the 'Salt-licks.' Under such a compulsion does the locust, under such a compulsion does the leeming, traverse its mysterious path. They are deaf to danger, deaf to the cry of battle, deaf to the trumpets of death. Let the sea cross their path, let armies with artillery bar the road, even these terrific powers can arrest only by destroying; and the most frightful abysses, up to the very last menace of engulfment, up to the very instant of absorption, have no power to alter or retard the line of their inexorable advance.

Such an instinct it was, such a rapturous command— even so potent, and alas! even so blind—that, under the whirl of tumultuous indignation and of new-born hope, suddenly transfigured my whole being. In the twinkling of an eye, I came to an adamantine resolution —not as if issuing from any act or any choice of my own, but as if passively received from some dark oracular legislation external to myself. That I would elope from Manchester—this was the resolution. *Abscond* would have been the word, if I had meditated anything criminal. But whence came the indignation, and the hope? The indignation arose naturally against my three tormentors (guardian, Archididascalus, and the professor of tigrology) for those who *do* substantially co-operate to one result, however little designing it, unavoidably the mind unifies as a hostile confederacy. But the hope—how shall I explain *that?* Was it the first-born of the resolution, or was the resolution the first-born of the hope? Indivisibly they went together, like thunder and lightning ; or each interchangeably ran before and after the other. Under that transcendent rapture which the prospect of sudden liberation let loose, all that natural anxiety which should otherwise have interlinked itself with my anticipations was actually drowned in the blaze of joy, as the light of the planet Mercury is lost and confounded on sinking too far within the blaze of the solar beams. Practically I felt no care at all stretching beyond two or three weeks. Not as being heedless and improvident ; my tendencies lay generally in the other direction. No ; the cause lurked in what Wordsworth, when describing the festal state of France during the happy morning-tide of her First Revolution (1788–1790), calls '*the senselessness of joy*': this it was, joy—headlong—frantic—irreflec-tive—and (as Wordsworth truly calls it), for that very reason, *sublime*[1]—which swallowed up all capacities of rankling care or heart-corroding doubt. I was, I had been long, a captive : I was in a house of bondage : one fulminating word—*Let there be freedom*—spoken from some hidden recess in my own will, had as by an earthquake rent asunder my prison gates. At any minute I could walk out. Already I trod by anti-cipation the sweet pastoral hills, already I breathed gales of the everlasting mountains, that to my feelings blew from the garden of Paradise ; and in that vestibule of an earthly heaven it was no more possible for me to see vividly or in any lingering detail the thorny cares which might hereafter multiply around me than amongst the roses of June, and on the loveliest of June mornings, I could gather depression from the glooms of the last December.

[1] '*The senselessness of joy was then sublime.*'—Wordsworth at Calais in 1802 (see his sonnets), looking back through thirteen years to the great era of social resurrection, in 1788–89, from a sleep of ten centuries.

To go was settled. But *when* and *whither*? *When* could have but one answer; for on more reasons than one I needed summer weather, and as much of it as possible. Besides that, when August came, it would bring along with it my own birth-day: now, one codicil in my general vow of freedom had been that my seventeenth birth-day should not find me at school. Still I needed some trifle of preparation. Especially I needed a little money. I wrote, therefore, to the only confidential friend that I had—viz., Lady Carbery. Originally, as early friends of my mother's, both she and Lord Carbery had distinguished me at Bath and elsewhere, for some years, by flattering attentions; and, for the last three years in particular, Lady Carbery, a young woman some ten years older than myself, and who was as remarkable for her intellectual pretensions as she was for her beauty and her benevolence, had maintained a correspondence with me upon questions of literature. She thought too highly of my powers and attainments, and everywhere spoke of me with an enthusiasm that, if I had been five or six years older, and had possessed any personal advantages, might have raised smiles at her expense. To her I now wrote, requesting the loan of five guineas. A whole week passed without any answer. This perplexed and made me uneasy: for her ladyship was rich by a vast fortune removed entirely from her husband's control; and, as I felt assured, would have cheerfully sent me twenty times the sum asked, unless her sagacity had suggested some suspicion (which seemed impossible) of the real purposes which I contemplated in the employment of the five guineas. Could I incautiously have said anything in my own letter tending that way? Certainly not; then why—— But at that moment my speculations were cut short by a letter bearing a coroneted seal. It was from Lady Carbery, of course, and enclosed ten guineas instead of five. Slow in those days were the mails; besides which, Lady Carbery happened to be down at the seaside, whither my letter had been sent after her. Now, then, including my own pocket-money, I possessed a dozen guineas; which seemed sufficient for my immediate purpose; and all ulterior emergencies, as the reader understands, I trampled under foot. This sum, however, spent at inns on the most economic footing, could not have held out for much above a calendar month; and, as to the plan of selecting secondary inns, these are not always cheaper; but the main objection is that in the solitary stations amongst the mountains (Cambrian no less than Cumbrian) there is often no choice to be found: the high-priced inn is the only one. Even this dozen of guineas it became necessary to diminish by three. The age of 'vails' and perquisites to three or four servants at any gentleman's house where you dined—this age, it is true, had passed away by thirty years perhaps. But that flagrant abuse had no connexion at all with the English custom of distributing money amongst that part of the domestics whose daily labours may have been increased by a visitor's residence in the family for some considerable space of time. This custom (almost peculiar, I believe, to the English gentry) is honourable and just. I personally had been trained by my mother, who detested sordid habits, to look upon it as ignominious in a gentleman to leave a household without acknowledging the obliging services of those who cannot openly remind him of their claims. On this occasion, mere necessity compelled me to overlook the housekeeper: for to her I could not have offered less than two or three guineas; and, as she was a fixture, I reflected that I might send it at some future period. To three inferior servants I found that I ought not to give less than one guinea each: so much, therefore, I left in the hands of G——, the most honourable and upright of boys; since to have given it myself would have been prematurely to publish my purpose. These three guineas deducted, I still had nine, or thereabouts. And now all things were settled, except one: the *when* was settled, and the *how;* but not the *whither.* That was still *sub judice.*

My plan originally had been to travel northwards— viz., to the region of the English Lakes. That little mountainous district, lying stretched like a pavilion between four well-known points—viz., the small towns of Ulverstone and Penrith as its two poles, south and north ; between Kendal, again, on the east, and Egremont on the west—measuring on the one diameter about forty miles, and on the other perhaps thirty-five—had for me a secret fascination, subtle, sweet, fantastic, and even from my seventh or eighth year spiritually strong. The southern section of that district, about eighteen or twenty miles long, which bears the name of Furness, figures in the eccentric geography of English law as a section of Lancashire, though separated from that county by the estuary of Morecambe Bay : and therefore, as Lancashire happened to be my own native county, I had from childhood, on the strength of this mere legal fiction, cherished as a mystic privilege, slender as a filament of air, some fraction of denizenship in the fairy little domain of the English Lakes. The major part of these lakes lies in Westmoreland and Cumberland : but the sweet reposing little water of Esthwaite, with its few emerald fields, and the grander one of Coniston, with the sublime cluster of mountain groups, and the little network of quiet dells lurking about its head [1] all the way back to Grasmere, lie in or near the upper chamber of Furness ; and all these, together with the ruins of the once glorious

---

[1] 'Its head' :—That end of a lake which receives the rivulets and brooks feeding its waters is locally called its *head ;* and, in continuation of the same constructive image, the counter terminus, which discharges its surplus water, is called its *foot.* By the way, as a suggestion from this obvious distinction, I may remark that in all cases the very existence of a head and a foot to any sheet of water defeats the malice of Lord Byron's sneer against the lake poets, in calling them by the contemptuous designation of '*pond* poets' ; a variation which some part of the public readily caught up as a natural reverberation of that spitefulness, so petty and apparently so groundless, which notoriously Lord Byron cherished against Wordsworth steadily, and more fitfully against Southey. The effect of transforming a living image—an image of restless motion—into an image of foul stagnation was tangibly apprehensible. But was it that contradistinguished the ' *vivi lacus*' of Virgil from rotting ponds mantled with verdant slime ? To have, or *not* to have, a head and a foot (*i.e.* a principle of perpetual change) is at the very heart of this distinction ; and to substitute for *lake* a term which ignores and negatives the very differential principle that constitutes a lake—viz., its current and its eternal mobility—is to offer an insult in which the insulted party has no interest or concern.

abbey, had been brought out not many years before into sunny splendour by the great enchantress of that generation—Anne Radcliffe. But more even than Anne Radcliffe had the landscape painters, so many and so various, contributed to the glorification of the English lake district; drawing out and impressing upon the heart the sanctity of repose in its shy recesses—its alpine grandeurs in such passes as those of Wastdale-head, Langdale-head, Borrowdale, Kirkstone, Hawsdale, etc., together with the monastic peace which seems to brood over its peculiar form of pastoral life, so much nobler (as Wordsworth notices) in its stern simplicity and continual conflict with danger hidden in the vast draperies of mist overshadowing the hills, and amongst the armies of snow and hail arrayed by fierce northern winters, than the effeminate shepherd's life in the classical Arcadia, or in the flowery pastures of Sicily.

Amongst these attractions that drew me so strongly to the Lakes, there had also by that time arisen in this lovely region the deep deep magnet (as to me *only* in all this world it then was) of William Wordsworth. Inevitably this close connexion of the poetry which most of all had moved me with the particular region and scenery that most of all had fastened upon my affections, and led captive my imagination, was calculated, under ordinary circumstances, to impress upon my fluctuating deliberations a summary and decisive bias. But the very depth of the impressions which had been made upon me, either as regarded the poetry or the scenery, was too solemn and (unaffectedly I may say it) too spiritual, to clothe itself in any hasty or chance movement as at all adequately expressing its strength, or reflecting its hallowed character. If you, reader, were a devout Mahometan, throwing gazes of mystical awe daily towards Mecca, or were a Christian devotee looking with the same rapt adoration to St. Peter's at Rome, or to El Kodah, the Holy City of Jerusalem (so called even amongst the Arabs, who hate both Christian and Jew)— how painfully would it jar upon your sensibilities if some friend, sweeping past you upon a high road, with a train (according to the circumstances) of dromedaries or of wheel carriages, should suddenly pull up, and say, 'Come, old fellow, jump up alongside of me; I'm off for the Red Sea, and here's a spare dromedary,' or 'Off for Rome, and here's a well-cushioned barouche.' Seasonable and convenient it might happen that the invitation were; but still it would shock you that a journey which, with or without your consent, could not *but* assume the character eventually of a saintly pilgrimage, should arise and take its initial movement upon a casual summons, or upon a vulgar opening of momentary convenience. In the present case, under no circumstances should I have dreamed of presenting myself to Wordsworth. The principle of 'veneration' (to speak phrenologically) was by many degrees too strong in me for any such overture on my part. Hardly could I have found the courage to meet and to answer such an overture coming from *him*. I could not even tolerate the prospect (as a bare possibility) of Wordsworth's hearing my name first of all associated with some case of pecuniary embarrassment. And, apart from all *that*, it vulgarised the whole 'interest' (no other term can I find to express the case collectively)—the whole 'interest' of poetry and the enchanted land—equally it vulgarised person and thing, the vineyard and the vintage, the gardens and the ladies, of the Hesperides, together with all their golden fruitage, if I should rush upon them in a hurried and thoughtless state of excitement. I remembered the fine caution of this subject involved in a tradition preserved by Pausanias. Those (he tells us) who visited by night the great field of Marathon (where at certain times phantom cavalry careered, flying and pursuing) in a temper of vulgar sight-seeking, and under no higher impulse than the degrading one of curiosity, were met and punished severely in the dark, by the same sort of people, I presume, as those who handled Falstaff so roughly in the venerable shades of Windsor: whilst loyal visitors, who came bringing a true and filial sympathy with the grand deeds of their Athenian ancestors, who came as children of the same hearth, met with the most gracious acceptance, and fulfilled all the purposes of a pilgrimage or sacred mission. Under my present circumstances, I saw that the very motives of love and honour, which would have inclined the scale so powerfully in favour of the northern lakes, were exactly those which drew most heavily in the other direction—the circumstances being what they were as to hurry and perplexity. And just at that moment suddenly unveiled itself another powerful motive against taking the northern direction—viz., consideration for my mother—which made my heart recoil from giving her too great a shock; and in what other way could it be mitigated than by my personal presence in a case of emergency? For such a purpose North Wales would be the best haven to make for, since the road thither from my present home lay through Chester—where at that time my mother had fixed her residence.

If I had hesitated (and hesitate I did very sincerely) about such a mode of expressing the consideration due to my mother, it was not from any want of decision in my feeling, but really because I feared to be taunted with this act of tenderness, as arguing an exaggerated estimate of my own importance in my mother's eyes. To be capable of causing any alarming shock, must I not suppose myself an object of special interest? No: I did not agree to that inference. But no matter. Better to stand ten thousand sneers than one abiding pang, such as time could not abolish, of bitter self-reproach. So I resolved to face this taunt without flinching, and to steer a course for St. John's Priory,—my mother's residence near Chester. At the very instant of coming to this resolution, a singular accident occurred to confirm it. On the very day before my rash journey commenced, I received through the post-office a letter bearing this address in a foreign handwriting—*A Monsieur Monsieur de Quincy, Chester*. This iteration of the *Monsieur*, as a courteous French fashion [1] for effecting something

---

[1] '*As a courteous French fashion*':—And not at all a modern fashion. That famous Countess of Derby (Charlotte de Tremouille) who presided in the defence of Lathom House (which, and not Knowsley, was then

equivalent to our own *Esquire*, was to me at that time an unintelligible novelty. The best way to explain it was to read the letter; which, to the extent of *mon possible*, I did, but vainly attempted to decipher. So much, however, I spelled out as satisfied me that the letter could not have been meant for myself. The post-mark was, I think, *Hamburgh*: but the date within was from some place in Normandy; and eventually it came out that the person addressed was a poor emigrant, some relative of Quatremère de Quincy,[1] who had come to Chester, probably as a teacher of French, and now in 1802 found his return to France made easy by the brief and hollow peace of Amiens. Such an obscure person was naturally unknown to any English post-office; and the letter had been forwarded to myself, as the oldest male member of a family at that time necessarily well known in Chester.

I was astonished to find myself translated by a touch of the pen not only into a *Monsieur*, but even into a self-multiplied *Monsieur;* or, speaking algebraically, into the square of Monsieur; having a chance at some future day of being perhaps cubed into Monsieur. From the letter, as I had hastily torn it open, out dropped a draft upon Smith, Payne & Smith for somewhere about forty guineas. At this stage of the revelations opening upon me, it might be fancied that the interest of the case thickened: since undoubtedly, if this windfall could be seriously meant for myself, *and no mistake*, never descended upon the head of man, in the outset of a

the capital domicile of the Stanleys), when addressing Prince Rupert, sometimes superscribes her envelope *A Monseigneur le Prince Rupert*, but sometimes *A Monsieur Monsieur le Prince Rupert*. This was in 1644, the year of Marston Moor, and the penultimate year of the Parliamentary War.

1 ' *De Quincy*':—The family of De Quincey, or Quincy, or Quincie (spelt of course, like all proper names, under the anarchy prevailing as to orthography until the last one hundred and fifty years, in every possible form open to human caprice), was originally Norwegian. Early in the eleventh century this family emigrated from Norway to the South; and since then it has thrown off three separate swarms—French, English, and Anglo-American—each of which writes the name with its own slight variations. A brief outline of their migrations will be found in the Appendix.

perilous adventure, aid more seasonable, nay, more melodramatically critical. But alas! my eye is quick to value the logic of evil chances. Prophet of evil I ever am to myself: forced for ever into sorrowful auguries that I have no power to hide from my own heart, no, not through one night's solitary dreams. In a moment I saw too plainly that I was not Monsieur. I might be *Monsieur*, but not *Monsieur to the second power*. Who indeed could be *my* debtor to the amount of forty guineas? If there really *was* such a person, why had he been so many years in liquidating his debt? How shameful to suffer me to enter upon my seventeenth year before he made known his debt, or even his amiable existence! Doubtless, in strict morals, this dreadful procrastination could not be justified. Still, as the man was apparently testifying his penitence, and in the most practical form (viz., payment), I felt perfectly willing to grant him absolution for past sins, and a general release from all arrears, if any should remain, through all coming generations. But alas! the mere seasonableness of the remittance floored my hopes. A five-guinea debtor might have been a conceivable being: such a debtor might exist in the flesh: *him* I could believe in; but further my faith would not go; and, if the money were, after all, *bonâ fide* meant for myself, clearly it must come from the Fiend: in which case it became an open question whether I ought to take it. At this stage the case had become a Sphinx's riddle; and the solution, if any, must be sought in the letter. But, as to the letter, O heaven and earth! if the Sphinx of old conducted her intercourse with Oedipus by way of letter, and propounded her wicked questions through the post-office of Thebes, it strikes me that she needed only to have used French penmanship in order to baffle that fatal decipherer of riddles for ever and ever. At Bath, where the French emigrants mustered in great strength (six thousand, I have heard) during the three closing years of the last century, I, through my mother's acquaintance with several leading families amongst them, had gained a large experience of French caligraphy. From this ex-

perience I had learned that the French aristocracy still
persisted (*did* persist at that period, 1797–1800) in a
traditional contempt for all accomplishments of that
class as clerkly and plebeian, fitted only (as Shakspere
says, when recording similar prejudices amongst his own
countrymen) to do 'yeoman's service.' One and all,
they delegated the care of their spelling to *valets* and
*femmes-de-chambre;* sometimes even those persons who
scoured their blankets and counterpanes scoured their
spelling—that is to say, their week-day spelling; but, as
to their Sunday spelling, that superfine spelling which
they reserved for their efforts in literature, this was consigned to the care of compositors. Letters written by
the royal family of France in 1792–93 still survive, in
the memoirs of Cléry and others amongst their most
faithful servants, which display the utmost excess of
ignorance as to grammar and orthography. Then, as
to the penmanship, all seemed to write the same hand,
and with the same piece of most ancient wood, or
venerable skewer; all alike scratching out stiff perpendicular letters, as if executed (I should say) with a pair
of snuffers. I do not speak thus in any spirit of derision.
Such accomplishments were *wilfully* neglected, and even
ambitiously, as if in open proclamation of scorn for the
arts by which humbler people oftentimes got their bread.
And a man of rank would no more conceive himself
dishonoured by any deficiencies in the snobbish accomplishments of penmanship, grammar, or correct
orthography, than a gentleman amongst ourselves by
inexpertness in the mystery of cleaning shoes, or of
polishing furniture. The result, however, from this
systematic and ostentatious neglect of caligraphy is
oftentimes most perplexing to all who are called upon
to decipher their MSS. It happens, indeed, that the
product of this carelessness thus far differs : always it
is coarse and inelegant, but sometimes (say in 1-20th
of the cases) it becomes specially legible. Far otherwise
was the case before me. Being greatly hurried on this
my farewell day, I could not make out two consecutive sentences. Unfortunately, one-half of a sentence

sufficed to show that the enclosure belonged to some needy Frenchman living in a country not his own, and struggling probably with the ordinary evils of such a condition—friendlessness and exile. Before the letter came into my hands, it had already suffered some days' delay. When I noticed this, I found my sympathy with the poor stranger naturally quickened. Already, and unavoidably, he had been suffering from the vexation of a letter delayed; but henceforth, and continually more so, he must be suffering from the anxieties of a letter gone astray. Throughout this farewell day I was unable to carve out any opportunity for going up to the Manchester Post-office; and, without a distinct explanation in my own person, exonerating myself, on the written acknowledgment of the post-office, from all further responsibility, I was most reluctant to give up the letter. It is true that the necessity of committing a forgery (which crime in those days was punished inexorably with death) before the money could have been fraudulently appropriated would, *if made known to the public*, have acquitted any casual holder of the letter from all suspicion of dishonest intentions. But the danger was that, during the suspense and progress of the case whilst awaiting its final settlement, ugly rumours should arise and cling to one's name amongst the many that would hear only a fragmentary version of the whole affair.

At length all was ready. Midsummer, like an army with banners, was moving through the heavens; already the longest day had passed; those arrangements, few and imperfect, through which I attempted some partial evasion of disagreeable contingencies likely to arise, had been finished: what more remained for me to do of things that I was able to do? None; and yet, though now at last free to move off, I lingered; lingered as under some sense of dim perplexity, or even of relenting love for the very captivity itself which I was making so violent an effort to abjure, but more intelligibly for all the external objects, living or inanimate, by which that captivity had been surrounded and gladdened. What I was hastening to desert, nevertheless I grieved to desert; and, but for the foreign letter, I might have long continued to loiter and procrastinate. That, however, through various and urgent motives which it suggested, quickened my movements; and the same hour which brought this letter into my hands witnessed my resolution (uttered *audibly* to myself in my study) that early on the next day I would take my departure. A day, therefore, had at length arrived, had somewhat suddenly arrived, which would be the last, the very last, on which I should make my appearance in the school.

It is a just and a feeling remark of Dr. Johnson's that we never do anything consciously for the last time (of things, that is to say, which we have been long in the habit of doing) without sadness of heart. The secret sense of a farewell or testamentary act I carried along with me into every word or deed of this memorable day. Agent or patient, singly or one of a crowd, I heard for ever some sullen echo of valediction in every change, casual or periodic, that varied the revolving hours from morning to night. Most of all, I felt this valedictory sound as a pathetic appeal when the closing hour of five P.M. brought with it the solemn evening service of the English Church—read by Mr. Lawson; read now, as always, under a reverential stillness of the entire school. Already in itself, without the solemnity of prayers, the decaying light of the dying day suggests a mood of pensive and sympathetic sadness. And, if the changes in the light are less impressively made known so early as five o'clock in the depth of summer-tide, not the less we are sensible of being as near to the hours of repose, and to the secret dangers of the night, as if the season were mid-winter. Even thus far there was something that oftentimes had profoundly impressed me in this evening liturgy, and its special prayer against the perils of darkness. But greatly was that effect deepened by the symbolic treatment which this liturgy gives to this darkness and to these perils. Naturally, when contemplating that treatment, I had been led vividly to feel the memorable *rhabdomancy*[1] or magical power of evocation which Christianity has put forth here and in parallel cases. The ordinary physical rhabdomantist, who undertakes to evoke from the dark chambers of our earth wells of water lying far below its surface, and more rarely to evoke minerals, or hidden deposits of jewels and gold, by some magnetic sympathy between his rod and the occult object of his divination, is able to indicate the spot at which this object can be hopefully sought for. Not otherwise has the marvellous magnetism of Christianity called up from darkness sentiments the most august, previously inconceivable, formless, and without life; for previously there had been no religious philosophy equal to the task of ripening such sentiments; but also, at the same time, by incarnating these sentiments in images of corresponding grandeur, it has so

---

[1] '*Rhabdomancy*':—The Greek word *manteia* (μαντεία), represented by the English form *mancy*, constitutes the stationary element in a large family of compounds: it means *divination*, or the art of magically deducing some weighty inference (generally prophetic) from any one of the many dark sources sanctioned by Pagan superstition. And universally the particular source relied on is expressed in the prior half of the compound. For instance, *oneiros* is the Greek word for a dream; and therefore *oneiromancy* indicates that mode of prophecy which is founded upon the interpretation of dreams. *Ornis*, again (in the genitive case *ornithos*), is the common Greek word for a bird; accordingly, *ornithomancy* means prophecy founded on the particular mode of flight noticed amongst any casual gathering of birds. *Cheir* (χείρ) is Greek for the hand; whence *cheiromancy* expresses the art of predicting a man's fortune by the lines in his hand, or (under its Latin form from *palma*) *palmistry*: *Nekros*, a dead man, and consequently *necromancy*, prophecy founded on the answer extorted either from phantoms, as by the Witch of Endor, or from the corpse itself, as by Lucan's witch Erichtho. I have allowed myself to wander into this ample illustration of the case, having for many years been taxed by ingenious readers (confessing their own classical ignorance) with too scanty explanations of my meaning. I go on to say that the Greek word *rhabdos* (ῥάβδος), a rod—not that sort of rod which the Roman lictors carried, viz., a bundle of twigs, but a wand about as thick as a common cedar pencil, or at most, as the ordinary brass rod of stair-carpets—this, when made from a willow-tree, furnished of old, and furnishes to this day in a southern county of England, a potent instrument of divination. But let it be understood that *divination* expresses an idea ampler by much than the word *prophecy*: whilst even this word *prophecy*, already more limited than divination, is most injuriously narrowed in our received translation of the Bible. To unveil or decipher what is hidden—that is, in effect, the meaning of divination. And, accordingly, in the writings of St.

exalted their character as to lodge them eternally in human hearts.

Flowers, for example, that are so pathetic in their beauty, frail as the clouds, and in their colouring as gorgeous as the heavens, had through thousands of years been the heritage of children—honoured as the jewellery of God only by *them*—when suddenly the voice of Christianity, counter-signing the voice of infancy, raised them to a grandeur transcending the Hebrew throne, although founded by God himself, and pronounced Solomon in all his glory not to be arrayed like one of these. Winds again, hurricanes, the eternal breathings, soft or loud, of Æolian power, wherefore had they, raving or sleeping, escaped all moral arrest and detention? Simply because vain it were to offer a nest for the reception of some new moral birth whilst no religion is yet moving amongst men that can furnish

Paul the phrase *gifts of prophecy* never once indicates what the English reader supposes, but *exegetic* gifts, gifts of analysis applied to what is dark, of analysis applied to what is logically perplexed, of expansion applied to what is condensed, of practical improvement applied to what might else be overlooked as purely speculative. In Somersetshire, which is a county the most ill-watered of all in England, upon building a house, there arises uniformly a difficulty in selecting a proper spot for sinking a well. The remedy is to call in a set of local rhabdomantists. These men traverse the adjacent ground, holding the willow rod horizontally: wherever that dips, or inclines itself spontaneously to the ground, *there* will be found water. I have myself not only seen the process tried with success, but have witnessed the enormous trouble, delay, and expense, accruing to those of the opposite faction who refused to benefit by this art. To pursue the tentative plan (*i.e.* the plan of trying for water by boring at haphazard) ended, so far as I was aware, in multiplied vexation. In reality, these poor men are, after all, more philosophic than those who scornfully reject their services. For the artists obey unconsciously the logic of Lord Bacon: *they* build upon a long chain of induction, upon the uniform results of their life-long experience. But the counter faction do not deny this experience: all they have to allege is that agreeably to any laws known to themselves *a priori*, there ought not to be any such experience. Now, a sufficient course of facts overthrows all antecedent plausibilities. Whatever science or scepticism may say, most of the tea-kettles in the vale of Wrington are filled by *rhabdomancy*. And, after all, the supposed *a priori* scruples against this rhabdomancy are only such scruples as would, antecedently to a trial, have pronounced the mariner's compass impossible. There is in both cases alike a blind sympathy of some unknown force, which no man can explain, with a passive index that practically guides you aright—even if Mephistopheles should be at the bottom of the affair.

such a birth. Vain is the image that should illustrate
a heavenly sentiment, if the sentiment is yet unborn.
Then, first, when it had become necessary to the purposes of a spiritual religion that the spirit of man, as the
fountain of all religion, should in some commensurate
reflex image have its grandeur and its mysteriousness
emblazoned, suddenly the pomp and mysterious path of
winds and tempests, blowing whither they list, and from
what fountains no man knows, are cited from darkness
and neglect, to give and to receive reciprocally an impassioned glorification, where the lower mystery enshrines
and illustrates the higher. Call for the grandest of all
earthly spectacles, what is *that*? It is the sun going to
his rest. Call for the grandest of all human sentiments,
what is *that*? It is that man should forget his anger
before he lies down to sleep. And these two grandeurs,
the mighty sentiment and the mighty spectacle, are by
Christianity married together.

Here again, in his prayer 'Lighten our darkness,
we beseech thee, O Lord!' were the darkness and the
great shadows of night made symbolically significant:
these great powers, Night and Darkness, that belong to
aboriginal Chaos, were made representative of the perils
that continually menace poor afflicted human nature.
With deepest sympathy I accompanied the prayer against
the perils of darkness—perils that I seemed to see, in
the ambush of midnight solitude, brooding around the
beds of sleeping nations; perils from even worse forms
of darkness shrouded within the recesses of blind human
hearts; perils from temptations weaving unseen snares
for our footing; perils from the limitations of our own
misleading knowledge.

Prayers had finished. The school had dissolved itself.
Six o'clock came, seven, eight. By three hours nearer
stood the dying day to its departure. By three hours
nearer, therefore, stood we to that darkness which our
English liturgy calls into such symbolic grandeur, as
hiding beneath its shadowy mantle all perils that besiege
our human infirmity. But in summer, in the immediate
suburbs of midsummer, the vast scale of the heavenly

movements is read in their slowness. Time becomes
the expounder of Space. And now, though eight o'clock
has struck, the sun was still lingering above the horizon :
the light, broad and gaudy, having still two hours of
travel to face before it would assume that tender fading
hue prelusive to the twilight.[1] Now came the last official
ceremony of the day : the students were all mustered ;
and the names of all were challenged according to the
order of precedence. My name, as usual, came first.[2]
Stepping forward, I passed Mr. Lawson, and bowed to
him, looking earnestly in his face, and saying to myself,
' He is old and infirm, and in this world I shall not see
him again.' I was right ; I never *did* see him again,
nor ever shall. He looked at me complacently ; smiled
placidly ; returned my salutation (not knowing it to be

---

[1] ' *To the twilight* ' :—*i.e.* to the second twilight : for I remember to
have read in some German work upon Hebrew antiquities, and also in
a great English divine of 1630 (namely, Isaac Ambrose), that the Jews
in elder times made two twilights, first and second ; the first they
called the dove's twilight, or crepusculum of the day ; the second they
called the raven's twilight, or crepusculum of the night.

[2] ' *First* ' :—Within the school I should *not* have been first : for in
the trinity which composed the head class there was no absolute or
meritorious precedence, but simply a precedence of chance. Our dignity,
as leaders of the school, raised us above all petty competitions ; yet, as
it was unavoidable to stand in some order, this was regulated by seniority. I, therefore, as junior amongst the three, was *tertius inter
pares.* But my two seniors happened to be day-scholars : so that, in
Mr. Lawson's house, I rose into the supreme place. *There*, I was
*princeps senatûs.* Such trivial circumstantialities I notice, as checks
upon all openings to inaccuracy, great or small. It would vitiate the
interest which any reader might otherwise take in this narrative, if for
one moment it were supposed that any feature of the case were var-
nished or distorted. From the very first, I had been faithful to the
most rigorous law of accuracy—even in absolute trifles. But I became
even more jealous over myself, after an Irish critic, specially brilliant
as a wit and as a scholar, but also specially malicious, had attempted
to impeach the accuracy of my narrative, in its London section, upon
alleged internal grounds.

I wish it could have been said with truth, that we of the leading
form were, not a triad, but a duad. The facts, however, of the case
will not allow me to say this. Facts, as people generally remark, are
stubborn things. Yes, and too often very spiteful things ; as in this
case, where, if it were not for *them*, I might describe myself as having
one sole assessor in the class, and in that case he and I might have
been likened to Castor and Pollux, who went up and down like alternate buckets—one rising with the dawn (or Phosphorus), and the other
(viz., myself) rising with Hesperus, and reigning all night long.

my valediction); and we parted for ever. Intellectually, I might not have seen cause to reverence him in any emphatic sense. But very sincerely I respected him as a conscientious man, faithful to his duties, and as, even in his latter ineffectual struggle with these duties, inflicting more suffering upon himself than upon others: finally, I respected him as a sound and accurate (though not brilliant) scholar. Personally I owed him much gratitude; for he had been uniformly kind to me, and had allowed me such indulgences as lay in his power; and I grieved at the thought of the mortification I should inflict upon him.

The morning came which was to launch me into the world; that morning from which, and from its consequences, my whole succeeding life has, in many important points, taken its colouring. At half after three I rose, and gazed with deep emotion at the ancient collegiate church, ' dressed in earliest light,' and beginning to crimson with the deep lustre of a cloudless July morning. I was firm and immovable in my purpose, but yet agitated by anticipation of uncertain danger and troubles. To this agitation the deep peace of the morning presented an affecting contrast, and in some degree a medicine. The silence was more profound than that of midnight: and to me the silence of a summer morning is more touching than all other silence, because, the light being broad and strong as that of noonday at other seasons of the year, it seems to differ from perfect day chiefly because man is not yet abroad, and thus the peace of nature, and of the innocent creatures of God, seems to be secure and deep only so long as the presence of man, and his unquiet spirit, are not there to trouble its sanctity. I dressed myself, took my hat and gloves, and lingered a little in the room. For nearly a year and a half this room had been my ' pensive citadel': here I had read and studied through all the hours of night; and, though true it was that, for the latter part of this time, I had lost my gaiety and peace of mind during the strife and fever of contention with my guardian, yet, on the other hand, as a boy passionately

fond of books, and dedicated to intellectual pursuits, I
could not fail to have enjoyed many happy hours in the
midst of general dejection.

Happy hours? Yes; and was it certain that ever
again I should enjoy hours *as* happy? At this point it
is not impossible that, left to my own final impressions,
I might have receded from my plan. But it seemed to
me, as too often happens in such cases, that no retreat
was now open. The confidence which unavoidably I
had reposed in a groom of Mr. Lawson's made it dangerous. The effect of this distracted view was, not to
alter my plan, but to throw despondency for one sad
half hour over the whole prospect before me. In that
condition, with my eyes open, I dreamed. Suddenly a
sort of trance, a frost as of some deathlike revelation,
wrapped round me; and I found renewed within me a
hateful remembrance derived from a moment that I had
long left behind. Two years before, when I wanted
about as much of my fifteenth birthday as now of my
seventeenth, I happened to be in London for part of
a single day, with a friend of my own age. Naturally,
amongst some eight or ten great spectacles which challenged our earnest attention, St. Paul's Cathedral had
been one. This we had visited, and consequently the
Whispering Gallery.[1] More than by all beside I had
been impressed by this: and some half-hour later, as we
were standing beneath the dome, and I should imagine
pretty nearly on the very spot where rather more than
five years subsequently Lord Nelson was buried,—a
spot from which we saw, pompously floating to and fro
in the upper spaces of a great aisle running westwards
from ourselves, many flags captured from France, Spain,
and Holland,—I, having my previous impressions of
awe deepened by these solemn trophies of chance and
change amongst mighty nations, had suddenly been

[1] To those who have never visited the Whispering Gallery, nor
have read any account of it amongst other acoustic phenomena described in scientific treatises, it may be proper to mention, as the
distinguishing feature of the case, that a word or a question, uttered
at one end of the gallery in the gentlest of whispers, is reverberated at
the other end in peals of thunder.

surprised by a dream, as profound as at present, in which a thought that often had persecuted me figured triumphantly. This thought turned upon the fatality that must often attend an evil choice. As an oracle of fear I remembered that great Roman warning, *Nescit vox missa reverti* (that a word once uttered is irrevocable), a freezing arrest upon the motions of hope too sanguine that haunted me in many shapes. Long before that fifteenth year of mine, I had noticed, as a worm lying at the heart of life and fretting its security, the fact that innumerable acts of choice change countenance and are variously appraised at varying stages of life—shift with the shifting hours. Already, at fifteen, I had become deeply ashamed of judgments which I had once pronounced, of idle hopes that I had once encouraged, false admirations or contempts with which once I had sympathised. And, as to the acts which I surveyed with any doubts at all, I never felt sure that after some succession of years I might not feel withering doubts about them, both as to principle and as to inevitable results.

This sentiment of nervous recoil from any word or deed that could not be recalled had been suddenly re-awakened on that London morning by the impressive experience of the Whispering Gallery. At the earlier end of the gallery had stood my friend, breathing in the softest of whispers a solemn but not acceptable truth. At the further end, after running along the walls of the gallery, that solemn truth reached me as a deafening menace in tempestuous uproars. And now in these last lingering moments, when I dreamed ominously with open eyes in my Manchester study, once again that London menace broke angrily upon me as out of a thick cloud with redoubled strength; a voice, too late for warning, seemed audibly to say, 'Once leave this house, and a Rubicon is placed between thee and all possibility of return. Thou wilt not say that what thou doest is altogether approved in thy secret heart. Even now thy conscience speaks against it in sullen whispers; but at the other end of thy long life-gallery that same conscience will speak to thee in volleying thunders.'

A sudden step upon the stairs broke up my dream, and recalled me to myself. Dangerous hours were now drawing near, and I prepared for a hasty farewell.

I shed tears as I looked round on the chair, hearth, writing-table, and other familiar objects, knowing too certainly that I looked upon them for the last time. Whilst I write this, it is nineteen[1] years ago; and yet, at this moment, I see, as if it were but yesterday, the lineaments and expressions of the object on which I fixed my parting gaze. It was the picture of a lovely lady, which hung over the mantelpiece; the eyes and mouth of which were so beautiful, and the whole countenance so radiant with divine tranquillity, that I had a thousand times laid down my pen, or my book, to gather consolation from it, as a devotee from his patron saint.[2] Whilst I was yet gazing upon it, the deep tones of the old church clock proclaimed that it was six o'clock. I went up to the picture, kissed it, then gently walked out, and closed the door for ever.

.    .    .    .    .    .    .

So blended and intertwisted in this life are occasions of laughter and of tears that I cannot yet recall without smiling an incident which occurred at that time, and which had nearly put a stop to the immediate execution of my plan. I had a trunk of immense weight; for, besides my clothes, it contained nearly all my library. The difficulty was to get this removed to a carrier's, my

[1] Written in the August of 1821.

[2] The housekeeper was in the habit of telling me that the lady had *lived* (meaning, perhaps, had been *born*) two centuries ago; that date would better agree with the tradition that the portrait was a copy from Vandyke. All that she knew further about the lady was that either to the grammar school, or to that particular college at Oxford with which the school was connected, or else to that particular college at Oxford with which Mr. Lawson personally was connected, or else, fourthly, to Mr. Lawson himself as a private individual, the unknown lady has been a special benefactress. She was also a special benefactress to me, through eighteen months, by means of her sweet Madonna countenance. And in some degree it serves to spiritualise and to hallow this service that of her who unconsciously rendered it I know neither the name, nor the exact rank or age, nor the place where she lived and died. She was parted from me by perhaps two centuries; I from her by the gulf of eternity.

room being at an aerial elevation in the house; and (what was worse) the staircase which communicated with this angle of the building was accessible only by a gallery, which passed the head-master's chamber-door. I was a favourite with all the servants; and, knowing that any of them would screen me, and act confidentially, I communicated my embarrassment to a groom of the head-master's. The groom declared his readiness to do anything I wished; and, when the time arrived, went upstairs to bring the trunk down. This I feared was beyond the strength of any one man: however, the groom was a man 'of Atlantean shoulders,' and had a back as spacious as Salisbury Plain. Accordingly he persisted in bringing down the trunk alone, whilst I stood waiting at the foot of the last flight, in great anxiety for the event. For some time I heard him descending with steps slow and steady; but, unfortunately, from his trepidation, as he drew near the dangerous quarter, within a few steps of the gallery, his foot slipped; and the mighty burden, falling from his shoulders, gained such increase of impetus at each step of the descent, that on reaching the bottom, it trundled, or rather leaped, right across, with the noise of twenty devils, against the very bedroom-door of Archididascalus. My first thought suggested that all was lost, and that my sole chance for effecting a retreat was to sacrifice my baggage. However, on reflection, I determined to abide the issue. The groom, meantime, was in the utmost alarm, both on his own account and mine: but, in spite of this, so irresistibly had the sense of the ludicrous, in this unhappy *contretemps*, taken possession of his fancy that he sang out a long, loud, and canorous peal of laughter, that might have wakened the 'Seven Sleepers.' At the sound of this resonant merriment, within the very ears of insulted authority, I could not forbear joining in it; subdued to this, not so much by the comic wilfulness of the trunk, trundling down from step to step with accelerated pace and multiplying uproar, like the λᾶας ἀναιδής[1] (the contumacious stone)

---

[1] 'Αὖτις ἔπειτα πεδόνδε κυλίνδετο λᾶας ἀναιδής.'—Hom. *Odyss.*

of Sisyphus, as by the effect it had upon the groom. We both expected, as a matter of course, that Mr. Lawson would sally out of his room; for, in general, if but a mouse stirred, he sprang out like a mastiff from his kennel. Strange to say, however, on this occasion, when the noise of laughter had subsided, no sound, or rustling even, was to be heard in the bedroom. Mr. Lawson had a painful complaint, which, oftentimes keeping him awake, made him sleep, when it *did* come, peculiarly deep. Gathering courage from the silence, the groom hoisted his burden again, and accomplished the remainder of his descent without accident. I waited until I saw the trunk placed on a wheel-barrow, and on its road to the carrier's: then, 'with Providence my guide,' or more truly it might be said, with my own headstrong folly for law and impulse, I set off on foot; carrying a small parcel with some articles of dress under my arm, a favourite English poet in one pocket, and an odd volume, containing about one-half of Canter's *Euripides*, in the other.

On leaving Manchester, by a south-western route, towards Chester and Wales, the first town that I reached (to the best of my remembrance) was Altrincham—colloquially called *Awtrigem*. When a child of three years old, and suffering from the hooping-cough, I had been carried for a change of air to different places on the Lancashire coast; and in order to benefit by as large a compass as possible of varying atmospheres, I and my nurse had been made to rest for the first night of our tour at this cheerful little town of Altrincham. On the next morning, which ushered in a most dazzling day of July, I rose earlier than my nurse fully approved: but in no long time she found it advisable to follow my example; and after putting me through my morning's drill of ablutions and the Lord's prayer, no sooner had she fully arranged my petticoats than she lifted me up in her arms, threw open the window, and let me suddenly look down upon the gayest scene I had ever beheld—viz., the little market-place of Altrincham at eight o'clock in the morning. It happened to be the market-day; and I, who till then had never consciously been in any town whatever, was equally astonished and delighted with the novel gaiety of the scene. Fruits, such as can be had in July, and flowers were scattered about in profusion: even the stalls of the butchers, from their brilliant cleanliness, appeared attractive: and the bonny young women of Altrincham were all tripping about in caps and aprons coquettishly disposed. The general hilarity of the scene at this early hour, with the low murmurings of pleasurable conversation and laughter, that rose up like a fountain to the open window, left so profound an impression upon me that I never lost it. All this occurred, as I have said, about eight o'clock on a superb July morning. Exactly at that time of the morning, on exactly such another heavenly day of July, did I, leaving Manchester at six A.M., naturally enough find myself in the centre of Altrincham market-place. Nothing had altered. There were the very same fruits and flowers; the same bonny young women tripping up and down in the same (no, *not* the same) coquettish bonnets; everything was apparently the same: perhaps the window of my bedroom was still open, only my nurse and I were not looking out; for alas! on recollection, fourteen years precisely had passed since then. Breakfast-time, however, is always a cheerful stage of the day; if a man can forget his cares at any season, it is then; and after a walk of seven miles it is doubly so. I felt it at the time, and have stopped, therefore, to notice it, as a singular coincidence, that twice, and by the merest accident, I should find myself, precisely as the clocks on a July morning were all striking eight, drawing inspiration of pleasurable feelings from the genial sights and sounds in the little market-place of Altrincham. There I breakfasted; and already by the two hours' exercise I felt myself half restored to health. After an hour's rest, I started again upon my journey: all my gloom and despondency were already retiring to the rear; and, as I left Altrincham, I said to myself, 'All places, it seems, are not Whispering Galleries.'

The distance between Manchester and Chester *was*

about forty miles. What it *is* under railway changes I know not. This I planned to walk in two days: for, though the whole might have been performed in one, I saw no use in exhausting myself; and my walking powers were rusty from long disuse. I wished to bisect the journey; and, as nearly as I could expect—*i.e.* within two or three miles—such a bisection was attained in a clean roadside inn, of the class so commonly found in England. A kind, motherly landlady, easy in circumstances, having no motive for rapacity, and looking for her livelihood much less to her inn than to her farm, guaranteed to me a safe and profound night's rest. On the following morning there remained not quite eighteen miles between myself and venerable Chester. Before I reached it, so mighty now (as ever before and since) had become the benefit from the air and the exercise that oftentimes I felt inebriated and crazy with ebullient spirits. But for the accursed letter, which sometimes

> 'Came over me,
> As doth the raven o'er the infected house,'

I should have too much forgot my gravity under this new-born health. For two hours before reaching Chester, from the accident of the south-west course which the road itself pursued, I saw held up aloft before my eyes that matchless spectacle,

> 'New, and yet as old
> As the foundations of the heavens and earth,'

an elaborate and pompous sunset hanging over the mountains of North Wales. The clouds passed slowly through several arrangements, and in the last of these I read the very scene which six months before I had read in a most exquisite poem of Wordsworth's, extracted entire into a London newspaper (I think the *St. James's Chronicle*). It was a Canadian lake,

> 'With all its fairy crowds
> Of islands that together lie
> As quietly as spots of sky
> Amongst the evening clouds.'

The scene in the poem ('Ruth'), that had been originally mimicked by the poet from the sky, was here re-mimicked and rehearsed to the life, as it seemed, by the sky from the poet. Was I then, in July 1802, really quoting from Wordsworth? Yes, reader; and I only in all Europe. In 1799 I had become acquainted with 'We are Seven' at Bath. In the winter of 1801–2 I had read the whole of 'Ruth'; early in 1803 I had written to Wordsworth. In May 1803 I had received a very long answer from Wordsworth.

The next morning after reaching Chester, my first thought on rising was directed to the vexatious letter in my custody. The odious responsibility, thrust upon me in connexion with this letter, was now becoming every hour more irritating, because every hour more embarrassing to the freedom of my own movements, since it must by this time have drawn the post-office into the ranks of my pursuers. Indignant I was that this letter should have the power of making myself an accomplice in causing anxiety, perhaps even calamity, to the poor emigrant—a man doubly liable to unjust suspicion; first, as by his profession presumably poor, and, secondly, as an alien. Indignant I was that this most filthy of letters should also have the power of forcing me into all sorts of indirect and cowardly movements at inns; for beyond all things it seemed to me important that I should not be arrested, or even for a moment challenged, as the wrongful holder of an important letter, before I had testified, by my own spontaneous transfer of it, that I had not dallied with any idea of converting it to my own benefit. In some way I must contrive to restore the letter. But was it not then the simplest of all courses to take my hat before sitting down to breakfast, present myself at the post-office, tender my explanation, and then (like Christian in Bunyan's allegory) to lay down my soul-wearying burden at the feet of those who could sign my certificate of absolution? Was not *that* simple? Was not *that* easy? Oh yes, beyond a doubt. And, if a favourite fawn should be carried off by a lion, would it not be a very simple and easy course to walk after the robber, follow him into his den, and reason with the wretch on the indelicacy of his conduct? In my particular circumstances, the post-office was in relation to myself simply a lion's den. Two separate parties, I felt satisfied, must by this time be in chase of me; and the two chasers would be confluent at the post-office. Beyond all other objects which I had to keep in view, paramount was that of fencing against my own re-capture. Anxious I was on behalf of the poor foreigner; but it did not strike me that to this anxiety I was bound to sacrifice myself. Now, if I went to the post-office, I felt sure that nothing else would be the result; and afterwards it turned out that in this anticipation I had been right. For it struck me that the nature of the enclosure in the French letter—viz., the fact that without a forgery it was not negotiable—could not be known certainly to anybody but myself. Doubts upon that point must have quickened the anxieties of all connected with myself, or connected with the case. More urgent consequently would have been the applications of 'Monsieur Monsieur' to the post-office; and consequently of the post-office to the Priory; and consequently more easily suggested and concerted between the post-office and the Priory would be all the arrangements for stopping me, in the event of my taking the route of Chester—in which case it was natural to suppose that I might *personally* return the letter to the official authorities. Of course, none of these measures was certainly known to myself; but I guessed at them as reasonable probabilities; and it was evident that the fifty and odd hours since my elopement from Manchester had allowed ample time for concerting all the requisite preparations. As a last resource, in default of any better occurring, it is likely enough that my anxiety would have tempted me into this mode of surrendering my abominable trust, which by this time I regarded with such eyes of burning malice as Sinbad must have directed at intervals towards the venerable ruffian that sat astride upon his shoulders. But things had not yet come to Sinbad's state of desperation; so, immediately after breakfast, I took

my hat, determining to review the case and adopt some
final decision in the open air. For I have always found
it easier to think over a matter of perplexity whilst walking in wide open spaces, under the broad eye of the
natural heavens, than whilst shut up in a room. But at
the very door of the inn I was suddenly brought to a
pause by the recollection that some of the servants from
the Priory were sure on every forenoon to be at times
in the streets. The streets, however, could be evaded
by shaping a course along the city walls; which I did,
and descended into some obscure lane that brought me
gradually to the banks of the river Dee. In the infancy
of its course amongst the Denbighshire mountains, this
river (famous in our pre-Norman history for the earliest
parade[1] of English monarchy) is wild and picturesque;
and even below my mother's Priory it wears a character
of interest. But, a mile or so nearer to its mouth,
when leaving Chester for Parkgate, it becomes miserably
tame; and the several reaches of the river take the
appearance of formal canals. On the right bank[2] of
the river runs an artificial mound, called the Cop. It
was, I believe, originally a Danish work; and certainly
its name is Danish (*i.e.* Icelandic, or old Danish), and
the same from which is derived our architectural word
*coping*. Upon this bank I was walking, and throwing
my gaze along the formal vista presented by the river.
Some trifle of anxiety might mingle with this gaze at the

[1] ' *Earliest parade* ':—It was a very scenical parade, for somewhere
along this reach of the Dee—viz. immediately below St. John's Priory
—Edgar, the first sovereign of all England, was rowed by nine vassal
*reguli*.

[2] ' *Right bank* ':—But which bank *is* right, and which left, under
circumstances of position varying by possibility without end? This is a
reasonable demur; but yet it argues an inexperienced reader. For
always the position of the spectator is conventionally fixed. In military
tactics, in philosophic geography, in history, etc. the uniform assumption is that you are standing with your back to the source of the river,
and your eyes travelling along with its current. That bank of the river
which under these circumstances lies upon your right is the right bank
*absolutely*, and not *relatively* only (as would be the case if a room, and
not a river, were concerned). Hence it follows that the Middlesex side
of the Thames is always the left bank, and the Surrey side always the
right bank, no matter whether you are moving from London to Oxford,
or reversely from Oxford to London.

first, lest perhaps Philistines might be abroad; for it was just possible that I had been watched. But I have generally found that, if you are in quest of some certain escape from Philistines of whatsoever class—sheriff-officers, bores, no matter what—the surest refuge is to be found amongst hedgerows and fields, amongst cows and sheep: in fact, cows are amongst the gentlest of breathing creatures; none show more passionate tenderness to their young when deprived of them; and, in short, I am not ashamed to profess a deep love for these quiet creatures. On the present occasion there were many cows grazing in the fields below the Cop: but all along the Cop itself I could descry no person whatever answering to the idea of a Philistine: in fact, there was nobody at all, except one woman, apparently middle-aged (meaning by *that* from thirty-five to forty-five), neatly dressed, though perhaps in rustic fashion, and by no possibility belonging to any class of my enemies; for already I was near enough to see so much. This woman might be a quarter of a mile distant, and was steadily advancing towards me—face to face. Soon, therefore, I was beginning to read the character of her features pretty distinctly; and her countenance naturally served as a mirror to echo and reverberate my own feelings, consequently my own horror (horror without exaggeration it was), at a sudden uproar of tumultuous sounds rising clamorously ahead. *Ahead* I mean in relation to myself, but to *her* the sound was from the rear. Our situation was briefly this. Nearly half-a-mile behind the station of the woman, that reach of the river along which we two were moving came to an abrupt close; so that the next reach, making nearly a right-angled turn, lay entirely out of view. From this unseen reach it was that the angry clamour, so passionate and so mysterious, arose: and I, for *my* part, having never heard such a fierce battling outcry, nor even heard *of* such a cry, either in books or on the stage, in prose or verse, could not so much as whisper a guess to myself upon its probable cause. Only this I felt, that blind, unorganised nature it must be—and nothing in human or in brutal wrath—that could utter itself by such an anarchy of sea-like roars. What was it? Where was it? Whence was it? Earthquake was it? convulsion of the steadfast earth? or was it the breaking loose from ancient chains of some deep morass like that of Solway? More probable it seemed that the ἄνω ποτάμων of Euripides (the flowing backwards of rivers to their fountains) now, at last, after ages of expectation, had been suddenly realised. Not long I needed to speculate; for within half a minute, perhaps, from the first arrest of our attention, the proximate cause of this mystery declared itself to our eyes, although the remote cause (the hidden cause of that visible cause) was still as dark as before. Round that right-angled turn which I have mentioned as wheeling into the next succeeding reach of the river, suddenly as with the trampling of cavalry—but all dressing accurately—and the water at the outer angle sweeping so much faster than that at the inner angle, as to keep the front of advance rigorously in line, violently careered round into our own placid watery vista a huge charging block of waters, filling the whole channel of the river, and coming down upon us at the rate of forty miles an hour. Well was it for us, myself and that respectable rustic woman, us the Deucalion and Pyrrha of this perilous moment, sole survivors apparently of the deluge (since by accident there was at that particular moment on that particular Cop nothing else to survive), that by means of this Cop, and of ancient Danish hands (possibly not yet paid for their work), we *could* survive. In fact, this watery breastwork, a perpendicular wall of water carrying itself as true as if controlled by a mason's plumb-line, rode forward at such a pace, that obviously the fleetest horse or dromedary would have had no chance of escape. Many a decent railway even, among railways since born its rivals, would not have had above the third of a chance. Naturally, I had too short a time for observing much or accurately; and universally I am a poor hand at observing; else I should say, that this riding block of crystal waters did not gallop, but went at a long trot;

yes, long trot—that most frightful of paces in a tiger, in a buffalo, or in a rebellion of waters. Even a ghost, I feel convinced, would appal me more if coming up at a long diabolical trot, than at a canter or gallop. The first impulse to both of us was derived from cowardice; cowardice the most abject and selfish. Such is man, though a Deucalion elect; such is woman, though a decent Pyrrha. Both of us ran like hares; neither did I, Deucalion, think of poor Pyrrha at all for the first sixty seconds. Yet, on the other hand, why *should* I? It struck me seriously that St. George's Channel (and, if so, beyond a doubt, the Atlantic Ocean) had broke loose, and was, doubtless, playing the same insufferable gambols upon all rivers along a seaboard of six to seven thousand miles; in which case, as all the race of woman must be doomed, how romantic a speculation it was for me, sole relic of literature, to think specially of one poor Pyrrha, probably very illiterate, whom I had never yet spoken to. That idea pulled me up. *Not spoken to her?* Then I *would* speak to her; and the more so, because the sound of the pursuing river told me that flight was useless. And, besides, if any reporter or sub-editor of some Chester chronicle should, at this moment, with his glass be sweeping the Cop, and discover me flying under these unchivalrous circumstances, he might gibbet me to all eternity. Halting, therefore (and really I had not run above eighty or a hundred steps), I waited for my solitary co-tenant of the Cop. She was a little blown by running, and could not easily speak; besides which, at the very moment of her coming up, the preter-natural column of waters, running in the very opposite direction to the natural current of the river, came up with us, ran by with the ferocious uproar of a hurricane, sent up the sides of the Cop a salute of waters, as if hypocritically pretending to kiss our feet, but secretly understood by all parties as a vain treachery for pulling us down into the flying deluge; whilst all along both banks the mighty refluent wash was heard as it rode along, leaving memorials, by sight and by sound, of its victorious power. But my female associate in this

terrific drama, what said she, on coming up with me?
Or what said I? For, by accident, I it was that spoke
first; notwithstanding the fact, notorious and undeniable, that *I had never been introduced to her*. Here,
however, be it understood, as a case now solemnly
adjudicated and set at rest, that, in the midst of any
great natural convulsion—earthquake, suppose, water-
spout, tornado, or eruption of Vesuvius—it shall and
may be lawful in all time coming (any usage or tradition
to the contrary notwithstanding), for two English people
to communicate with each other, although, by affidavit
made before two justices of the peace, it shall have been
proved that no previous introduction had been possible;
in all other cases the old statute of non-intercourse holds
good. Meantime, the present case, in default of more
circumstantial evidence, might be regarded, if not as
an earthquake, yet as ranking amongst the first-fruits
or blossoms of an earthquake. So I spoke without
scruple. All my freezing English reserve gave way
under this boiling sense of having been so recently
running for life: and then, again, suppose the water
column should come back—riding *along with* the
current, and no longer riding *against* it—in that case,
we and all the County Palatine might soon have to
run for our lives. Under such threatenings of common
peril, surely the παρρησία, or unlimited license of speech,
ought spontaneously to proclaim itself without waiting
for sanction.

So I asked her the meaning of this horrible tumult in
the waters: how did she read the mystery? Her answer
was, that though she had never before seen such a thing,
yet from her grandmother she had often heard of it;
and, if she had run before it, *that* was because *I* ran;
and a little, perhaps, because the noise frightened her.
What was it, then? I asked. 'It was,' she said, 'the
*Bore;* and it was an affection to which only some few
rivers here and there were liable; and the Dee was one
of these.' So ignorant was I, that, until that moment, I
had never heard of such a nervous affection in rivers.
Subsequently I found that, amongst English rivers, the

neighbouring river Severn, a far more important stream, suffered at spring-tides the same kind of hysterics, and, perhaps, some few other rivers in this British Island; but amongst Indian rivers, only the Ganges.

At last, when the *Bore* had been discussed to the full extent of our united ignorance, I went off to the subject of that other curse, far more afflicting than any conceivable bore—viz., the foreign letter in my pocket. The *Bore* had certainly alarmed us for ninety or a hundred seconds, but the letter would poison my very existence, like the bottle-imp, until I could transfer it to some person truly qualified to receive it. Might not my fair friend on the Cop be marked out by Fate as 'the coming woman' born to deliver me from this pocket curse? It is true that she displayed a rustic simplicity somewhat resembling that of Audrey in *As you like it.* *Her*, in fact, not at all more than Audrey, had the gods been pleased to make 'poetical.' But, for my particular mission, *that* might be amongst her best qualifications. At any rate, I was wearied in spirit under my load of responsibility: personally to liberate myself by visiting the post-office, too surely I felt as the ruin of my enterprise in its very outset. Some agent *must* be employed; and where could one be found promising by looks, words, manners, more trustworthiness than this agent, sent by accident? The case almost explained itself. She readily understood how the resemblance of a name had thrown the letter into my possession; and that the simple remedy was—to restore it to the right owner through the right channel, which channel was the never-enough-to-be-esteemed General Post-office, at that time pitching its tents and bivouacking nightly in Lombard Street, but for this special case legally represented by the Chester head-office: a service of no risk to *her*, for which, on the contrary, all parties would thank her. I, to begin, begged to put *my* thanks into the shape of half-a-crown: but, as some natural doubts arose with respect to her precise station in life (for she might be a farmer's wife, and not a servant), I thought it advisable to postulate the existence of some youthful daughter: to which mythological person I begged to address my offering, when incarnated in the shape of a doll.

I therefore, Deucalion that was or had been provisionally through a brief interval of panic, took leave of my Pyrrha, sole partner in the perils and anxieties of that astounding Bore, dismissing her—Thessalian Pyrrha—not to any Thessalian vales of Tempe, but—O ye powers of moral anachronism !—to the Chester Post-office ; and warning her on no account to be prematurely wheedled out of her secret. Her position, diplomatically speaking, was better (as I made her understand) than that of the Post-office : she having something in her gift—viz., an appointment to forty guineas ; whereas in the counter-gift of the proud post-office was nothing ; neither for instant fruition nor in far-off reversion. Her, in fact, one might regard as a Pandora, carrying a box with something better than hope at the bottom ; for hope too often betrays ; but a draft upon Smith, Payne, & Smith, which never betrays, and for a sum which, on the authority of Goldsmith, makes an English clergyman ' passing rich' through a whole twelvemonth, entitled her to look scornfully upon every second person that she met.

In about two hours the partner of my solitary kingdom upon the Cop re-appeared, with the welcome assurance that Chester had survived the Bore, that all was right, and that anything which ever *had* been looking crooked was now made straight as the path of an arrow. She had given ' my love' (so she said) to the post-office ; had been thanked by more than either one or two amongst the men of letters who figured in the equipage of that establishment ; and had been assured that, long before daylight departed, one large cornucopia of justice and felicity would be emptied out upon the heads of all parties in the drama. I myself, not the least afflicted person on the roll, was already released—suddenly released, and fully—from the iniquitous load of responsibility thrust upon me ; the poor emigrant was released from his conflict with fears that were uncertain, and creditors too certain ; the post-office was released from the scandal and embarrassment of a gross irregularity, that might eventually have brought the postmaster-general down upon their haunches; and the household at the Priory were released from all anxieties, great and small, sound and visionary, on the question of my fancied felony.

In those anxieties, one person there was that never had condescended to participate. This was my eldest sister Mary—just eleven months senior to myself. She was among the gentlest of girls, and yet from the very first she had testified the most incredulous disdain of all who fancied *her* brother capable of any thought so base as that of meditating a wrong to a needy exile. At present, after exchanging a few parting words, and a few final or farewell farewells with my faithful female [1] agent, further business I had none to detain me in Chester, except what concerned this particular sister. My business with *her* was not to thank her for the resolute justice which she had done me, since as yet I could not know of that service, but simply to see her, to learn the domestic news of the Priory, and, according to the possibilities of the case, to concert with her some plan of regular correspondence. Meantime it happened that a maternal uncle, a military man on the Bengal establishment, who had come to England on a three-years' leave of absence (according to the custom in those days), was at this time a visitor at the Priory. My mother's establishment of servants was usually limited to five persons—all, except one, elderly and torpid. But my uncle, who had brought to England some beautiful Arab and Persian horses, found it necessary to gather about his stables an extra body of men and boys. These were all alert and active; so that, when I reconnoitred the windows of the Priory in the dusk,

---

[1] Some people are irritated, or even fancy themselves insulted, by overt acts of 'alliteration, as many people are by puns. On their account, let me say, that, although there are here eight separate f's in less than half a sentence, this is to be held as pure accident. In fact, at one time there were nine f's in the original cast of the sentence, until I, in pity of the affronted people, substituted *female agent* for *female friend*.

hoping in some way to attract my sister's attention, I
not only failed in that object, seeing no lights in any
room which could naturally have been occupied by her,
but I also found myself growing into an object of special
attention to certain unknown servants, who, having no
doubt received instructions to look out for me, easily
inferred from my anxious movements that I must be the
person 'wanted.'   Uneasy at all the novel appearances
of things, I went away, and returned, after an hour's
interval, armed with a note to my sister, requesting her
to watch for an opportunity of coming out for a few
minutes under the shadows of the little ruins in the
Priory garden,[1] where I meantime would be waiting.
This note I gave to a stranger, whose costume showed
him to be a groom, begging him to give it to the young
lady whose address it bore.   He answered, in a respectful tone, that he would do so; but he could not
sincerely have meant it, since (as I soon learned) it was
impossible.   In fact, not one minute had I waited,
when in glided amongst the ruins—not my fair sister,
but my bronzed Bengal uncle!   A Bengal tiger would
not more have startled me.   Now, to a dead certainty,
I said, here comes a fatal barrier to the prosecution of
my scheme.   I was mistaken.   Between my mother and

----

[1] '*The little ruins in the Priory garden*' :—St. John's Priory had
been part of the monastic foundation attached to the very ancient
church of St. John, standing beyond the walls of Chester.   Early in
the seventeenth century, this Priory, or so much of it as remained, was
occupied as a dwelling-house by Sir Robert Cotton the antiquary.
And there, according to tradition, he had been visited by Ben Jonson.
All that remained of the Priory when used as a domestic residence by
Cotton was upon a miniature scale, except only the kitchen—a noble
room, with a groined roof of stone, exactly as it had been fitted to the
uses of the monastic establishment.   The little hall of entrance, the
dining-room, and principal bedroom, were in a modest style of
elegance, fitted by the scale of accommodation for the abode of a
literary bachelor, and pretty nearly as Cotton had left them two
centuries before.   But the miniature character of the Priory, which
had dwindled by successive abridgments from a royal quarto into a
pretty duodecimo, was seen chiefly in the beautiful ruins which adorned
the little lawn, across which access was gained to the house through
the hall.   These ruins amounted at the most to three arches—which,
because round and not pointed, were then usually called Saxon, as
contradistinguished from Gothic.   What might be the exact classification of the architecture I do not know.   Certainly the very ancient

my uncle there existed the very deepest affection; for they regarded each other as sole reliques of a household once living together in memorable harmony. But in many features of character no human beings could stand off from each other in more lively repulsion. And this was seen on the present occasion. My dear excellent mother, from the eternal quiet of her decorous household, looked upon every violent or irregular movement, and therefore upon mine at present, much as she would have done upon the opening of the seventh seal in the Revelations. But my uncle was thoroughly a man of the world, and what told even more powerfully on my behalf in this instance, he was a man of even morbid activity. It was so exquisitely natural in his eyes that any rational person should prefer moving about amongst the breezy mountains of Wales, to a slavish routine of study amongst books grim with dust and masters too probably still more dusty, that he seemed disposed to regard my conduct as an extraordinary act of virtue. On his advice, it was decided that there could be no hope in any contest with my main wishes, and that I should be left to pursue my original purpose of walking amongst the Welsh mountains; provided I chose to do so upon the slender allowance of a guinea a-week. My uncle, whose Indian

church of St. John, to which at one time the Priory must have been an appendage, wore a character of harsh and naked simplicity tha' was repulsive. But the little ruins were really beautiful, and drew continual visits from artists and sketchers through every successive summer. Whether they had any architectural enrichments, I do not remember. But they interested all people—first by their miniature scale, which would have qualified them (if portable) for a direct introduction amongst the 'properties' and *dramatis personæ* on our London opera boards; and, secondly, by the exquisite beauty of the shrubs, wild-flowers, and ferns, that surmounted the arches with natural coronets of the richest composition. In this condition of attractiveness my mother saw this little Priory, which was then on sale. As a residence, it had the great advantage of standing somewhat aloof from the city of Chester, which however (like all cathedral cities), was quiet and respectable in the composition of its population. My mother bought it, added a drawing-room, eight or nine bedrooms, dressing-rooms, etc., all on the miniature scale corresponding to the original plan; and thus formed a very pretty residence, with the grace of monastic antiquity hanging over the whole little retreat.

munificence ran riot upon all occasions, would gladly
have had a far larger allowance made to me, and would
himself have clandestinely given me anything I asked.
But I myself, from general ignorance (in which accomplishment I excelled), judged this to be sufficient; and
at this point my mother, hitherto passively acquiescent
in my uncle's proposals, interfered with a decisive rigour
that in my own heart I could not disapprove.    Any
larger allowance, most reasonably she urged, what was it
but to 'make proclamation to my two younger brothers
that rebellion bore a premium, and that mutiny was the
ready road to ease and comfort'?    My conscience
smote me at these words: I felt something like an
electric shock on this sudden reference, so utterly unexpected, to my brothers; for, to say the truth, I never
once admitted them to my thoughts in forecasting the
eventual consequences that might possibly unroll themselves from my own headstrong act.    Here now, within
three days, rang like a solemn knell, reverberating from
the sounding-board within my awakened conscience, one
of those many self-reproaches so dimly masked, but not
circumstantially prefigured, by the secret thought under
the dome of St. Paul's Cathedral about its dread
Whispering Gallery.    In this particular instance, I
know that the evil consequences from my own example
never did take effect.    But at the moment of my
mother's sorrowful suggestion, the fear that they *might*
take effect thrilled me with remorse.    My next brother,
a boy of generous and heroic temper, was at a school
governed by a brutal and savage master.    This brother,
I well know, had justifying reasons, ten times weightier
than any which I could plead, for copying my precedent.
Most probable it was that he would do so; but I learned
many years subsequently from himself that in fact he did
not.    The man's diabolical malice at last made further
toleration impossible.    Without thinking of my example,
under very different circumstances my brother won his
own emancipation in ways suggested by his own views
and limited by his own resources: he got afloat upon
the wide, wide world of ocean; ran along a perilous

seven-years' career of nautical romance; had his name almost blotted out from all memories in England; became of necessity a pirate amongst pirates; was liable to the death of a pirate wherever taken; then suddenly, on a morning of battle, having effected his escape from the bloody flag, he joined the English storming party at Monte Video, fought under the eye of Sir Home Popham, the commodore, and within twenty-four hours after the victory was rated as a midshipman on board the *Diadem* (a 64-gun ship), which bore Sir Home's flag. All this I have more circumstantially narrated elsewhere. I repeat the sum of it here, as showing that his elopement from a brutal tyrant was not due to any misleading of mine. I happen to know this now—but then I could not know it. And if I had so entirely overlooked one such possible result, full of calamity to my youthful brothers, why might I not have overlooked many hundreds beside, equally probable —equally full of peril? That consideration saddened me, and deepened more and more the ominous sugges-tion—the oracle full of woe—that spoke from those Belshazzar thunderings upon the wall of the Whispering Gallery. In fact, every intricate and untried path in life, where it was from the first a matter of arbitrary choice to enter upon it or avoid it, is effectually a path through a vast Hercynian forest, unexplored and unmapped, where each several turn in your advance leaves you open to new anticipations of what is next to be expected, and consequently open to altered valuations of all that has been already traversed. Even the character of your own absolute experience, past and gone, which (if any-thing in this world) you might surely answer for as sealed and settled for ever—even this you must submit to hold in suspense, as a thing conditional and con-tingent upon what is yet to come—liable to have its provisional character affirmed or reversed, according to the new combinations into which it may enter with elements only yet perhaps in the earliest stages of development.

Saddened by these reflections, I was still more

saddened by the chilling manner of my mother. If I could presume to descry a fault in my mother, it was—that she turned the chilling aspects of her high-toned character too exclusively upon those whom, in any degree, she knew or supposed to be promoters of evil. Sometimes her austerity might seem even unjust. But at present the whole artillery of her displeasure seemed to be unmasked, and *justly* unmasked, against a moral aberration, that offered for itself no excuse that was obvious in one moment, that was legible at one glance, that could utter itself in one word. My mother was predisposed to think ill of all causes that required many words : I, predisposed to subtleties of all sorts and degrees, had naturally become acquainted with cases that could not unrobe their apparellings down to that degree of simplicity. If in this world there is one misery having no relief, it is the pressure on the heart from the *Incommunicable*. And if another Sphinx should arise to propose another enigma to man—saying, What burden is that which only is insupportable by human fortitude ? I should answer at once—*It is the burden of the Incommunicable*. At this moment, sitting in the same room of the Priory with my mother, knowing how reasonable she was—how patient of explanations—how candid—how open to pity—not the less I sank away in a hopelessness that was immeasurable from all effort at explanation. She and I were contemplating the very same act ; but she from one centre, I from another. Certain I was, that if through one half minute she could realise in one deadly experience the suffering with which I had fought through more than three months, the amount of physical anguish, the desolation of all genial life, she would have uttered a rapturous absolution of that which else must always seem to her a mere explosion of wilful insubordination. 'In this brief experience,' she would exclaim, 'I read the record of your acquittal ; in this fiery torment I acknowledge the gladiatorial resistance.' Such in the case supposed would have been her revised verdict. But this case was exquisitely impossible. Nothing which offered itself to my rhetoric gave any but the feeblest and most childish reflection of my past sufferings. Just so helpless did I feel, disarmed into just the same languishing impotence to face (or make an effort at facing) the difficulty before me, as most of us have felt in the dreams of our childhood when lying down without a struggle before some all-conquering lion. I felt that the situation was one without hope; a solitary word, which I attempted to mould upon my lips, died away into a sigh; and passively I acquiesced in the apparent confession spread through all the appearances—that in reality I had no palliation to produce.

One alternative, in the offer made to me, was, that I had permission to stay at the Priory. The Priory, or the mountainous region of Wales, was offered freely to my choice. Either of the two offered an attractive abode. The Priory, it may be fancied, was clogged with the liability to fresh and intermitting reproaches. But this was not so. I knew my mother sufficiently to be assured that, once having expressed her sorrowful condemnation of my act, having made it impossible for me to misunderstand her views, she was ready to extend her wonted hospitality to me, and (as regarded all practical matters) her wonted kindness; but not that sort of kindness which could make me forget that I stood under the deepest shadows of her displeasure, or could leave me for a moment free to converse at my ease upon any and every subject. A man that is talking on simple toleration, and, as it were, under permanent protest, cannot feel himself morally at his ease, unless very obtuse and coarse in his sensibilities.

Mine, under any situation approaching to the present, were so far from being obtuse that they were morbidly and extravagantly acute. I had erred: that I knew, and did not disguise from myself. Indeed, the rapture of anguish with which I had recurred involuntarily to my experience of the Whispering Gallery, and the symbolic meaning which I had given to that experience, manifested indirectly my deep sense of error through the dim misgiving which attended it—that in some mysterious way the sense and the consequences of this error would magnify themselves at every stage of life, in proportion as they were viewed retrospectively from greater and greater distances. I had, besides, through the casual allusion to my brothers, suddenly become painfully aware of another and separate failure in the filial obligations resting on myself. Any mother, who is a widow, has especial claims on the co-operation of her eldest son in all means of giving a beneficial bias to the thoughts and purposes of the younger children: and, if *any* mother, then by a title how special could my own mother invoke such co-operation, who had on *her* part satisfied all the claims made upon her maternal character, by self-sacrifices as varied, as privately I knew them to be exemplary. Whilst yet comparatively young, not more than thirty-six, she had sternly refused all countenance, on at least two separate occasions, to distinguished proposals of marriage, out of pure regard to the memory of my father, and to the interests of his children. Could I fail to read, in such unostentatious exemplifications of maternal goodness, a summons to a corresponding earnestness on my part in lightening, as much as possible, the burden of her responsibilities? Alas! too certainly, as regarded *that* duty, I felt my own failure: one opportunity had been signally lost, and yet, on the other hand, I also felt that more might be pleaded on my behalf than could by possibility be apparent to a neutral bystander. But this, to be pleaded effectually, needed to be said—not by myself, but by a disinterested advocate: and no such advocate was at hand. In blind distress of mind, conscience-stricken and heart-stricken, I stretched out my arms, seeking for my one sole auxiliary; that was my eldest sister Mary; for my younger sister Jane was a mere infant. Blindly and mechanically, I stretched out my arms as if to arrest her attention; and giving utterance to my labouring thoughts, I was beginning to speak, when all at once I became sensible that Mary was not there. I had heard a step behind me, and supposed it hers: since the groom's ready acceptance of my letter to her had preoccupied me with the belief that I should see her in a few moments.  But she was far away, on a mission of anxious, sisterly love.  Immediately after my elopement, an express had been sent off to the Priory from Manchester ; this express, well mounted, had not spent more than four hours on the road.  He must have passed me on my first day's walk ; and, within an hour after *his* arrival, came a communication from the post-office, explaining the nature and value of the letter that had been so vexatiously thrust into my hands.  Alarm spread through the Priory : for it must be confessed that the coincidence of my elopement with this certified delivery of the letter to myself, gave but too reasonable grounds for connecting the two incidents.  I was grateful to dear Mary for resisting such strong plausibilities against me ; and yet I could not feel entitled to complain of those who had *not* resisted.  The probability seemed that I must have violated the laws to some extent, either by forgery or by fraudulent appropriation.  In either case, the most eligible course seemed to be my instant expatriation.  France (this being the year of peace) or Holland would offer the best asylum until the affair should be settled ; and, as there could be no anxieties in any quarter as to the main thing concerned in the issue—viz., the money—in any case there was no reason to fear a vindictive pursuit, even on the worst assumption as regarded the offence.  An elderly gentleman, long connected with the family, and in many cases an agent for the guardians, at this moment offered his services as counsellor and protector to my sister Mary.  Two hours therefore from the arrival of the Manchester express (who, starting about 11 A.M., had reached Chester at 3 P.M.), all the requisite steps having been concerted with one of the Chester banks for getting letters of credit, etc., a carriage-and-four was at the Priory gate, into which stepped my sister Mary, with one female attendant and her friendly escort.  And thus, the same day, on which I had made my exit from Mr. Lawson's, saw the chase after me commencing.  Sunset saw the pursuers crossing the Mersey, and trotting into Liverpool.  Thence to Ormskirk, thirteen miles, and thence to *proud Preston*, about twenty more. Within a trifle, these three stages make fifty miles; and so much did my chasers, that pursued when no man fled, accomplish before sleeping. On the next day, long and long before the time when I, in my humble pedestrian character, reached Chester, my sister's party had reached Ambleside—distant about ninety-two miles from Liverpool, consequently somewhere about a hundred and seven miles from the Priory. This chasing party, with good reason, supposed themselves to be on my traces ever after reaching 'proud Preston,' which is the point of confluence for the Liverpool and Manchester roads northwards. For I myself, having originally planned my route for the English Lakes, purposely suffered some indications of that plan to remain behind me, in the hope of thus giving a false direction to any pursuit that might be attempted.

The further course of this chase was disagreeably made known to me about four years later, on attaining my majority, by a 'little account' of about £150 against my little patrimonial fortune. Of all the letters from the Priory (which, however, from natural oversight were not thought of until the day after my own arrival at the Priory—*i.e.*, the third day after my sister's departure), not one caught them: which was unfortunate. For the journey to and from the Lakes, together with a circuit of more than one hundred and fifty miles amongst the Lakes, would at any rate have run up to nearly four hundred miles. But it happened that my pursuers, not having time to sift such intelligence as they received, were misled into an excursus of full two hundred miles more, by chasing an imaginary '*me*' to the caves, thence to Bolton Abbey, thence nearly to York. Altogether, the journey amounted to above six hundred miles, all performed with four horses. Now at that time the cost of four horses—which in the cheapest hay and corn seasons was three shillings a-mile, and in dear seasons four—was three-and-sixpence a mile; to which it was usual to compute an average addition of one shilling a-mile for gates, postilions, ostlers; so that the total amount, with the natural expenses of the three travellers at the inns, ran up to five shillings a-mile. Consequently, five shillings being the quarter of a pound, six hundred miles cost the quarter of £600. The only item in this long account which consoled me to the amount of a solitary smile for all this money thrown away, was an item in a bill at Patterdale (head of Ulleswater)—

| | |
|---|---|
| To an echo, first quality . . . . . . . | £0 10 0 |
| To do., second quality . . . . . | 0 5 0 |

It seems the price of echoes varied, reasonably enough, with the amount of gunpowder consumed. But at Low-wood, on Windermere, half-crown echoes might be had by those base snobs who would put up with a vile Brummagem substitute for 'the genuine article.'

Trivial, meantime, as regarded any permanent consequences, would have been this casual inroad upon my patrimony. Had I waited until my sister returned home, which I might have been sure could only have been delayed through the imperfectly concerted system of correspondence, all would have prospered. From her I should have received the cordiality and the genial sympathy which I needed; I could have quietly pursued my studies; and my Oxford matriculation would have followed as a matter of course. But, unhappily, having for so long a time been seriously shaken in health, any interruption of my wild open-air system of life instantly threw me back into nervous derangements. Past all doubt it had now become that the *al fresco* life, to which I had looked with so much hopefulness for a sure and rapid restoration to health, was even more potent than I had supposed it. Literally irresistible it seemed in re-organising the system of my languishing powers. Impatient, therefore, under the absence of my sister, and agitated every hour so long as my home wanted its central charm in some household countenance, some σύντροφον ὅμμα, beaming with perfect sympathy, I resolved to avail myself of those wild mountainous and sylvan attractions which at present lay nearest to me. Those parts, indeed, of Flintshire, or even of Denbighshire, which lay near to Chester, were not in any very eminent sense attractive. The vale of Gressford, for instance, within the Flintshire border, and yet not more than seven miles distant, offered a lovely little seclusion ; and to this I had a privileged access ; and at first I tried it ; but it was a dressed and ornamented pleasure-ground : and two ladies of some distinction, nearly related to each other, and old friends of my mother, were in a manner the ladies paramount within the ring fence of this Arcadian vale. But this did not offer what I wanted. Everything was elegant, polished, quiet, throughout the lawns and groves of this verdant retreat : no rudeness was allowed here ; even the little brooks were trained to ' behave themselves ' ; and the two villas of the reigning ladies (Mrs. Warrington and Mrs. Parry) showed the perfection of good taste. For both ladies had cultivated a taste for painting, and [had] I believe some executive power. Here my introductions were rather too favourable ; since they forced me into society. From Gressford, however, the character of the scene, considered as a daily residence, very soon repelled me, however otherwise fascinating by the accomplishments of its two possessors. Just two-and-twenty miles from Chester, meantime, lay a far grander scene, the fine vale of Llangollen in the centre of Denbighshire. Here, also, the presiding residents were two ladies, whose romantic retirement from the world at an early age had attracted for many years a general interest to their persons, habits, and opinions. These ladies were Irish—Miss Ponsonby, and Lady Eleanor Butler, a sister of Lord Ormond. I had twice been formally presented to them by persons of a rank to stamp a value upon this introduction. But, naturally, though high-bred courtesy concealed any such open expressions of feeling, they must have felt a very slight interest in myself or my opinions.[1] I grieve to

[1] It is worthy of notice that, when I, in this year 1802, and again in after years, endeavoured to impress them favourably with regard to Wordsworth as a poet (that subject having not been introduced by myself, but by one of the ladies, who happened to have a Cambridge friend intimate with the man, and perhaps with his works), neither of them was disposed to look with any interest or hopefulness upon his

say that my own feelings were not more ardent towards *them*. Nevertheless, I presented myself at their cottage as often as I passed through Llangollen; and was always courteously received when they happened to be in the country. However, as it was not ladies that I was seeking in Wales, I now pushed on to Carnarvonshire; and for some weeks took a very miniature suite of rooms— viz., one room and a closet—at Bangor.

My landlady had been a lady's-maid, or a nurse, or something of that sort, in the Bishop of Bangor's family; and had but lately married away from that family, or (to use her own expression) had 'settled.' In a little town like Bangor, barely to have lived in the bishop's family conferred some distinction; and my good landlady had rather more than her share of the pride natural to that glorious advantage. What 'my lord' said, and what 'my lord' did, how useful he was in Parliament, and how indispensable at Oxford, formed the daily burden of her talk. All this I bore very well; for it cost no great effort to make allowance for the garrulity of an old servant; and luckily nothing in our daily routine of life brought us often into each other's company. Sometimes, however, we met; and of necessity, on such occasions, I must have appeared in her eyes very inadequately impressed with the bishop's importance, and with the grandeur of having lived in a palace; and, perhaps, to punish me for my indifference, or it might, after all, be mere accident, she one day repeated to me a conversation in which I was indirectly a party concerned. She had been to the palace; and, dinner being over, she had been summoned into the dining-room. In giving an account of her household economy, she happened to mention that she had let what she styled

pretensions. But, at a period long subsequent to this, when the House of Commons had rung with applause on Sergeant Talfourd's mention of his name, and when all American tourists of any distinction flocked annually to Rydal Mount, Wordsworth's own poems bear witness that a great revolution had been worked at Llangollen. I mention this anecdote, because I have good reason to think that a large proportion of the 'conversions' in the case of Wordsworth took place under the same influence.

somewhat magnificently her 'apartments.' The good bishop (it seemed) had thence taken occasion to caution her as to her selection of inmates; 'for,' said he, 'you must recollect, Betty, that Bangor is in the high road to the Head' (*the Head* was the common colloquial expression for Holyhead); 'so that multitudes of Irish swindlers, running away from their debts into England, and of English swindlers, running away from their debts to the Isle of Man, are likely to take this place in their route.' Such advice was certainly not without reasonable grounds, but rather fitted to be stored up for Mrs. Betty's private meditations, than specially reported to me. What followed was worse:—'O my lord,' answered my landlady (according to her own representation of the matter), 'I really don't think that this young gentleman is a swindler; because——'—'You don't *think* me a swindler?' said I, interrupting her, in a tumult of indignation; 'for the future I shall spare you the trouble of thinking about it.' And without delay I prepared for my departure. Some concessions the good woman seemed disposed to make; but a harsh and contemptuous expression, which I fear that I applied to the learned dignitary himself, roused *her* indignation in turn; and reconciliation then became impossible. I was, indeed, greatly irritated at the bishop's having suggested any grounds of suspicion, however remotely, against a person whom he had never seen; and I thought of letting him know my mind in Greek; which, at the same time that it would furnish some presumption in behalf of my respectability, might also (I hoped) compel the bishop to answer in the same language; and in that case I doubted not to make good my superiority as a versatile wielder of arms, rarely managed with effect, against all the terrors of his lordship's wig.

I was wrong if I said anything in my anger that was disparaging or sceptical as to the bishop's intellectual pretensions; which were not only very sound, but very appropriate to the particular stations which he filled. For the Bishop of Bangor (at that time Dr. Cleaver) was also the head of Brasenose, Oxford—which college was indebted to him for its leadership[1] at that era in scholarship and discipline. In this academic character I learned afterwards that he might be called almost a reformer : a wise, temperate, and successful reformer ; and, as a scholar, I saw many years later that he had received the laudatory notice of Porson. But, on the other hand, the bishop was not altogether without blame in unchaining his local influence, were it only by hint or insinuation, against a defenceless stranger. For so great a man, in so small a town as Bangor, was really as much of an autocrat as a post-captain on the quarter-deck of his own vessel. A 'sea-lawyer' in such a case

---

[1] The rank to which Brasenose had suddenly risen in the estimation of the world was put to the test in the following year. The leading family in the house (the *gens*) of Grenville was, at this time, that of the Marquis of Buckingham, not long after elevated to the ducal rank. The second son of this nobleman—viz., Lord George Grenville (subsequently succeeding to the peerage of Nugent, and known in his literary character only as Lord Nugent)—happened, in this or the following year, to be ripe for college ; which means, in England, that he was a young man, and not a boy ; generally, at the very least, eighteen years old. According to all known precedent, he should have gone to Christ Church. But, on such a question arising, naturally his uncle, Lord Grenville, under whose patronage the Grenville *Homer* had been published, and who was reputed an accomplished scholar, assisted at the family council ; and by *his* advice, to the astonishment of Oxford, Brasenose was selected in preference to Christ Church ; and, I believe, on the one sole ground of deference for the administrative talents (combined with singular erudition) of Dr. Cleaver. This casual precedency, however, of Brasenose, resting (as it did) on a mere *personal* basis, ran down as suddenly as it had run up, and has long since been forgotten. The fact is, that rustic families, at a distance from Oxford, naturally presume some superior dignity in any college that should happen to have a bishop for its ruler ; not knowing that, in Oxford and Cambridge, all heads of considerable colleges hold themselves (and *are* held) equals in rank and dignity to the bench of bishops. In Oxford more especially, this doctrine receives a standing illustration ; for *there* the dean of the diocese is necessarily and *ex officio* the head of Christ Church, which (by the number and the rank of its population) is beyond all competition the supreme college in the whole university. In that character, therefore (of college head), Mr. Dean is a very much greater man than my lord the Bishop. This virtual inferiority in the face of an ostensible superiority was, until the new regulations for somewhat equalising the bishoprics, further reinforced by the poverty of Oxford as an episcopal see. It ought to be added, that to hold the headship of a college in combination with a bishopric, considering the burdensomeness of irreconcilable functions attached to each of the offices, is a scandalous violation of public duty, such as ought never to have won an hour's toleration.

must contrive to pocket his wrongs, until he finds himself and the captain on shore. Yet, after all, my scheme was not altogether so absurd; and the anger, in which perhaps it might begin, all melted away in the fun which would have accompanied its execution. It will strike the reader that my plan of retaliation must have failed by arming against me the official pride of the bishop. Any man, it will be thought, occupying so dignified a place in public life—a lord of Parliament, holder of a prize in the episcopal lottery (for Bangor was worth six thousand a-year), a leading Don at Oxford—in short, a splendid pluralist, armed with diocesan thunder and lightning—would never stoop from his Jovian altitude to notice any communication whatever from a boy. But it would make all the difference in the world that this communication by the supposition was to be in Greek. Mere curiosity in such a case would compel the Bishop to read it. And then, shockingly irregular as such a course would be, a fatal temptation would arise to the hazardous experiment of answering it in Greek. It would not be pleasant to shrink from the sort of silent challenge thrown out by such an eccentric form of epistle, when worded in the tone of respect due to the bishop's age and spiritual office. And certainly the degradation would be conspicuously less in replying even to a boy, if armed with that sort of accomplishment. But was not the bishop a learned man, well qualified to answer, whose reading must naturally be greater by a score of times than mine? I had heard so; and I was told also, but long after, that he had written well and learnedly (*but not in Greek*) on the Arundel marbles; even to attempt which, in our days, when the forestalling labours of two centuries have so much narrowed the field open to original sagacity, argues an erudition far from common. But I have already given it as my opinion, that there is no proportion held between a man's general knowledge of Greek, and the special art of writing Greek; that is, using it as a vehicle for ordinary and familiar intercourse. This advantage, not necessarily or usually belonging to the most exquisite

Greek scholarship, I myself wielded with a preternatural address for varying the forms of expression, and for bringing the most refractory ideas within the harness of Grecian phraseology. Had the bishop yielded to the temptation of replying, then I figured to myself the inevitable result—the episcopal hulk lying motionless on the water like a huge three-decker, not able to return a gun, whilst I, as a light agile frigate, should have sailed round and round him, and raked him at pleasure, as opportunity offered. He could have had no opening for his erudition (as, for instance, upon the Arundel marbles), without too flagrantly recalling the cosmogony man in the *Vicar of Wakefield*, with his ἄναρχον ἄρα καὶ ἀτελεύταιον τὸ πᾶν. Once falling into the snare of replying at all, his lordship would not be at liberty either to break off the correspondence abruptly, or to continue it without damage to his episcopal pomp. My anger, meantime, sudden and fiery, as under a sense of real injury, had not been malicious; and it was already propitiated beforehand by the mere fun and comic effect of the picture which I thus prefigured as arising between us. In no case could I have found pleasure in causing any mortifications to the bishop—mortifications which the Methodists (by this time swarming in Carnarvonshire) would exultingly have diffused. In the end I should probably have confined myself to a grave and temperate remonstrance, simply stating the distressing consequences which were likely to result to me from the too unguarded insinuations of his lordship.

But these consequences travelled fast upon the traces of those insinuations; and already upon the very day when my foolish landlady (more, perhaps, in thoughtlessness than with any purpose of mischief) had repeated the bishop's words in what seemed to me so insulting a tone, and so entirely without provocation (since there never had been the smallest irregularity in our little weekly settlements), one of those consequences was, that I became houseless. For I disdained to profit by the shelter of a house from which truth and courtesy seemed alike banished. And from that one consequence naturally enough flowed others; for, having, at any rate, to seek a new home, I left Bangor[1] at once, and rambled away to Carnarvon—distant about two-and-a-half hours' smart walking. At Carnarvon I found no lodging that altogether suited my purposes; hired lodgings being then thinly sown in North Wales; and for some time, therefore, having a small reserve of guineas, I lived very much at inns.

This change of abode naturally drew my thoughts away from the bishop. And thus gradually all my thoughts of expostulation faded away. This I am disposed to regard as an unfortunate solution of the affair, which otherwise would probably have taken the following course. The bishop, as I afterwards heard when resident myself at Oxford and personally acquainted with men of Brasenose (to which college, indeed, subsequently, my own youngest brother belonged), was a reasonable and even amiable man. On receiving, therefore, my Greek remonstrance, he was sure as a scholar to have taken some interest in the writer; and he was too equitable to have neglected any statement, Greek or not Greek, which reflected, with some apparent justice, upon his own conduct as not sufficiently considerate. He would, therefore, almost certainly have replied to me in courteous terms; regretting the accident which had made me houseless; but reminding me that all communications made to a dependant within a man's own gates, and never meant as grounds of action, but simply as cautions—general and not special

---

[1] In this, except for what concerned the cheapness and the brilliant cleanliness of the lodgings, under the management of an English house-maid approved by an English bishop's housekeeper, there was little to regret. Bangor, indeed, had few attractions, fewer than any other spot in Carnarvonshire. And yet, was there not the cathedral? Certainly there was; and that might have been a great resource to me, had there been the regular choir services, but there were none. Indeed, there could be none; for, so far as I ever heard, there was no choir. The cathedral cemetery was at that time famous as the most beautiful in the whole kingdom. But the beauty was scarcely appropriate: it was the beauty of a well-kept shrubbery, and not of a cemetery. It contrived to look smiling and attractive by the entire dissembling of its real purposes.

—are in law and usage held to be privileged communications, and equally whether written or spoken. The insulting use made of this caution, he would have treated as due simply to the woman's coarseness, but in part, perhaps, as due to a cause which has much to do with the harsh and uncivil expressions of uneducated people—viz., their very limited command of language. They use phrases much stronger than naturally belong to their thoughts and meaning, simply because the narrowness of their vocabulary oftentimes suggests to their embarrassed choice no variation of expression wearing a character less offensive. To such a letter I should have made a suitable reply; and, thenceforward, it is probable that, until the Michaelmas term drew the bishop's family away to Oxford, I should have found my abode in Bangor, or its neighbourhood, much improved as regards the command of books. That advantage would have been fugitive. But other and remoter advantages might have been more serious. It happened that the college to which the Manchester Grammar School would have consigned me as a privileged *alumnus*, was that very college over which the bishop presided. I have no reason to think that the bishop would have had power to retrieve for me any part of the privileges which by my elopement I had wilfully forfeited: but he would have had it abundantly in his power to place the ordinary college advantages of Fellowships, etc., within my reach: whereas afterwards, going under erroneous counsel to a college disconnected from my own country and my own schools, I never enjoyed those ordinary opportunities of advancement, and consequently of literary leisure, which the English universities open to almost every man who qualifies himself duly to obtain them. All this, however, was thrown into the world of dreams and fable by my hasty movement to Carnarvon, and that region which Pennant first distinguished by the name of Snowdonia.

There were already, even in those days of 1802, numerous inns, erected at reasonable distances from each other, for the accommodation of tourists: and no sort of disgrace attached in Wales, as too generally upon the great roads of England, to the pedestrian style of travelling. Indeed, the majority of those whom I met as fellow-tourists in the quiet little cottage-parlours of the Welsh posting-houses were pedestrian travellers. All the way from Shrewsbury through Llangollen, Llanrwst,[1] Conway, Bangor, then turning to the left at right angles through Carnarvon, and so on to Dolgelly (the chief town of Merionethshire), Tan-y-Bwlch, Harlech, Barmouth, and through the sweet solitudes of Cardiganshire, or turning back sharply towards the English border through the gorgeous wood scenery of Montgomeryshire—everywhere at intermitting distances of twelve to sixteen miles, I found the most comfortable inns. One feature indeed of repose in all this chain of solitary resting-houses—viz., the fact that none of them rose above two storeys in height—was due to the modest scale on which the travelling system of the Principality had moulded itself in correspondence to the calls of England, which then (but be it remembered this *then* was in 1802, a year of peace) threw a very small proportion of her vast migratory population annually into this sequestered channel. No huge Babylonian centres of commerce towered into the clouds on these sweet sylvan routes : no hurricanes of haste, or fever-stricken armies of horses and flying chariots, tormented the echoes in these mountain recesses. And it has often struck me that a world-wearied man, who sought for the peace of monasteries separated from their gloomy captivity—peace and silence such as theirs combined with the large liberty of nature—could not do better than revolve amongst these modest inns in the five northern Welsh counties of Denbigh, Montgomery, Carnarvon, Merioneth, and Cardigan. Sleeping, for instance, and breakfasting at Carnarvon; then, by an easy nine-mile walk, going forwards to dinner at Bangor, thence to Aber—nine miles ; or to Llanberris ; and so on

---

[1] '*Llanrwst*' :—This is an alarming word for the eye ; one vowel to what the English eye counts as seven consonants: but it is easily pronounced as *Tlanrōōst*.

for ever, accomplishing seventy to ninety or one hundred miles in a week. This, upon actual experiment, and for week after week, I found the most delightful of lives. Here was the eternal motion of winds and rivers, or of the Wandering Jew liberated from the persecution which compelled him to move, and turned his breezy freedom into a killing captivity. Happier life I cannot imagine than this vagrancy, if the weather were but tolerable, through endless successions of changing beauty, and towards evening a courteous welcome in a pretty rustic home—that having all the luxuries of a fine hotel (in particular some luxuries [1] that are almost sacred to Alpine regions), was at the same time liberated from the inevitable accompaniments of such hotels in great cities or at great travelling stations—viz., the tumult and uproar.

Life on this model was but too delightful; and to myself especially, that am never thoroughly in health unless when having pedestrian exercise to the extent of fifteen miles at the most, and eight to ten miles at the least. Living thus, a man earned his daily enjoyment. But what did it cost? About half a guinea a day: whilst my boyish allowance was not a third of this. The flagrant health, health boiling over in fiery rapture, which ran along, side by side, with exercise on this scale, whilst all the while from morning to night I was inhaling mountain air, soon passed into a hateful scourge. Perquisites to servants and a bed would have absorbed the whole of my weekly guinea. My policy therefore was, if the autumnal air was warm enough, to save this expense of a bed and the chambermaid by sleeping amongst ferns or furze upon a hillside; and perhaps with a cloak of sufficient *weight* as well as compass, or an Arab's burnoose, this would have been no great hardship. But then in the daytime what an oppressive burden to carry! So perhaps it was as well that I had no cloak at all. I did, however, for some weeks try the plan of carrying a canvas tent manufac-

---

[1] But a luxury of another class, and quite peculiar to Wales, was in those days (I hope in these) the Welsh harp, in attendance at every inn.

tured by myself, and not larger than an ordinary umbrella: but to pitch this securely I found difficult; and on windy nights it became a troublesome companion. As winter drew near, this bivouacking system became too dangerous to attempt. Still one may bivouack decently, barring rain and wind, up to the end of October. And I counted, on the whole, that in a fortnight I spent nine nights abroad. There are, as perhaps the reader knows by experience, no jaguars in Wales — nor pumas — nor anacondas — nor (generally speaking) any Thugs. What I feared most, but perhaps only through ignorance of zoology, was, lest, whilst my sleeping face was upturned to the stars, some one of the many little Brahminical-looking cows on the Cambrian hills, one or other, might poach her foot into the centre of my face. I do not suppose any fixed hostility of that nature to English faces in Welsh cows: but everywhere I observe in the feminine mind something of beautiful caprice, a floral exuberance of that charming wilfulness which characterises our dear human sisters I fear through all worlds. Against Thugs I had Juvenal's license to be careless in the emptiness of my pockets (*cantabit vacuus* [1] *coram latrone viator*). But I fear that Juvenal's license will not always hold water. There are people bent upon cudgelling one who will persist in excusing one's having nothing but a bad shilling in one's purse, without reading in that Juvenalian *vacuitas* any privilege or license of exemption from the general fate of travellers that intrude upon the solitude of robbers.

Dr. Johnson, upon some occasion, which I have forgotten, is represented by his biographers as accounting for an undeserving person's success in these terms: 'Why, I suppose that *his* nonsense suited *their* nonsense.' Can *that* be the humiliating solution of my own colloquial success at this time in Carnarvonshire

---

[1] '*Vacuus*':—I am afraid, though many a year has passed since I read Juvenal, that the true classical sense of *vacuus* is, *careless, clear from all burden of anxiety*, so that *vacuitas* will be the *result* of immunity from robbery. But suffer me to understand it in the sense of *free from the burden of property*, in which sense *vacuitas* would be the *cause* of such an immunity.

inns? Do not suggest such a thought, most courteous
reader. No matter: won in whatsoever way, success *is*
success; and even nonsense, if it is to be victorious
nonsense—victorious over the fatal habit of yawning in
those who listen, and in some cases over the habit of
disputing—must involve a deeper art or more effective
secret of power than is easily attained. Nonsense, in
fact, is a very difficult thing. Not every seventh son
of a seventh son (to use Milton's words) is equal to the
task of keeping and maintaining a company of decent
men in orthodox nonsense for a matter of two hours.
Come from what fountain it may, all talk that succeeds
to the extent of raising a wish to meet the talker again,
must contain *salt*; must be seasoned with some flavour-
ing element pungent enough to neutralise the natural
tendencies of all mixed conversation, not vigilantly
tended, to lose itself in insipidities and platitudes.
Above all things, I shunned, as I would shun a pestilence, Coleridge's capital error, which through life he
practised, of keeping the audience in a state of passiveness. Unjust this was to others, but most of all to
himself. This eternal stream of talk which never for
one instant intermitted, and allowed no momentary
opportunity of reaction to the persecuted and bated
auditor, was absolute ruin to the interests of the talker
himself. Always passive—always acted upon, never
allowed to react, into what state did the poor afflicted
listener—he that played the *rôle* of listener—collapse?
He returned home in the exhausted condition of one
that has been drawn up just before death from the
bottom of a well occupied by foul gases; and, of course,
hours before he had reached that perilous point of
depression, he had lost all power of distinguishing,
understanding, or connecting. I, for my part, without
needing to think of the unamiable arrogance involved
in such a habit, simply on principles of deadliest selfishness, should have avoided thus incapacitating my hearer
from doing any justice to the rhetoric or the argument
with which I might address him.

Some great advantages I had for colloquial purposes,

and for engaging the attention of people wiser than myself. Ignorant I was in a degree past all imagination of daily life—even as it exists in England. But, on the other hand, having the advantage of a prodigious memory, and the far greater advantage of a logical instinct for feeling in a moment the secret analogies or parallelisms that connected things else apparently remote, I enjoyed these two peculiar gifts for conversation : first, an inexhaustible fertility of topics, and therefore of resources for illustrating or for varying any subject that chance or purpose suggested; secondly, a prematurely awakened sense of *art* applied to conversation. I had learned the use of vigilance in evading with civility the approach of wearisome discussions, and in impressing, quietly and oftentimes imperceptibly, a new movement upon dialogues that loitered painfully, or see-sawed unprofitably. That it was one function of art to hide and mask itself (*artis est artem celare*), this I well knew. Neither was there much art required. The chief demand was for new facts, or new views, or for views newly-coloured impressing novelty upon old facts. To throw in a little of the mysterious every now and then was useful, even with those that by temperament were averse to the mysterious ; pointed epigrammatic sayings and jests—even somewhat worn—were useful; a seasonable quotation in verse was always effective; and illustrative anecdotes diffused a grace over the whole movement of the dialogue. It would have been coxcombry to practise any elaborate or any conspicuous art : few and simple were any artifices that I ever employed ; but, being hidden and seasonable, they were often effective. And the whole result was, that I became exceedingly popular within my narrow circle of friends. This circle was necessarily a fluctuating one, since it was mainly composed of tourists that happened to linger for a few weeks in or near Snowdonia, making their headquarters at Bethgellert or Carnarvon, or at the utmost roaming no farther than the foot of Cader Idris. Amongst these fugitive members of our society, I recollect with especial pleasure Mr. De Haren, an accomplished young German, who held, or *had* held, the commission of lieutenant in our British navy, but now, in an interval of peace, was seeking to extend his knowledge of England, and also of the English language; though in *that*, as regarded the fullest command of it colloquially, he had little, indeed, to learn. From him it was that I obtained my first lessons in German, and my first acquaintance with German literature. Paul Richter I then first heard of, together with Hippel, a humorist admired by Kant, and Hamann, also classed as a humorist, but a nondescript writer, singularly obscure, whom I have never since seen in the hands of any Englishman, except once of Sir William Hamilton. With all these writers Mr. De Haren had the means of making me usefully acquainted in the small portable library which filled one of his trunks. But the most stationary members of this semi-literary circle were Welshmen; two of them lawyers, one a clergyman. This last had been regularly educated at Oxford—as a member of Jesus (the Welsh college)—and was a man of extensive information. The lawyers had not enjoyed the same advantages, but they had read diligently, and were interesting companions. Wales, as is pretty well known, breeds a population somewhat litigious. I do not think the worse of them for *that*. The martial Butlers and the heroic Talbots of the fifteenth century, having no regular opening for their warlike fury in the seventeenth century, took to quarrelling with each other; and no letters are more bitter than those which to this day survive from the hostile correspondence of the brother Talbots contemporary with the last days of Shakspere.[1] One channel being closed against their martial propensities, naturally they opened such others as circumstances made available. This temper, widely spread amongst the lower classes of the Welsh, made it a necessity that the lawyers should itinerate on market-days through all the principal towns in their districts. In those towns continually I met them; and continually we renewed our literary friendship.

[1] See especially a book written by Sir Egerton Brydges (I forget the title) on the Peerage in the reign of James I.

Meantime alternately I sailed upon the high-priced
and the low-priced tack. So exceedingly cheap were
provisions at that period, when the war taxation of Mr.
Pitt was partially intermitting, that it was easy beyond
measure upon any three weeks' expenditure, by living
with cottagers, to save two guineas out of the three.
Mr. De Haren assured me that even in an inn, and not
in a poor man's cottage (but an unpretending rustic inn,
where the mistress of the house took upon herself the
functions of every possible servant in turn—cook, waiter,
chambermaid, boots, ostler), he had passed a day or
two; and for what he considered a really elegant dinner,
as regarded everything except the table equipage (that
being rude and coarse), he had paid only sixpence.
This very inn, about ten or twelve miles south of
Dolgelly, I myself visited some time later; and I found
Mr. De Haren's account in all points confirmed: the
sole drawback upon the comfort of the visitor being that
the fuel was chiefly of green wood, and with a chimney
that smoked. I suffered so much under this kind of
smoke, which irritates and inflames the eyes more than
any other, that on the following day reluctantly I took
leave of that obliging pluralist the landlady, and really
felt myself blushing on settling the bill, until I bethought
me of the green wood, which, upon the whole, seemed to
balance the account. I could not then, nor can I now,
account for these preposterously low prices; which same
prices, strange to say, ruled (as Wordsworth and his sister
often assured me) among the same kind of scenery—*i.e.*,
amongst the English lakes—at the very same time. To
account for it, as people often do, by alleging the want
of markets for agricultural produce, is crazy political
economy; since the remedy for paucity of markets, and
consequent failure of competition, is, certainly not to
sell at losing rates, but to forbear producing, and consequently not to sell at all.[1]

[1] Thirteen years later—viz., in the year of Waterloo—happening to
walk through the whole Principality from south to north, beginning at
Cardiff, and ending at Bangor, I turned aside about twenty-five miles
to inquire after the health of my excellent hostess, that determined

So cheap in fact were all provisions, which one had any chance of meeting with in a labouring man's house, that I found it difficult under such a roof to spend sixpence a-day. Tea or coffee there was none: and I did not at that period very much care for either. Milk, with bread (coarse, but more agreeable by much than the insipid *whity-grey* bread of towns), potatoes if one wished, and also a little goat's, or kid's, flesh—these composed the cottager's choice of viands; not luxurious, but palatable enough to a person who took much exercise. And, if one wished, fresh-water fish could be had cheap enough; especially trout of the very finest quality. In these circumstances, I never found it easy to spend even five shillings (no, not three shillings, unless whortleberries or fish had been bought) in one week. And thus it was easy enough to create funds for

pluralist and intense antipole of all possible sinecurists. I found her cleaning a pair of boots and spurs, and purposing (I rather think) to enter next upon the elegant office of greasing a horse's heels. In that design, however, she was thwarted for the present by myself and another tourist, who claimed her services in three or four other characters previously. I inquired after the chimney—was it still smoking? She seemed surprised that it had ever been suspected of anything criminal; so, as it was not a season for fires, I said no more. But I saw plenty of green wood, and but a small proportion of peats. I fear, therefore, that this, the state-room of the whole concern, still poisons the peace of the unhappy tourists. One personal indemnification, meantime, I must mention which this little guilty room made to me on that same night for all the tears it had caused me to shed. It happened that there was a public dance held at this inn on this very night. I therefore retired early to my bedroom, having had so long a walk, and not wishing to annoy the company, or the excellent landlady, who had, I dare say, to play the fiddle to the dancers. The noise and uproar were almost insupportable; so that I could not sleep at all. At three o'clock all became silent, the company having departed in a body. Suddenly from the little parlour, separated from my bedroom overhead by the slightest and most pervious of ceilings, arose with the rising dawn the very sweetest of female voices perhaps that ever I had heard, although for many years an *habitué* of the opera. She was a stranger; a visitor from some distance; and (I was told in the morning) a Methodist. What she sang, or at least sang last, were the beautiful verses of Shirley, ending—

> 'Only the actions of the just
> Smell sweet, and blossom in the dust.'

This incident caused me to forget and forgive the wicked little chimney.

my periodical transmigrations back into the character of gentleman-tourist. Even the half of five shillings I could not always find means to spend: for in some families, raised above dependence upon daily wages, when I performed any services in the way of letter-writing, I found it impossible at times to force any money at all upon them. Once, in particular, near the small lake of Talyllyn (so written, I believe, but pronounced Taltlyn), in a sequestered part of Merionethshire, I was entertained for upwards of three days by a family of young people, with an affectionate and fraternal kindness that left an impression upon my heart not yet impaired. The family consisted, at that time, of four sisters and three brothers, all grown-up, and remarkable for elegance and delicacy of manners. So much beauty, or so much native good breeding and refinement, I do not remember to have seen before or since in any cottage, except once or twice in Westmoreland and Devonshire. They spoke English; an accomplishment not often met with in so many members of one Welsh family, especially in villages remote from the high road. Here I wrote, on my first introduction, a letter about prize-money for one of the brothers, who had served on board an English man-of-war; and, more privately, two letters to sweethearts for two of the sisters. They were both interesting in appearance; and one of uncommon loveliness. In the midst of their confusion and blushes, whilst dictating, or rather giving me general instructions, it did not require any great penetration to discover that they wished their letters to be as kind as was consistent with proper maidenly reserve. I contrived so to temper my expressions as to reconcile the gratification of both feelings; and they were as much pleased with the way in which I had given expression to their thoughts, as (in their simplicity) they were astonished at my having so readily discovered them. The reception one meets with from the women of a family generally determines the tenor of one's whole entertainment. In this case I had discharged my confidential duties as secretary so much to the general satisfaction, perhaps also amusing them with my conversation, that I was pressed to stay; and pressed with a cordiality which I had little inclination to resist. I slept unavoidably with the brothers, the only unoccupied bed standing in the chamber of the young women: but in all other points they treated me with a respect not usually paid to purses as light as mine; making it evident that my scholarship and courteous demeanour were considered sufficient arguments of gentle blood. Thus I lived with them for three days, and great part of a fourth; and, from the undiminished kindness which they continued to show me, I believe that I might have stayed with them up to this time, if their power had corresponded with their wishes. On the last morning, however, I perceived upon their countenances, as they sat at breakfast, the approach of some unpleasant communication; and soon after, one of the brothers explained to me that, on the day before my arrival, their parents had gone to an annual meeting of Methodists, held at Carnarvon,[1] and in the course of that day were expected to return; 'and if they should not be so civil as they ought to be,' he begged, on the part of all the young people, that I would not take it amiss. The parents returned with churlish faces, and '*Dym Sassenach*' (*no English*) in answer to all my addresses. I saw how matters stood; and so, taking an affectionate leave of my kind and interesting young hosts, I went my way. For, though they spoke warmly to their parents on my behalf, and often excused the manner of the old people by saying that it was 'only their way,' yet I easily understood that my talent for writing love-letters would do as little to recommend me with two sexagenarian Welsh Methodists as my Greek Sapphics or Alcaics; and what had been hospitality,

---

[1] '*At Carnarvon*':—It was on this occasion that I learned how vague are the ideas of *number* in unpractised minds. 'What number of people do you think,' said I to an elderly person, 'will be assembled this day at Carnarvon?'—'What number?' rejoined the person addressed—'what number? Well, really now, I should reckon—perhaps a matter of four millions.' Four millions of *extra* people in little Carnarvon, that could barely find accommodation (I should calculate) for an extra four hundred.

when offered with the gracious courtesy of my young friends, would become charity, when connected with the harsh demeanour of their parents.

About this time—just when it was becoming daily more difficult to eke out the weekly funds for high-priced inns by the bivouacking system—as if some over-mastering fiend, some instinct of migration, sorrowful but irresistible, were driving me forth to wander like the unhappy Io of the Grecian mythus, some oestrum of hidden persecution that bade me fly when no man pursued ; not in false hope—for my hopes whispered but a doubtful chance, not in reasonable fear—for all was sweet pastoral quiet and autumnal beauty around me, suddenly I took a fierce resolution to sacrifice my weekly allowance, to slip my anchor, and to throw myself in desperation upon London. Not to make the case more frantic than it really was, let the reader remember what it was that I found grievous in my present position, and upon what possibilities it was that I relied for bettering it. With a more extended knowledge of life than I at that time had, it would not have been so hopeless a speculation for a boy, having my accomplishments, to launch himself on the boundless ocean of London. I possessed attainments that bore a money value. For instance, as a ' *Reader*' to the Press in the field of Greek re-publications, I might perhaps have earned a livelihood. But these chances, which I really had, never occurred to me in the light of useful resources ; or, to speak the truth, they were unknown to me : and those, which I chiefly relied on, were most unlikely to prove available. But what, meantime, was it that I complained of in the life that I was at present living? It was this : the dilemma proposed to my choice was—that if I *would*—positively *would*—have society, I must live at inns. But if I reconciled myself to a quiet stationary abode in some village or hamlet, in that case for *me*, so transcendently careless about diet, my weekly guinea would have procured all that I wanted : and in some houses the advantage, quite indispensable to my comfort, of a private sitting-room. Yet even here the expense was most needlessly enhanced by the aristocratic luxuriousness of our English system, which presumes it impossible for a gentleman to sleep in his sitting-room. On this footing, however, I might perhaps have commanded clean and comfortable accommodations in some respectable families, to whom my noiseless habits, and my respectful courtesy to women, would have recommended me as a desirable inmate. But the deadly drawback on this scheme was—the utter want of access to books, or (generally speaking) to any intellectual intercourse. I languished all the day through, and all the week through—with nothing whatever, not so much as the county newspaper once in seven days to relieve my mortal ennui.

I have told the reader how inexplicably cheap was the life in poor men's cottages. But this did not affect the prices at the first-class hotels, where only I had any chance of meeting society. Those, and chiefly on the plea that the season was so brief, charged London prices. To meet such prices, it would no longer be possible, as winter came on, to raise one-half the funds by passing half the time in a less costly mode. There was an end of any feasible plan for interleaving days of hardship with days of ease and intellectual luxury. Meantime, whilst this perplexity was resounding in one ear, in the other were continually echoing the kind offers of my Welsh friends, especially the two lawyers, to furnish me with any money which I might think necessary for my visit to London. Twelve guineas, at length, I mentioned as probably enough. This they lent me on the spot. And now, all at once, I was—ready for London.

My farewell to the Principality was in the same unassuming character of pedestrian tourist as that in which I had entered it. *Impedimenta* of any kind—that is, the encumbrances of horse or baggage—I had none even to the last. Where I pleased, and *when* I pleased, I could call a halt. My last halt of any duration was at Oswestry; mere accident carried me thither, and accident very naturally in so small a town threw me across the path of the very warmest amongst my Welsh friends, who, as it turned out, resided there. He, by mere coercion of kindness, detained me for several days; for denial he would not take. Being as yet unmarried, he could not vivify the other attractions of his most hospitable abode by the reinforcement of female society. His own, however, coming recommended as it did by the graces of a youthful frankness and a kindling intellect, was all-sufficient for the beguiling of the longest day. This Welsh friend was one of many whom I have crossed in life, chained by early accident or by domestic necessity to the calls of a professional service, whilst all the while his whole nature, wild and refractory, ran headlong into intellectual channels that could not be trained into reconciliation with his hourly duties. His library was already large, and as select as under the ordinary chances of provincial book-collection could be reasonably expected. For generally one-half, at the least, of a young man's library in a provincial town may be characterised as a mere dropping or deposition from local accidents, a casual windfall of fruits stripped and strewed by the rough storms of bankruptcy. In many cases, again, such a provincial library will represent simply that part of the heavy baggage which many a family, on removing to some distant quarter, has shrunk from the cost of transporting, books being amongst the heaviest of household goods. Sometimes also, though more rarely, it happens that an ancient family dying out, having unavoidably left to executors the duty of selling every chattel attached to its ancient habits of life, suddenly with meteoric glare there emerges from its hiding-place of centuries some great jewel of literature, a First Folio of the 1623 Shakspere, an uncastrated *Decamerone*, or other dazzling κειμήλιον. And thus it is that a large provincial library, though naturally and peacefully accumulated, yet sometimes shows mute evidence of convulsions and household tragedies; speaks as if by records of storms, and through dim mementoes of half-forgotten shipwrecks. Real shipwrecks present often such incoherent libraries on the floors of the hungry sea. Magnificent is the library that sleeps unvexed by criticism at the bottom of the ocean, Indian or Atlantic, from the mere annual contributions and keepsakes, the never-ending *Forget-me-nots*, of mighty English India-men. The *Halsewell*, with its sad parting between the captain and his daughters, the *Grosvenor*, the *Winterton*, the *Abergavenny*, and scores of vessels on the same scale, with populations varying by births, deaths, and marri-ages, populations large as cities, and rich as gold mines, capable of factions and rebellions, all and each have liberally patronised, by the gift of many *Large-Paper* copies, that vast submarine Bodleian, which stands in far less risk from fire than the insolent Bodleian of the upper world. This private Oswestry library wore some-thing of the same wild tumultuary aspect, fantastic and disordinate, but was not for that reason the less attractive; everything was there that you never expected to meet anywhere, but certainly not to meet in company ; so that, what between the library and the mercurial conversation of its proprietor, elated by the rare advantage of fraternal sympathy, I was in danger of finding attractions strong enough to lay me asleep over the proprieties of the case, or even to set me a-dreaming over imaginary cases. In fact, I had some excuse for doing so ; since I knew very imperfectly the common routine of my friend's life ; and from *his* lofty Castilian sense of the obligations imposed by the great goddess Hospitality, I never should have been suffered to guess at the extent in which I was now gradually and unconsciously coming daily into collision with the regular calls upon his time. To ride off, under mask of 'business,' upon a circuit of a week, would, in *his* eyes, have been *virtually*, as regards the result, meanly and evasively, as regards the mode, to turn me out of his house. He would sooner have died. But in the mean-time an accident, which revealed to me the true state of things, or at least revealed a suspicion of it, all at once armed my sense of delicacy against any further lingering. Suddenly and peremptorily I announced my departure—*that* and the mode of it. For a long time he fought with unaffected zeal against my purpose, as nowise essential to his own free action. But at last, seeing that

I was in earnest, he forbore to oppose my plan, contenting himself with guiding and improving its details. My plan had been, to walk over the border into England, as far as Shrewsbury (distant from Oswestry, I think, about eighteen miles), and there to ascend any of the heavy stages which would convey me cheaply to Birmingham—the grand focus to which all the routes of England in its main central area converge. Any such plan moved on the assumption that rain would be falling steadily and heavily—a reasonable assumption at the close of November. But, in the possible event of fair weather lasting over four or five days, what should prevent me from traversing the whole distance on foot? It is true, that the aristocratic scowl of the landlord might be looked for as a customary salutation at the close of each day's journey; but, unless at solitary posting-houses, this criminal fact of having advanced by base pedestrian methods, known only to patriarchs of older days and to modern '*tramps*' (so they are called in solemn acts of Parliament), is easily expiated and cleansed, by distributing your dust, should you fortunately have any to show, amongst the streets that you have invaded as a stranger. Happily the scandal of pedestrianism is in one respect more hopefully situated than that of scrofula or leprosy; it is not in any case written in your face. The man who is guilty of pedestrianism, on entering any town whatever, by the simple artifice of diving into the crowds of those untainted by that guilt, will emerge, for all practical purposes, washed and re-baptized. The landlord, indeed, of any one inn knows that you did not reach *him* on horseback, or in a carriage; but you may have been visiting for weeks at the house of some distinguished citizen, whom it might be dangerous to offend; and you may even be favourably known at some other inn. Else, as a general imputation, undoubtedly pedestrianism, in the estimate of English landlords, carries with it the most awful shadow and shibboleth of the pariah. My Welsh friend knew this, and strongly urged me to take advantage of the public carriages, both on that motive and others.

A journey of a hundred and eighty miles, as a pedestrian, would cost me nine or ten days; for which extent the mere amount of expenses at inns would more than defray the fare of the dearest carriage. To this there was no sound reply, except that corresponding expenses would arise, at any rate, on these nine or ten days, wherever I might be—in London, or on the road. However, as it seemed ungracious to offer too obstinate a resistance to suggestions prompted so entirely by consideration for my own comfort, I submitted to my friend's plan in all its details; one being that I should go by the Holyhead Mail, and not by any of the heavy coaches. This stipulation pointed to a novel feature in the machinery of travelling just then emerging. The light coaches charged almost mail prices. But the heavy coaches were at that time beginning to assume a new and dreadful form. Locomotion was so prodigiously on the increase, that, in order to meet its demands, the old form of coach (carrying at most six insides) was exchanging itself, on all great roads, for a long, boatlike vehicle, very much resembling our modern detestable *omnibus*, but without our modern improvements. This carriage was called a '*long coach*,' and the passengers, twelve or fourteen insides, sat along the sides; and, as ventilation was little regarded in those days—the very existence of an atmosphere being usually ignored—it followed that the horrors of Governor Holwell's black cage at Calcutta were every night repeated, in smaller proportions, upon every great English road. It was finally agreed that I should leave Oswestry on foot, simply with a view to the best enjoyment of the lovely weather; but that, as the mail passed through Oswestry, my friend should secure a place for me the whole way to London, so as to shut out competitors.

The day on which I left Oswestry (convoyed for nearly five miles by my warm-hearted friend) was a day of golden sunshine amongst the closing days of November. As truly as Jessica's moonlight (*Merchant of Venice*), this golden sunshine might be said to *sleep* upon the woods and the fields; so awful was the universal silence, so

profound the death-like stillness. It was a day belonging
to a brief and pathetic season of farewell summer resurrection, which, under one name or other, is known almost
everywhere. In North America it is called the 'Indian
Summer.' In North Germany and Midland Germany
it is called the 'Old Wives' Summer,' and more rarely
the 'Girls' Summer.' It is that last brief resurrection of
summer in its most brilliant memorials, a resurrection
that has no root in the past, nor steady hold in the
future, like the lambent and fitful gleams from an ex-
piring lamp, mimicking what is called the 'lightning
before death' in sick patients, when close upon their
end. There is the feeling of a conflict that has been
going on between the lingering powers of summer and
the strengthening powers of winter, not unlike that
which moves by antagonist forces in some deadly in-
flammation hurrying forwards through fierce struggles
into the final repose of mortification. For a time the
equilibrium has been maintained between the hostile
forces; but at last the antagonism is overthrown; the
victory is accomplished for the powers that fight on the
side of death; simultaneously with the conflict, the pain
of conflict has departed: and thenceforward the gentle
process of collapsing life, no longer fretted by counter-
movements, slips away with holy peace into the noiseless
deeps of the Infinite. So sweet, so ghostly, in its soft,
golden smiles, silent as a dream, and quiet as the dying
trance of a saint, faded through all its stages this departing day, along the whole length of which I bade farewell
for many a year to Wales, and farewell to summer.
In the very aspect and the sepulchral stillness of the
motionless day, as solemnly it wore away through
morning, noontide, afternoon, to meet the darkness
that was hurrying to swallow up its beauty, I had a
fantastic feeling as though I read the very language
of resignation when bending before some irresistible
agency. And at intervals I heard—in how different a
key!—the raving, the everlasting uproar of that dreadful
metropolis, which at every step was coming nearer, and
beckoning (as it seemed) to myself for purposes as dim,

for issues as incalculable, as the path of cannon-shots fired at random and in darkness.

It was not late, but it was at least two hours after nightfall, when I reached Shrewsbury. Was I not liable to the suspicion of pedestrianism? Certainly I was: but, even if my criminality had been more unequivocally attested than it could be under the circumstances, still there is a *locus penitentiæ* in such a case. Surely a man may repent of *any* crime; and therefore of pedestrianism. I might have erred; and a court of *pié poudré* (dusty foot) might have found the evidences of my crime on my shoes. Yet secretly I might be forming good resolutions to do so no more. Certainly it looked like this, when I announced myself as a passenger 'booked' for that night's mail. This character at once installed me as rightfully a guest of the inn, however profligate a life I might have previously led as a pedestrian. Accordingly I was received with special courtesy; and it so happened that I was received with something even like pomp. Four wax-lights carried before me by obedient mutes, these were but ordinary honours, meant (as old experience had instructed me) for the first engineering step towards effecting a lodgment upon the stranger's purse. In fact the wax-lights are used by innkeepers, both abroad and at home, to 'try the range of their guns.' If the stranger submits quietly, as a good anti-pedestrian ought surely to do, and fires no counter gun by way of protest, then he is recognised at once as passively within range, and amenable to orders. I have always looked upon this fine of five or seven shillings (for wax that you do not absolutely need) as a sort of inaugural *honorarium* entrance-money, what in jails used to be known as *smart* money, proclaiming me to be a man *comme il faut;* and no toll in this world of tolls do I pay so cheerfully. This, meantime, as I have said, was too customary a form to confer much distinction. The wax-lights, to use the magnificent Grecian phrase ἐπομπεύε, moved pompously before me, as the holy—holy fire, the inextinguishable fire and its golden hearth, moved before Cæsar *semper Augustus,* when he made his official or ceremonial *avatars.*

Yet still this moved along the ordinary channels of glorification: it rolled along ancient grooves: I might say, indeed, like one of the twelve Cæsars when dying, *Ut puto, Deus fio* (It's my private opinion that at this very moment I am turning into a god), but still the metamorphosis was not complete. *That* was accomplished when I stepped into the sumptuous room allotted to me. It was a ball-room[1] of noble proportions—lighted, if I chose to issue orders, by three gorgeous chandeliers, not basely wrapped up in paper, but sparkling through all their thickets of crystal branches, and flashing back the soft rays of my tall waxen lights. There were, moreover, two orchestras, which money would have filled within thirty minutes. And, upon the whole, one thing only was wanting—viz., a throne—for the completion of my *apotheosis*.

It might be seven P.M. when first I entered upon my kingdom. About three hours later I rose from my chair, and with considerable interest looked out into the night. For nearly two hours I had heard fierce winds arising; and the whole atmosphere had, by this time, become one vast laboratory of hostile movements in all directions. Such a chaos, such a distracting wilderness of dim sights, and of those awful 'sounds that live in darkness' (Wordsworth's *Excursion*), never had I consciously witnessed. Rightly, and by a true instinct, had I made my farewell adieus to summer. All through the day, Wales and her grand mountain ranges—Penmaenmawr, Snowdon, Cader Idris—had divided my thoughts with London. But now rose London—sole, dark, infinite—brooding over the whole capacities of my heart. Other object— other thought—I could not admit. Long before midnight, the whole household (with the exception of a solitary waiter) had retired to rest. Two hours, at least, were left to me, after twelve o'clock had struck, for heart-

---

1 '*It was a ball-room*':—The explanation of the case was simply, that the hotel was under some extensive process of purification, adornment, and, I believe, extension: and, under the accident of being myself on that particular night the sole visitor of the house, I slipped unavoidably into the honours of a semi-regal reception.

shaking reflections.  More than ever I stood upon the
brink of a precipice ; and the local circumstances around
me deepened and intensified these reflections, impressed
upon them solemnity and terror, sometimes even horror.
It is all but inconceivable to men of unyielding and
callous sensibilities, how profoundly others find their
reveries modified and overruled by the external characters of the immediate scene around them.  Many a
suicide that hung dubiously in the balances has been
ratified, and carried into summary effect, through the
forlorn, soul-revolting aspect of a crazy, dilapidated home.
Oftentimes, without extravagance, the whole difference
between a mind that spurns life and the same mind
reconciled to life, turns upon the outside features of that
particular domestic scenery which hourly besieges the
eyes.  I, in this Shrewsbury hotel, naturally contemplated a group of objects tending to far different results.
And yet in some respects they agreed.

The unusual dimensions of the rooms, especially their
towering height, brought up continually and obstinately,
through natural links of associated feelings or images,
the mighty vision of London waiting for me afar off.
An altitude of nineteen or twenty feet showed itself
unavoidably upon an exaggerated scale in some of the
smaller side-rooms—meant probably for cards or for
refreshments.  This single feature of the rooms—their
unusual altitude, and the echoing hollowness which had
become the exponent of that altitude—this one terrific
feature (for terrific it was in the effect), together with
crowding and evanescent images of the flying feet that
so often had spread gladness through these halls on the
wings of youth and hope at seasons when every room
rang with music—all this, rising in tumultuous vision,
whilst the dead hours of night were stealing along, all
around me—household and town—sleeping, and whilst
against the windows more and more the storm outside
was raving, and to all appearance endlessly growing,
threw me into the deadliest condition of nervous emotion
under contradictory forces, high over which predomi-
nated horror recoiling from that unfathomed abyss in

London into which I was now so wilfully precipitating myself. Often I looked out and examined the night. Wild it was beyond all description, and dark as 'the inside of a wolf's throat.' But at intervals, when the wind, shifting continually, swept in such a direction as to clear away the vast curtain of vapour, the stars shone out, though with a light unusually dim and distant. Still, as I turned inwards to the echoing chambers, or outwards to the wild, wild night, I saw London expanding her visionary gates to receive me, like some dreadful mouth of Acheron (*Acherontis avari*). Thou also, Whispering Gallery! once again in those moments of conscious and wilful desolation didst to my ear utter monitorial sighs. For once again I was preparing to utter an irrevocable word, to enter upon one of those fatally tortuous paths of which the windings can never be unlinked.

Such thoughts, and visions without number corresponding to them, were moving across the *camera obscura* of my fermenting fancy, when suddenly I heard a sound of wheels; which, however, soon died off into some remote quarter. I guessed at the truth—viz., that it was the Holyhead Mail [1] wheeling off on its primary duty of delivering its bags at the post-office. In a few minutes it was announced as having changed horses; and off I was to London.

All the mails in the kingdom, with one solitary exception (that of Liverpool), in those days, were so arranged as to reach London early in the morning. Between the

[1] The Holyhead Mail, depending in its earliest stages upon winds and waters (though not upon tides), could not realise the same exquisite accuracy as mails that moved exclusively upon land. Sixty miles of watery transit between Dublin and Holyhead were performed with miraculous precision. The packets were intrusted by the General Post-office to none but post-captains, who had commanded frigates. And the salaries were so high as to make these commands confessedly prizes in nautical life, and objects of keen competition. No evil, therefore, which care, foresight, and professional skill could remedy, was suffered to exist. Yet, after all, baffling winds would now and then (especially in three or four weeks *after* the equinox) make it impossible for the very ablest man, under the total defect of steam resources, to keep his time. Six hours, I believe, were allowed by the Post-office for the sixty miles· but at times this must have proved a very inadequate allowance.

hours of four and six A.M., one after the other, according to their station upon the roll, all the mails from the N[orth]—the E[ast]—the W[est]—the S[outh]—whence, according to some curious etymologists, comes the magical word *NEWS*—drove up successively to the post-office, and rendered up their heart-shaking budgets; none earlier than four o'clock, none later than six. I am speaking of days when all things moved slowly. The condition of the roads was then such, that, in order to face it, a corresponding build of coaches hyperbolically massive was rendered necessary: the mails were upon principle made so strong as to be the heaviest of all carriages known to the wit or the experience of man; and from these joint evils of ponderous coaches and roads that were quagmires, it was impossible for even the picked breed of English-coach-horses, all bone and blood, to carry forward their huge tonnage at a greater rate than six-and-a-half miles an hour. Consequently, it cost eight-and-twenty massy hours for us, leaving Shrewsbury at two o'clock in the dead of night, to reach the General Post-office, and faithfully to deposit upon the threshing-floors of Lombard Street, all that weight of love and hatred which Ireland had found herself able to muster through twenty-four hours in the great depôt of Dublin, by way of donation to England.

On reflection, I have done myself some injustice. Not altogether without a plan had I been from the first; and in coming along I had matured it. My success in such a plan would turn upon my chance of borrowing on personal security. £200, without counting any interest upon it, would subdivide into four sums of £50. Now, what interval was it that divided me from my majority? Simply an interval of four years. London, I knew or believed, was the dearest of all cities for three items of expenditure: (1) servants' wages; (2) lodgings;[1] (3) dairy produce. In other

[1] Not universally. Glasgow, if you travel from Hammerfest southwards (that is, from the northernmost point of Norway, or Swedish Lapland, traversing all latitudes of Europe to Gibraltar on the west, or Naples on the east), is the one dearest place for lodgings known to

things, London was often cheaper than most towns. Now, in a London street, having no pretensions beyond those of decent respectability, it has always been possible for the last half century to obtain two furnished rooms at a weekly cost of half a guinea. This sum (or say £25) deducted would leave me annually about the same sum for my other expenses. Too certainly I knew that this would suffice. If, therefore, I could obtain the £200, my plan was to withdraw from the knowledge of all my connections until I should become *mei juris* by course of law. In such a case, it is true that I must have waived all the advantages, fancied or real, small or great, from residence at a university. But, as in fact I never drew the slightest advantage or emolument from any university, my scheme when realised would have landed me in the same point which finally I attained by its failure. The plan was simple enough, but it rested on the assumption that I could melt the obduracy of money-lenders. On this point I had both hopes and fears. But more irritating than either was the *delay*, which eventually I came to recognise as an essential element in the policy of all money-lenders: in that way only can they raise up such claims on behalf of their law agents as may be fitted for sustaining their zeal.

. . . . . . .

I lost no time in opening the business which had brought me to London. By ten A.M., an hour when all men of business are presumed to be at their posts, personally or by proxy, I presented myself at the money-lender's office. My name was already known there: for I had, by letters from Wales, containing very plain and very accurate statements of my position in life and my pecuniary expectations (some of which statements it afterwards appeared that he had personally investigated and verified), endeavoured to win his favourable attention.

man. A decent lodging for a single person, in Edinburgh, which could be had readily for half-a-guinea a-week, will in Glasgow cost a guinea. Glasgow, except as to servants, is a dearer abode than London.

The money-lender, as it turned out, had one fixed rule of action. He never granted a personal interview to any man; no, not to the most beloved of his clients. One and all—myself, therefore, among the crowd—he referred for information, and for the means of prosecuting any kind of negotiation, to an attorney, who called himself, on most days of the week, by the name of Brunell, but occasionally (might it perhaps be on *red-letter* days?) by the more common name of Brown. Mr. Brunell-Brown, or Brown-Brunel, had located his hearth (if ever he had possessed one), and his household gods (when they were not in the custody of the sheriff), in Greek Street, Soho. The house was not in itself, supposing that its face had been washed now and then, at all disrespectable. But it wore an unhappy countenance of gloom and unsocial fretfulness, due in reality to the long neglect of painting, cleansing, and in some instances of repairing. There were, however, no fractured panes of glass in the windows; and the deep silence which invested the house, not only from the absence of all visitors, but also of those common household functionaries, bakers, butchers, beer-carriers, sufficiently accounted for the desolation, by suggesting an excuse not strictly true—viz., that it might be tenantless. The house already had tenants through the day, though of a noiseless order, and was destined soon to increase them. Mr. Brown-Brunell, after reconnoitring me through a narrow side-window (such as is often attached to front-doors in London), admitted me cheerfully, and conducted me, as an honoured guest, to his private *officina diplomatum* at the back of the house. From the expression of his face, but much more from the contradictory and self-counteracting play of his features, you gathered in a moment that he was a man who had much to conceal, and much, perhaps, that he would gladly forget. His eye expressed wariness against surprise, and passed in a moment into irrepressible glances of suspicion and alarm. No smile that ever his face naturally assumed, but was pulled short up by some freezing counteraction, or was chased by some close-following expression of sadness. One feature there was of relenting goodness and nobleness in Mr. Brunell's character, to which it was that subsequently I myself was most profoundly indebted for an asylum that saved my life. He had the deepest, the most liberal, and unaffected love of knowledge, but, above all, of that specific knowledge which we call literature. His own stormy (and no doubt oftentimes disgraceful) career in life, that had entangled him in perpetual feuds with his fellow-men, he ascribed, with bitter imprecations, to the sudden interruption of his studies consequent upon his father's violent death, and to the necessity which threw him, at a boyish age, upon a professional life in the lower branches of law—threw him, therefore, upon daily temptations, by surrounding him with opportunities for taking advantages not strictly honourable, before he had formed any fixed principles at all. From the very first, Mr. Brunell had entered zealously into such conversations with myself as either gave openings for reviving his own delightful remembrances of classic authors, or brought up sometimes doubts for solution, sometimes perplexities and cases of intricate construction for illustration and disentanglement. Hunger-bitten as the house and the household genius seemed, wearing the legend of *Famine* upon every mantelpiece or 'coigne of vantage,' and vehemently protesting, as it must have done through all its echoes, against the introduction of supernumerary mouths, nevertheless there was (and, I suppose, of necessity) a clerk, who bore the name of Pyment, or Pyemont, then first of all, then last of all, made known to me as a possible surname. Mr. Pyment had no *alias*—or not to my knowledge—except, indeed, in the vituperative vocabulary of Mr. Brunell, in which most variegated nomenclature he bore many scores of opprobrious names, having no reference whatever to any real habits of the man, good or bad. At two rooms' distance, Mr. Brunel always assumed a minute and circumstantial knowledge of what Pyment was doing then, and what he was going to do next. All which Pyment gave himself little

trouble to answer, unless it happened (as now and
then it did) that he could do so with ludicrous effect.
What made the necessity for Pyment was the continual
call for 'an appearance' to be put in at some of the
subordinate courts in Westminster—courts of conscience,
sheriff courts, &c. But it happens often that he who
is most indispensable, and gets through most work at
one hour, becomes a useless burden at another; as the
hardest-working reaper seems, in the eyes of an igno-
ramus, on a wet, wintry day, to be a luxurious idler.
Of these ups and downs in Pyment's working life, Mr.
Brunell made a most cynical use; making out that
Pyment not only did nothing, but also that he created
much work for the afflicted Brunell. However, it happened occasionally that the truth vindicated itself, by
making a call upon Pyment's physics—aggressive or
defensive—that needed an instant attention. 'Pyment,
I say; this way, Pyment—you're wanted, Pyment.' In
fact, both were big, hulking men, and had need to be
so; for sometimes, whether with good reason or none,
clients at the end of a losing suit, or of a suit nominally
gained, but unexpectedly laden with heavy expenses, became refractory, showed fight, and gave Pyment reason
for saying that at least on this day he had earned his
salary by serving an ejectment on a client whom on
any other plan it might have been hard to settle with.

But I am anticipating. I go back, therefore, for a few
explanatory words, to the day of my arrival in London.
How beneficial to me would a little candour have been
at that early period! If (which was the simple truth,
known to all parties but myself) I had been told that
nothing would be brought to a close in less than six
months, even assuming the ultimate adoption of my
proposals, I should from the first have dismissed all
hopes of this nature, as being unsuited to the prac-
ticabilities of my situation. It will be seen further on,
that there was a real and sincere intention of advancing
the money wanted. But it was then too late. And
universally I believe myself entitled to say, that even
honourable lawyers will not in a case of this nature

move at a faster pace: they will all alike loiter upon varied allegations through six months; and for this reason, that any shorter period, they fancy, will hardly seem to justify, in the eyes of their client, the sum which they find themselves entitled to charge for their trouble and their preliminary correspondence. How much better for both sides, and more honourable, as more frank and free from disguises, that the client should say, 'Raise this sum' (of, suppose, £400) 'in three weeks, which can be done, if it can be done in three years, and here is a *bonus* of £100. Delay for two months, and I decline the whole transaction.' Treated with that sort of openness, how much bodily suffering of an extreme order, and how much of the sickness from hope deferred, should I have escaped! Whereas, under the system (pursued with me as with all clients) of continually refreshing my hopes with new delusions, whiling me on with pretended preparation of deeds, and extorting from me, out of every little remittance I received from old family friends casually met in London, as much as possible for the purchase of imaginary stamps, the result was, that I myself was brought to the brink of destruction through pure inanition; whilst, on the other hand, those concerned in these deceptions gained nothing that might not have been gained honourably and rightfully under a system of plain dealing. As it was, subject to these eternal deceptions, I continued for seven or eight weeks to live most parsimoniously in lodgings. These lodgings, though barely decent in my eyes, ran away with at the least two-thirds of my remaining guineas. At length, whilst it was yet possible to reserve a solitary half-guinea towards the more urgent interest of finding daily food, I gave up my rooms; and, stating exactly the circumstances in which I stood, requested permission of Mr. Brunell to make use of his large house as a nightly asylum from the open air. Parliament had not then made it a crime, next door to a felony, for a man to sleep out-of-doors (as some twenty years later was done by our benign legislators); as yet *that* was no crime. By the law I came to know sin; and looking back to the Cambrian hills from distant years, discovered to my surprise what a parliamentary wretch I had been in elder days, when I slept amongst cows on the open hillsides. Lawful as yet this was; but not, therefore, less full of misery. Naturally, then, I was delighted when Mr. Brunell not only most readily assented to my request, but begged of me to come that very night, and turn the house to account as fully as I possibly could. The cheerfulness of such a concession brought with it one drawback. I now regretted that I had not, at a much earlier period, applied for this liberty; since I might thus have saved a considerable fund of guineas, applicable, of course, to all urgent necessities, but at this particular moment to one of clamorous urgency —viz., the purchase of blankets. O ancient women, daughters of toil and suffering, amongst all the hardships and bitter inheritances of flesh that ye are called upon to face, not one—not even hunger—seems in my eyes comparable to that of nightly cold. To seek a refuge from cold in bed, and then, from the thin, gauzy texture of the miserable, worn-out blankets, 'not to sleep a wink,' as Wordsworth records of poor old women in Dorsetshire, where coals, from local causes, were at the very dearest—what a terrific enemy was *that* for poor old grandmothers to face in fight! How feelingly I learned at this time, as heretofore I had learned on the wild hillsides in Wales, what an unspeakable blessing is that of warmth! A more killing curse there does not exist for man or woman, than that bitter combat between the weariness that prompts sleep, and the keen, searching cold that forces you from the first access of sleep to start up horror-stricken, and to seek warmth vainly in renewed exercise, though long since fainting under fatigue. However, even without blankets, it was a fine thing to have an asylum from the open air; and to be assured of this asylum as long as I was likely to want it.

Towards nightfall I went down to Greek Street; and found, on taking possession of my new quarters, that the house already contained one single inmate, a poor, friendless child, apparently ten years old; but she seemed hunger-bitten; and sufferings of that sort often make children look older than they are. From this forlorn child I learnt that she had slept and lived there alone for some time before I came; and great joy the poor creature expressed, when she found that I was in future to be her companion through the hours of darkness. The house could hardly be called large—that is, it was not large on each separate storey; but, having four storeys in all, it was large enough to impress vividly the sense of its echoing loneliness; and, from the want of furniture, the noise of the rats made a prodigious uproar on the staircase and hall; so that, amidst the real fleshly ills of cold and hunger, the forsaken child had found leisure to suffer still more from the self-created one of ghosts. Against these enemies I could promise her protection; human companionship was in itself protection; but of other and more needful aid I had, alas! little to offer. We lay upon the floor, with a bundle of law-papers for a pillow, but with no other covering than a large horseman's cloak; afterwards, however, we discovered in a garret an old sofa-cover, a small piece of rug, and some fragments of other articles, which added a little to our comfort. The poor child crept close to me for warmth, and for security against her ghostly enemies. When I was not more than usually ill, I took her into my arms, so that, in general, she was tolerably warm, and often slept when I could not; for, during the last two months of my sufferings I slept much in the daytime, and was apt to fall into transient dozings at all hours. But my sleep distressed me more than my watching; for, besides the tumultuousness of my dreams (which were only not so awful as those which I shall have hereafter to describe as produced by opium), my sleep was never more than what is called *dog-sleep*; so that I could hear myself moaning; and very often I was awakened suddenly by my own voice. About this time, a hideous sensation began to haunt me as soon as I fell into a slumber, which has since returned upon me at different periods of my life—viz., a sort of twitching (I knew not where, but apparently about the region of the stomach), which compelled me violently to throw out my feet for the sake of relieving it. This sensation coming on as soon as I began to sleep, and the effort to relieve it constantly awaking me, at length I slept only from exhaustion; and through increasing weakness (as I said before), I was constantly falling asleep, and constantly awaking. Too generally the very attainment of any deep repose seemed as if mechanically linked to some fatal necessity of self-interruption. It was as though a cup were gradually filled by the sleepy overflow of some natural fountain, the fulness of the cup expressing symbolically the completeness of the rest: but then, in the next stage of the process, it seemed as though the rush and torrent-like babbling of the redundant waters, when running over from every part of the cup, interrupted the slumber which in their earlier stage of silent gathering they had so naturally produced. Such and so regular in its swell and its collapse—in its tardy growth and its violent dispersion—did this endless alternation of stealthy sleep and stormy awaking travel through stages as natural as the increments of twilight, or the kindlings of the dawn: no rest that was not a prologue to terror; no sweet tremulous pulses of restoration that did not suddenly explode through rolling clamours of fiery disruption. Meantime, the master of the house sometimes came in upon us suddenly, and very early; sometimes not till ten o'clock; sometimes not at all. He was in constant fear of arrest. Improving on the plan of Cromwell, every night he slept in a different quarter of London; and I observed that he never failed to examine, through a private window, the appearance of those who knocked at the door, before he would allow it to be opened. He breakfasted alone; indeed, his tea equipage would hardly have admitted of his hazarding an invitation to a second person, any more than the quantity of esculent *material*, which, for the most part, was little more than a roll, or a few biscuits, purchased on his road from the place where he had slept. Or, if he *had* asked a party, as I once learnedly observed to him, the several members of it must have *stood* in the relation to each other (not *sat* in any relation whatever) of succession, and not of co-existence; in the relation of parts of time, and not of the parts of space. During his breakfast, I generally contrived a reason for lounging in; and, with an air of as much indifference as I could assume, took up such fragments as might chance to remain; sometimes, indeed, none at all remained. In doing this, I committed no robbery, except upon Mr. Brunell himself, who was thus obliged, now and then, to send out at noon for an extra biscuit; but he, through channels subsequently explained, was repaid a thousandfold; and, as to the poor child, *she* was never admitted into his study (if I may give that name to his chief depository of parchments, law-writings, etc.); that room was to her the Bluebeard room of the house, being regularly locked on his departure to dinner, about six o'clock, which usually was his final departure for the day. Whether this child were an illegitimate daughter of Mr. Brunell, or only a servant, I could not ascertain; she did not herself know; but certainly she was treated altogether as a menial servant. No sooner did Mr. Brunell make his appearance than she went below-stairs, brushed his shoes, coat, etc.; and, except when she was summoned to run upon some errand, she never emerged from the dismal Tartarus of the kitchens to the upper air, until my welcome knock towards nightfall called up her little trembling footsteps to the front-door. Of her life during the daytime, however, I knew little but what I gathered from her own account at night; for, as soon as the hours of business commenced, I saw that my absence would be acceptable; and, in general, therefore, I went off and sat in the parks or elsewhere until the approach of twilight.

But who, and what, meantime, was the master of the house himself? Reader, he was one of those anomalous practitioners in lower departments of the law who, on prudential reasons, or from necessity, deny themselves all indulgence in the luxury of too delicate a conscience. In many walks of life, a conscience is a more expensive encumbrance than a wife or a carriage; and, as people talk of 'laying down' their carriages, so I suppose my friend Mr. Brunell had 'laid down' his conscience for a time; meaning, doubtless, to resume it as soon as he could afford it. He was an advertising attorney, who continually notified to the public, through the morning papers, that he undertook to raise loans for approved parties in what would generally be regarded as desperate cases—viz., where there was nothing better than *personal* security to offer. But, as he took good care to ascertain that there were ample funds in reversion to be counted on, or near connections that would not suffer the family name to be dishonoured, and as he insured the borrower's life over a sufficient period, the risk was not great; and even of this the whole rested upon the actual money-lender, who stood aloof in the back-ground, and never revealed himself to clients in his proper person, transacting all affairs through his proxies learned in the law—Mr. Brunell or others. The inner economy of such a man's daily life would present a monstrous picture. Even with my limited opportunities for observing what went on, I saw scenes of intrigue and complex chicanery, at which I sometimes smile to this day, and at which I smiled then, in spite of my misery. My situation, however, at that time, gave me little experience, in my own person, of any qualities in Mr. Brunell's character but such as did him honour; and of his whole strange composition I ought to forget everything, but that towards me he was obliging, and, to the extent of his power, generous.

That power was not, indeed, very extensive. However, in common with the rats, I sat rent free; and as Dr. Johnson has recorded that he never but once in his life had as much wall-fruit as he wished, so let me be grateful that, on that single occasion, I had as large a choice of rooms, or even of apartments, in a London mansion—viz., as I am now at liberty to add, at the north-west corner of Greek Street, being the house on that side the street nearest to Soho Square—as I could possibly desire. Except the Bluebeard room, which the poor child believed to be permanently haunted, and which, besides, was locked, all others, from the attics to the cellars, were at our service. 'The world was all before us,' and we pitched our tent for the night in any spot we might fancy. This house I have described as roomy and respectable. It stands in a conspicuous situation, and in a well-known part of London. Many of my readers will have passed it, I doubt not, within a few hours of reading this. For myself, I never fail to visit it when accident draws me to London. About ten o'clock this very night (August 15, 1821, being my birthday), I turned aside from my evening walk along Oxford Street, in order to take a glance at it. It is now in the occupation of some family, apparently respectable. The windows are no longer coated by a paste, composed of ancient soot and superannuated rain; and the whole exterior no longer wears an aspect of gloom. By the lights in the front drawing-room, I observed a domestic party, assembled, perhaps, at tea, and apparently cheerful and gay—marvellous contrast, in my eyes, to the darkness, cold, silence, and desolation, of that same house nineteen years ago, when its nightly occupants were one famishing scholar and a poor, neglected child. Her, by-the-bye, in after years, I vainly endeavoured to trace. Apart from her situation, she was not what would be called an interesting child. She was neither pretty, nor quick in understanding, nor remarkably pleasing in manners. But, thank God! even in those years I needed not the embellishments of elegant accessories to conciliate my affections. Plain human nature, in its humblest and most homely apparel, was enough for me; and I loved the child because she was my partner in wretchedness. If she is now living, she is probably a mother, with children of her own; but, as I have said, I could never trace her.

This I regret; but another person there was, at that time, whom I have since sought to trace with far deeper earnestness, and with far deeper sorrow at my failure.

This person was a young woman, and one of that unhappy class who belong to the outcasts and pariahs of our female population. I feel no shame, nor have any reason to feel it, in avowing that I was then on familiar and friendly terms with many women in that unfortunate condition. Smile not, reader too carelessly facile! Frown not, reader too unseasonably austere! Little call was there here either for smiles or frowns. A penniless schoolboy could not be supposed to stand within the range of such temptations; besides that, according to the ancient Latin proverb, ' *sine Cerere et Baccho*,' &c. These unhappy women, to me, were simply sisters in calamity; and sisters amongst whom, in as large measure as amongst any other equal number of persons, commanding more of the world's respect, were to be found humanity, disinterested generosity, courage that would not falter in defence of the helpless, and fidelity that would have scorned to take bribes for betraying. But the truth is, that at no time of my life have I been a person to hold myself polluted by the touch or approach of any creature that wore a human shape. I cannot suppose, I will not believe, that any creatures wearing the form of man or woman are so absolutely rejected and reprobate outcasts, that merely to talk with them inflicts pollution. On the contrary, from my very earliest youth, it has been my pride to converse familiarly, *more Socratico*, with all human beings—man, woman, and child—that chance might fling in my way; for a philosopher should not see with the eyes of the poor limitary creature calling himself a man of the world, filled with narrow and self-regarding prejudices of birth and education, but should look upon himself as a catholic creature, and as standing in an equal relation to high and low, to educated and uneducated, to the guilty and the innocent. Being myself, at that time, of necessity a peripatetic, or a walker of the streets, I naturally fell in more frequently with those peripatetics who are technically called street-walkers. Some of these women had occasionally taken my part against watchmen who wished to drive me off the steps of houses where I was sitting; others had protected me against more serious aggressions. But one amongst them —the one on whose account I have at all introduced this subject—yet no! let me not class thee, O noble-minded Ann ——, with that order of women; let me find, if it be possible, some gentler name to designate the condition of her to whose bounty and compassion —ministering to my necessities when all the world stood aloof from me—I owe it that I am at this time alive. For many weeks I had walked, at nights, with this poor friendless girl up and down Oxford Street, or had rested with her on steps and under the shelter of porticos. She could not be so old as myself: she told me, indeed, that she had not completed her sixteenth year. By such questions as my interest about her prompted, I had gradually drawn forth her simple history. Hers was a case of ordinary occurrence (as I have since had reason to think), and one in which, if London benefi-cence had better adapted its arrangements to meet it, the power of the law might oftener be interposed to protect and to avenge. But the stream of London charity flows in a channel which, though deep and mighty, is yet noiseless and underground;—not obvious or readily accessible to poor, houseless wanderers; and it cannot be denied that the outside air and framework of society in London, as in all vast capitals, is unavoid-ably harsh, cruel, and repulsive. In any case, however, I saw that part of her injuries might have been re-dressed; and I urged her often and earnestly to lay her complaint before a magistrate. Friendless as she was, I assured her that she would meet with immediate attention; and that English justice, which was no re-specter of persons, would speedily and amply avenge her on the brutal ruffian who had plundered her little property. She promised me often that she would; but she delayed taking the steps I pointed out, from time to time; for she was timid and dejected to a degree which showed how deeply sorrow had taken hold of her young heart; and perhaps she thought justly that the most upright judge and the most righteous tribunals could do nothing to repair her heaviest wrongs. Something, however, would perhaps have been done; for it had been settled between us at length (but, unhappily, on the very last time but one that I was ever to see her), that in a day or two I, accompanied by her, should state her case to a magistrate. This little service it was destined, however, that I should never realise. Meantime, that which she rendered to me, and which was greater than I could ever have repaid her, was this. One night, when we were pacing slowly along Oxford Street, and after a day when I had felt unusually ill and faint, I requested her to turn off with me into Soho Square. Thither we went; and we sat down on the steps of a house, which to this hour I never pass without a pang of grief, and an inner act of homage to the spirit of that unhappy girl, in memory of the noble act which she there performed. Suddenly, as we sat, I grew much worse. I had been leaning my head against her bosom, and all at once I sank from her arms, and fell backwards on the steps. From the sensations I then had, I felt an inner conviction of the liveliest kind, that, without some powerful and reviving stimulus, I should either have died on the spot, or should, at least, have sunk to a point of exhaustion from which all re-ascent, under my friendless circumstances, would soon have become hopeless. Then it was, at this crisis of my fate, that my poor orphan companion, who had herself met with little but injuries in this world, stretched out a saving hand to me. Uttering a cry of terror, but without a moment's delay, she ran off into Oxford Street, and, in less time than could be imagined, returned to me with a glass of port-wine and spices, that acted upon my empty stomach (which at that time would have rejected all solid food) with an instantaneous power of restoration; and for this glass the generous girl, without a murmur, paid out of her own humble purse, at a time, be it remembered when she had scarcely wherewithal to purchase the bare necessaries of life, and when she could have no reason to expect that I should ever be able to reimburse her.

O youthful benefactress! how often in succeeding years, standing in solitary places, and thinking of thee with grief of heart and perfect love—how often have I wished that, as in ancient times the curse of a father was believed to have a supernatural power, and to pursue its object with a fatal necessity of self-fulfilment, even so the benediction of a heart oppressed with gratitude might have a like prerogative; might have power given it from above to chase, to haunt, to waylay, to pursue thee into the central darkness of a London brothel, or (if it were possible) even into the darkness of the grave, there to awaken thee with an authentic message of peace and forgiveness, and of final reconciliation!

Some feelings, though not deeper or more passionate, are more tender than others; and often when I walk, at this time, in Oxford Street by dreamy lamp-light, and hear those airs played on a common street-organ which years ago solaced me and my dear youthful companion, I shed tears, and muse with myself at the mysterious dispensation which so suddenly and so critically separated us for ever. How it happened, the reader will understand from what remains of this introductory narration.

Soon after the period of the last incident I have recorded, I met in Albemarle Street a gentleman of his late Majesty's household. This gentleman had received hospitalities, on different occasions, from my family; and he challenged me upon the strength of my family likeness. I did not attempt any disguise, but answered his questions ingenuously; and, on his pledging his word of honour that he would not betray me to my guardians, I gave him my real address in Greek Street. The next day I received from him a ten-pound bank-note. The letter enclosing it was delivered, with other letters of business, to the attorney; but, though his look and manner informed me that he suspected its contents, he gave it up to me honourably, and without demur.

This present, from the particular service to which much of it was applied, leads me naturally to speak again of the original purpose which had allured me up to London, and which I had been without intermission prosecuting through Mr. Brunell from the first day of my arrival in London.

In so mighty a world as London, it will suprise my readers that I should not have found some means of staving off the last extremities of penury; and it will strike them that two resources, at least, must have been open to me: viz., either to seek assistance from the friends of my family, or to turn my youthful accomplishments, such as they were, into some channel of pecuniary emolument. As to the first course, I may observe, generally, that what I dreaded beyond all other evils was the chance of being reclaimed by my guardians; not doubting that whatever power the law gave them would have been enforced against me to the utmost; that is, to the extremity of forcibly restoring me to the school which I had quitted; a restoration which, as it would, in my eyes, have been a dishonour, even if submitted to voluntarily, could not fail, when extorted from me in contempt and defiance of my own known wishes and earnest resistance, to have proved a humiliation worse to me than death, and which would, indeed, have terminated in death. I was, therefore, shy enough of applying for assistance even in those quarters where I was sure of receiving it, if at any risk of furnishing my guardians with a clue for tracing me. My father's friends, no doubt, had been many, and were scattered all over the kingdom; but, as to London in particular, though a large section of these friends would certainly be found there, yet (as full ten years had passed since his death) I knew very few of them even by name; and never having seen London before—except once, in my fifteenth year, for a few hours—I knew not the address of even those few. To this mode of gaining help, therefore, in part the difficulty, but much more the danger which I have mentioned, habitually indisposed me. In regard to the other mode—that of turning any talents or knowledge that I might possess to a lucrative use—I now feel half inclined to join my reader in wondering

that I should have overlooked it. As a corrector of
Greek proofs (if in no other way), I might surely have
gained enough for my slender wants. Such an office
as this I could have discharged with an exemplary and
punctual accuracy that would soon have gained me the
confidence of my employers. And there was this great
preliminary advantage in giving such a direction to my
efforts, that the intellectual dignity and elegance associated with all ministerial services about the press would
have saved my pride and self-respect from mortification.
In an extreme case, such as mine had now become, I
should not have absolutely disdained the humble station
of 'devil.' A subaltern situation in a service inherently
honourable is better than a much higher situation in a
service pointing to ultimate objects that are mean or
ignoble. I am, indeed, not sure that I could adequately
have discharged the functions of this office. To the perfection of the diabolic character I fear that patience is
one of the indispensable graces; more, perhaps, than I
should be found on trial to possess for dancing attendance upon crotchety authors, superstitiously fastidious
in matters of punctuation. But why talk of my qualifications? Qualified or not, where could I obtain such
an office? For it must not be forgotten that even a
diabolic appointment requires interest. Towards *that*,
I must first of all have an introduction to some respectable publisher; and this I had no means of obtaining.
To say the truth, however, it had never once occurred
to me to think of literary labours as a source of profit.
No mode sufficiently speedy of obtaining money had
ever suggested itself, but that of borrowing it on the
strength of my future claims and expectations. This
mode I sought by every avenue to compass; and
amongst other persons I applied to a Jew named
D——.[1]

[1] At this period (autumn of 1856), when thirty-five years have elapsed
since the first publication of these memoirs, reasons of delicacy can no
longer claim respect for concealing the Jew's name, or at least the
name which he adopted in his dealings with the Gentiles. I say,
therefore, without scruple, that the name was Dell: and some years
later it was one of the names that came before the House of Commons

To this Jew, and to other advertising money-lenders, I had introduced myself, with an account of my expectations; which account they had little difficulty in ascertaining to be correct. The person there mentioned as the second son of ——, was found to have all the claims (or more than all) that I had stated: but one question still remained, which the faces of the Jews pretty significantly suggested,—was I that person? This doubt had never occurred to me as a possible one; I had rather feared, whenever my Jewish friends scrutinised me keenly, that I might be too well known to be that person, and that some scheme might be passing in their minds for entrapping me and selling me to my guardians.

In connection with something or other (I have long since forgotten *what*) growing out of the parliamentary movement against the Duke of York, in reference to Mrs. Clark, etc. Like all the other Jews with whom I have had negotiations, he was frank and honourable in his mode of conducting business. What he promised he performed; and, if his terms were high, as naturally they could not *but* be, to cover his risks, he avowed them from the first.

To this same Mr. Dell, by the way, some eighteen months afterwards, I applied again on the same business; and, dating at that time from a respectable college, I was fortunate enough to win his serious attention to my proposals. My necessities had not arisen from any extravagance or youthful levities (these my habits forbade), but simply from the vindictive malice of my guardian, who, when he found himself no longer able to prevent me from going to the university, had, as a parting token of his regard, refused to sign an order for granting me a shilling beyond the allowance made to me at school—viz., £100 per annum. Upon this sum it was, in my time (*i.e.*, in the first decennium of this century), barely possible to have lived at college; and not possible to a man who, though above the affectation of ostentatious disregard for money, and without any expensive tastes, confided, nevertheless, rather too much in servants, and did not delight in the petty details of minute economy. I soon, therefore, became embarrassed: in a movement of impatience, instead of candidly avowing my condition to my mother, or to some one of the guardians, more than one of whom would have advanced me the £250 wanted (not in his legal character of guardian, but as a private friend), I was so foolish as to engage in a voluminous negotiation with the Jew, and was put in possession of the sum I asked for, on the 'regular' terms of paying seventeen and a-half per cent. by way of annuity on all the money furnished; Israel, on his part, graciously resuming no more than about ninety guineas of the said money, on account of an attorney's bill (for what services, to whom rendered, and when—whether at the siege of Jerusalem, or at the building of the Second Temple—I have not yet discovered). How many perches this bill measured I really forget; but I still keep it in a cabinet of natural curiosities.

It was strange to me to find my own self, *materialiter* considered (so I expressed it, for I doted on logical accuracy of distinctions), suspected of counterfeiting my own self, *formaliter* considered. However, to satisfy their scruples, I took the only course in my power. Whilst I was in Wales, I had received various letters from young friends; these I produced, for I carried them constantly in my pocket. Most of these letters were from the Earl of Altamont, who was at that time, and had been for some years back, amongst my confidential friends. These were dated from Eton. I had also some from the Marquis of Sligo, his father; who, though absorbed in agricultural pursuits, yet having been an Etonian himself, and as good a scholar as a nobleman needs to be, still retained an affection for classical studies and for youthful scholars. He had, accordingly, from the time that I was fifteen, corresponded with me—sometimes upon the great improvements which he had made, or was meditating, in the counties of Mayo and Sligo, since I had been there; sometimes upon the merits of a Latin poet; at other times, suggesting subjects on which he fancied that I could write verses myself, or breathe poetic inspiration into the mind of my once familiar companion, his son.

On reading the letters, one of my Jewish friends agreed to furnish two or three hundred pounds on my personal security, provided I could persuade the young earl—who was, by the way, not older than myself—to guarantee the payment on our joint coming of age; the Jew's final object being, as I now suppose, not the trifling profit he could expect to make by me, but the prospect of establishing a connection with my noble friend, whose great expectations were well known to him. In pursuance of this proposal on the part of the Jew, about eight or nine days after I had received the £10, I prepared to visit Eton. Nearly three guineas of the money I had given to my money-lending friend in the background; or, more accurately, I had given that sum to Mr. Brunell, *alias* Brown, as representing Mr. Dell, the Jew; and a smaller sum I had given directly to himself, on his own separate account. What he alleged in excuse for thus draining my purse at so critical a moment was, that stamps must be bought, in order that the writings might be prepared whilst I was away from London. I thought in my heart that he was lying, but I did not wish to give him any excuse for charging his own delays upon me. About fifteen shillings I had employed in re-establishing (though in a very humble way) my dress. Of the remainder, I gave one-quarter (something more than a guinea) to Ann, meaning, on my return, to have divided with her whatever might remain. These arrangements made, soon after six o'clock, on a dark winter evening, I set off, accompanied by Ann, towards Piccadilly; for it was my intention to go down as far as the turn to Salt Hill and Slough on the Bath or Bristol mail. Our course lay through a part of the town which has now totally disappeared, so that I can no longer retrace its ancient boundaries—having been replaced by Regent Street and its adjacencies. *Swallow Street* is all that I remember of the names superseded by this large revolutionary usurpation. Having time enough before us, however, we bore away to the left, until we came into Golden Square. There, near the corner of Sherrard Street, we sat down, not wishing to part in the tumult and blaze of Piccadilly. I had told Ann of my plans some time before, and now I assured her again that she should share in my good fortune, if I met with any, and that I would never forsake her, as soon as I had power to protect her. This I fully intended, as much from inclination as from a sense of duty; for, setting aside gratitude (which in any case must have made me her debtor for life), I loved her as affectionately as if she had been my sister; and at this moment with sevenfold tenderness, from pity at witnessing her extreme dejection. I had apparently most reason for dejection, because I was leaving the saviour of my life; yet I, considering the shock my health had received, was cheerful and full of hope. She, on the contrary, who was parting with one who had had little means of serving her, except by kindness and brotherly treatment, was overcome by sorrow, so that, when I kissed her at our final farewell, she put her arms about my neck, and wept, without speaking a word. I hoped to return in a week, at furthest, and I agreed with her, that on the fifth night from that, and every night afterwards, she should wait for me, at six o'clock, near the bottom of Great Titchfield Street; which had formerly been our customary haven of rendezvous, to prevent our missing each other in the great Mediterranean of Oxford Street. This, and other measures of precaution, I took; one, only, I forgot. She had either never told me, or (as a matter of no great interest) I had forgotten, her surname. It is a general practice, indeed, with girls of humble rank in her unhappy condition, not (as novel-reading women of higher pretensions) to style themselves *Miss Douglas*, *Miss Montague*, etc., but simply by their Christian names, *Mary*, *Jane*, *Frances*, etc. Her surname, as the surest means of tracing her, I ought now to have inquired; but the truth is, having no reason to think that our meeting again could, in consequence of a short interruption, be more difficult or uncertain than it had been for so many weeks, I scarcely for a moment adverted to it as necessary, or placed it amongst my memoranda against this parting interview; and my final anxieties being spent in comforting her with hopes, and in pressing upon her the necessity of getting some medicine for a violent cough with which she was troubled, I wholly forgot this precaution until it was too late to recall her.

When I reached the Gloucester Coffee-house in Piccadilly, at which, in those days, all the western mails stopped for a few minutes in going out of London, it was already a quarter of an hour past eight o'clock; the Bristol Mail was on the point of going off, and I mounted on the outside. The fine fluent motion[1] of this mail soon laid me asleep. It

[1] The Bristol Mail was at that time the best appointed in the kingdom—owing that advantage, first of all, to an unusually good

is somewhat remarkable that the first easy or refreshing sleep which I had enjoyed for some months was on the outside of a mail-coach—a bed which, at this day, I find rather an uneasy one. Connected with this sleep was a little incident which served, as hundreds of others did at that time, to convince me how easily a man, who has never been in any great distress, may pass through life without knowing in his own person, and experimentally testing, the possible goodness of the human heart, or, as unwillingly I add, its possible churlishness. So thick a curtain of *manners* is drawn over the features and expression of men's natures, that, to the ordinary observer, the two extremities, and the infinite field of varieties which lie between them, are all confounded under one neutral disguise. The case was this. For the first four or five miles out of London, I annoyed my fellow-passenger on the roof by occasionally falling against him when the coach gave a lurch; and, indeed, if the road had been less smooth and level than it was, I should have fallen off from weakness. Of this annoyance he complained heavily; as, perhaps, in the same circumstances, most people would. He expressed his complaint, however, more morosely than the occasion seemed to warrant; and if I had parted with him at that moment, I should have thought of him as a surly and almost brutal fellow. Still I was conscious that I had given him some cause for complaint; and therefore I apologised, assuring him that I would do what I could to avoid falling asleep for the future; and, at the same time, in as few words as possible, I explained to him that I was ill, and in a weak state from long suffering, and that I could not afford to take an inside place. The man's manner changed upon hearing this explanation in an instant: and when I next woke for a minute, from the noise and lights of Hounslow (for, in spite of my efforts, I had again fallen asleep within two minutes), I

road,—and this advantage it shared with the Bath Mail (their route being exactly the same for a hundred and five miles); but, secondly, it had the separate advantage of an *extra* sum for expenses subscribed by the Bristol merchants.

found that he had put his arm round me to protect me from falling off; and for the rest of my journey he behaved to me with the gentleness of a woman. And this was the more kind, as he could not have known that I was not going the whole way to Bath or Bristol. Unfortunately, indeed, I *did* go further than I intended; for so genial and refreshing was my sleep, being in the open air, that, upon the sudden pulling up of the mail (possibly at a post-office), I found that we had reached some place six or seven miles to the west of Salt Hill. Here I alighted; and, during the half-minute that the mail stopped, I was entreated by my friendly companion (who, from the transient glimpse I had of him under the glaring lights of Piccadilly, might be a respectable upper servant) to go to bed without delay. This, under the feeling that some consideration was due to one who had done me so seasonable a service, I promised, though with no intention of doing so; and, in fact, I immediately moved forward on foot. It must then have been nearly eleven; but so slowly did I creep along that I heard a clock in a cottage strike four as I was on the point of turning down the road from Slough to Eton. The air and the sleep had both refreshed me; but I was weary, nevertheless. I remember a thought (obvious enough, and pointedly expressed by a Roman poet) which gave me some consolation, at that moment, under my poverty. There had been, some weeks before, a murder committed on Hounslow Heath, which at that time was really a heath, entirely unenclosed, and exhibiting a sea-like expanse in all directions, except one. I cannot be mistaken when I say that the name of the murdered person was *Steele*, and that he was the owner of a lavender plantation in that neighbourhood.[1]

[1] Two men, Holloway and Haggerty, were long afterwards convicted, upon very questionable evidence, as the perpetrators of this murder. The main testimony against them was that of a Newgate turnkey, who had imperfectly overheard a conversation between the two men. The current impression was that of great dissatisfaction with the evidence; and this impression was strengthened by the pamphlet of an acute lawyer, exposing the unsoundness and incoherency of the statements relied upon by the court. They were executed, however, in the teeth of all opposition. And as it happened that an enormous wreck of life

Every step of my regress (for I now walked with my face towards London) was bringing me nearer to the heath; and it naturally occurred to me, that I and the accursed murderer, if he were that night abroad, might, at every instant, be unconsciously approaching each other through the darkness; in which case, said I, supposing myself—instead of being little better than an outcast,

> ' Lord of my learning, and no land beside '—

like my friend Lord Altamont, heir, by general repute, to £30,000 per annum, what a panic should I be under at this moment about my throat! Indeed, it was not likely that Lord Altamont should ever be in my situation; but, nevertheless, the spirit of the remark remains true, that vast power and possessions make a man shamefully afraid of dying; and I am convinced that many of the most intrepid adventurers, who, being poor, enjoy the full use of their natural energies, would, if at the very instant of going into action news were brought to them that they had unexpectedly succeeded to an estate in England of £50,000 a-year, feel their dislike to bullets furiously sharpened,[1] and their efforts at self-possession proportionably difficult. So true it is, in the language of a wise man, whose own experience had made him acquainted equally with good and evil fortune, that riches are better fitted

> ' To slacken virtue, and abate her edge,
> Than tempt her to do aught may merit praise.'
> *Paradise Regained.*

I dally with my subject, because, to myself, the

occurred at the execution (not fewer, I believe, than sixty persons having been trampled under foot by the unusual pressure of some brewers' draymen forcing their way with linked arms to the space below the drop), this tragedy was regarded for many years by a section of the London mob as a providential judgment upon the passive metropolis.

[1] It will be objected that many men, of the highest rank and wealth, have, notwithstanding, in our own day, as well as throughout our history, been amongst the foremost in courting danger on the field of battle. True; but this is not the case supposed. Long familiarity with power and with wealth has, to them, deadened their effect and attractions.

remembrance of these times is profoundly interesting. But my reader shall not have any further cause to complain; for now I hasten to its close. In the road between Slough and Eton I fell asleep; and, just as the morning began to dawn, I was awakened by the voice of a man standing over me, and apparently studying my *physics*, whilst to me—upon so sudden an introduction to him in so suspicious a situation— his *morals* naturally suggested a more interesting subject of inquiry. I know not what he was. He was an ill-looking fellow, but not, therefore, of necessity, an ill-meaning fellow; or, if he were, I suppose he thought that no person sleeping out-of-doors in winter could be worth robbing. In which conclusion, however, as it regarded myself, I have the honour to assure him, supposing him ever to find himself amongst my readers, that he was entirely mistaken. I was not sorry at his disturbance, as it roused me to pass through Eton before people were generally astir. The night had been heavy and misty, but towards the morning it had changed to a slight frost, and the trees were now covered with rime. I slipped through Eton unobserved; washed myself, and as far as possible adjusted my dress, at a little public-house in Windsor; and. about eight o'clock, went down towards the precincts of the college, near which were congregated the houses of the 'Dames.' On my road I met some junior boys, of whom I made inquiries. An Etonian is always a gentleman; and, in spite of my shabby habiliments, they answered me civilly. My friend Lord Altamont was gone to Jesus College, Cambridge. 'Ibi omnis effusus labor!' I had, however, other friends at Eton; but it is not to all who wear that name in prosperity that a man is willing to present himself in distress. On recollecting myself, however, I asked for the Earl of Desert,[1] to whom

---

[1] I had known Lord Desert, the eldest son of a very large family, some years earlier, when bearing the title of Lord Castlecuffe. Cuffe was the family name; and I believe that they traced their descent from a person of some historic interest—viz., that Cuffe who was secretary to the unhappy Earl of Essex during his treasonable *émeute* against the government of Queen Elizabeth.

(though my acquaintance with him was not so intimate as with some others) I should not have shrunk from presenting myself under any circumstances. He was still at Eton, though, I believe, on the wing for Cambridge. I called, was received kindly, and asked to breakfast.

Lord Desert placed before me a magnificent breakfast. It was really such; but in my eyes it seemed trebly magnificent from being the first regular meal, the first ' good man's table,' that I had sat down to for months. Strange to say, I could scarcely eat anything. On the day when I first received my ten-pound bank-note, I had gone to a baker's shop and bought a couple of rolls; this very shop I had some weeks before surveyed with an eagerness of desire which it was humiliating to recollect. I remembered the story (which, however, I now believed to be a falsehood) about Otway; and feared that there might be danger in eating too rapidly. But there was no cause for alarm; my appetite was utterly gone, and I nauseated food of every kind. This effect, from eating what approached to a meal, I continued to feel for weeks. On the present occasion, at Lord Desert's table, I found myself not at all better than usual; and, in the midst of luxuries, appetite I had none. I had, however, unfortunately, at all times a craving for wine: I explained my situation, therefore, to Lord Desert, and gave him a short account of my late sufferings; with which he expressed deep sympathy, and called for wine. This gave me instantaneous relief and immoderate pleasure; and on all occasions, when I had an opportunity, I never failed to drink wine. Obvious it is, however, that this indulgence in wine would continue to strengthen my malady, for the tone of my stomach was apparently quite sunk; but, by a better regimen, it might sooner, and, perhaps, effectually, have been restored. I hope that it was not from this love of wine that I lingered in the neighbourhood of my Eton friends; I persuaded myself *then*, that it was from reluctance to ask Lord Desert, on whom I was conscious of having no sufficient claims, the particular service in quest of which I had come to Eton. I was, however, unwilling to lose my journey, and—I asked it. Lord Desert, whose good-nature was unbounded, and which, in regard to myself, had been measured rather by his compassion, perhaps, for my condition, and his knowledge of my intimacy with several of his relatives, than by an over-rigorous inquiry into the extent of my own direct claims, faltered, nevertheless, at this request. He acknowledged that he did not like to have any dealings with money-lenders, and feared lest such a transaction might come to the ears of his connections. Moreover, he doubted whether *his* signature, whose expectations were so much more bounded than those of his cousin, would avail with my unchristian friends. Still he did not wish, apparently, to mortify me by a refusal peremptory and absolute; for, after a little consideration, he promised, under certain conditions, which he pointed out, to give his security. Lord Desert was at this time not above eighteen years of age; but I have often doubted, on recollecting, since, the good sense and prudence which on this occasion he mingled with so much urbanity of manner (which in him wore the grace of youthful sincerity), whether any statesman—the oldest and the most accomplished in diplomacy—could have acquitted himself better under the same circumstances.

Re-comforted by this promise, which was not quite equal to the best, but far above the worst that I had anticipated, I returned in a Windsor coach to London three days after I had quitted it. And now I come to the end of my story. The Jews did not approve of Lord Desert's conditions, or so they said; whether they would in the end have acceded to them, and were only seeking time for making further inquiries, I know not; but many delays were made—time passed on—the small fragment of my bank-note had just melted away, and before any conclusion could have been put to the business, I must have relapsed into my former state of wretchedness. Suddenly, at this crisis, an opening was made, almost by accident, for reconciliation with my guardians. I quitted London in haste, and returned to the Priory; after some time, I proceeded to Oxford; and it was not until many months had passed away that I had it in my power again to revisit the ground which had become so interesting to me, and to this day remains so, as the chief scene of my youthful sufferings.

Meantime, what had become of Ann? Where was she? Whither had she gone? According to our agreement, I sought her daily, and waited for her every night, so long as I staid in London, at the corner of Titchfield Street; and during the last days of my stay in London I put into activity every means of tracing her that my knowledge of London suggested, and the limited extent of my power made possible. The street where she had lodged I knew, but not the house; and I remembered, at last, some account which she had given of ill-treatment from her landlord, which made it probable that she had quitted those lodgings before we parted. She had few acquaintance; most people, besides, thought that the earnestness of my inquiries arose from motives which moved their laughter or their slight regard; and others, thinking that I was in chase of a girl who had robbed me of some trifles, were naturally and excusably indisposed to give me any clue to her, if indeed they had any to give. Finally, as my despairing resource, on the day I left London I put into the hands of the only person who (I was sure) must know Ann by sight, from having been in company with us once or twice, an address to the Priory. All was in vain. To this hour I have never heard a syllable about her. This, amongst such troubles as most men meet with in this life, has been my heaviest affliction. If she lived, doubtless we must have been sometimes in search of each other, at the very same moment, through the mighty labyrinths of London; perhaps even within a few feet of each other—a barrier no wider, in a London street, often amounting in the end to a separation for eternity! During some years I hoped that she *did* live; and I suppose that, in the literal and unrhetorical use of the word *myriad*, I must, on my different visits to London, have looked into many myriads of female faces, in the hope of meeting Ann.

I should know her again amongst a thousand, and if seen but for a moment. Handsome she was not; but she had a sweet expression of countenance, and a peculiarly graceful carriage of the head. I sought her, I have said, in hope. So it was for years; but now I should fear to see her; and her cough, which grieved me when I parted with her, is now my consolation. Now I wish to see her no longer, but think of her, more gladly, as one long since laid in the grave—in the grave, I would hope, of a Magdalen; taken away before injuries and cruelty had blotted out and transfigured her ingenuous nature, or the brutalities of ruffians had completed the ruin they had begun.

. . . . . .

So then, Oxford Street, stony-hearted stepmother, thou that listenest to the sighs of orphans, and drinkest the tears of children, at length I was dismissed from thee! The time was come that I no more should pace in anguish thy never-ending terraces; no more should wake and dream in captivity to the pangs of hunger. Successors too many to myself and Ann have, doubtless, since then trodden in our footsteps, inheritors of our calamities. Other orphans than Ann have sighed; tears have been shed by other children; and thou, Oxford Street, hast since those days echoed to the groans of innumerable hearts. For myself, however, the storm which I had outlived seemed to have been the pledge of a long fair weather; the premature sufferings which I had paid down, to have been accepted as a ransom for many years to come, as a price of long immunity from sorrow; and if again I walked in London, a solitary and contemplative man (as oftentimes I did), I walked for the most part in serenity and peace of mind. And, although it is true that the calamities of my novitiate in London had struck root so deeply in my bodily constitution, that afterwards they shot up and flourished afresh, and grew into a noxious umbrage that has over-shadowed and darkened my latter years, yet these second assaults of suffering were met with a fortitude more confirmed, with the resources of a maturer

intellect, and with alleviations, how deep! from sympathising affection.

Thus, however, with whatsoever alleviations, years far
asunder were bound together by subtle links of suffering
derived from a common root. And herein I notice the
short-sightedness of human desires—that oftentimes, on
moonlight nights, during my first mournful abode in
London, my consolation was (if such it could be thought)
to gaze from Oxford Street up every avenue in succession which pierces northwards through the heart of
Marylebone to the fields and the woods; for *that*, said
I, travelling with my eyes up the long vistas which lay
part in light and part in shade—'*that* is the road to the
north, and, therefore, to Grasmere' (upon which, though
as yet unknown to me, I had a presentiment that I
should fix my choice for a residence); 'and if I had the
wings of a dove, *that* way I would fly for rest.' Thus I
said, and thus I wished in my blindness; yet, even in
that very northern region it was, in that very valley to
which my erroneous wishes pointed, that this second
birth of my sufferings began, and that they again threat-
ened to besiege the citadel of life and hope. There it
was that for years I was persecuted by visions as ugly,
and by phantoms as ghastly, as ever haunted the couch
of Orestes; and in this unhappier than he—that sleep,
which comes to all as a respite and a restoration, and to
him especially as a blessed balm for his wounded heart
and his haunted brain, visited me as my bitterest scourge.
Thus blind was I in my desires. And yet, if a veil inter-
poses between the dim-sightedness of man and his future
calamities, the same veil hides from him their alleviations; and a grief which had not been feared, is met by
consolations which had not been hoped. I, therefore,
who participated, as it were, in the troubles of Orestes
(excepting only in his agitated conscience), participated
no less in all his supports; my Eumenides, like his, were
at my bed-feet, and stared in upon me through the curtains; but, watching by my pillow, or defrauding herself
of sleep to bear me company through the heavy watches
of the night, sat my Electra; for thou, beloved M——,

dear companion of my later years, thou wast my Electra!
and neither in nobility of mind nor in long-suffering
affection wouldst permit that a Grecian sister should
excel an English wife. For thou thoughtest not much
to stoop to humble offices of kindness, and to servile
ministrations of tenderest affection; to wipe away for
years the unwholesome dews upon the forehead, or to
refresh the lips when parched and baked with fever;
nor even when thy own peaceful slumbers had by long
sympathy become infected with the spectacle of my
dread contest with phantoms and shadowy enemies,
that oftentimes bade me 'sleep no more!'—not even
then didst thou utter a complaint or any murmur, nor
withdraw thy angelic smiles, nor shrink from thy service
of love, more than Electra did of old. For she, too,
though she was a Grecian woman, and the daughter of
the king of men,[1] yet wept sometimes, and hid her face [2]
in her robe.

But these troubles are past, and thou wilt read these
records of a period so dolorous to us both as the legend
of some hideous dream that can return no more.
Meantime I am again in London; and again I pace
the terraces of Oxford Street by night; and oftentimes
—when I am oppressed by anxieties that demand all my
philosophy and the comfort of thy presence to support,
and yet remember that I am separated from thee by
three hundred miles and the length of three dreary
months—I look up the streets that run northward from
Oxford Street, upon moonlight nights, and recollect my
youthful ejaculation of anguish; but then, remembering
that thou art sitting alone in that same valley, and
mistress of that very house to which my heart turned

---

[1] Agamemnon—ἄναξ ἀνδρῶν.

[2] Ὄμμα θεῖς' εἰς πέπλον. The scholar will know that throughout
this passage I refer to the early scenes of the *Orestes*—one of the most
beautiful exhibitions of the domestic affections which even the dramas
of Euripides can furnish. To the unlearned reader, it may be necessary to say that the situation at the opening of the drama is that of a
brother attended only by his sister during the demoniacal possession
of a suffering conscience (or, in the mythology of the play, haunted by
the Furies), under circumstances of immediate danger from enemies,
and of desertion or cold regard from nominal friends.

in its blindness nineteen years ago, I think that, though blind indeed, and scattered to the winds of late, the promptings of my heart may yet have had reference to a remoter time, and may be justified if read in another meaning; and if I could allow myself to descend again to the impotent wishes of childhood, I should again say to myself, as I look to the north, 'Oh, that I had the wings of a dove!' and with how just a confidence in thy good and gracious nature might I add the other half of my early ejaculation—'and *that* way I would fly for comfort!'

## THE PLEASURES OF OPIUM

It is very long since I first took opium; *so* long, that if it had been a trifling incident in my life, I might have forgotten its date; but cardinal events are not to be forgotten; and, from circumstances connected with it, I remember that this inauguration into the use of opium must be referred to the spring or to the autumn of 1804; during which seasons I was in London, having come thither for the first time since my entrance at Oxford. And this event arose in the following way: from an early age I had been accustomed to wash my head in cold water at least once a day; being suddenly seized with toothache, I attributed it to some relaxation caused by a casual intermission of that practice; jumped out of bed, plunged my head into a basin of cold water, and with hair thus wetted went to sleep. The next morning, as I need hardly say, I awoke with excruciating rheumatic pains of the head and face, from which I had hardly any respite for about twenty days. On the twenty-first day I think it was, and on a Sunday, that I went out into the streets; rather to run away, if possible, from my torments, than with any distinct purpose of relief. By accident, I met a college acquaintance, who recommended opium. Opium! dread agent of unimaginable pleasure and pain! I had heard of it as I had heard of manna or of ambrosia, but no further.

How unmeaning a sound was opium at that time! what
solemn chords does it now strike upon my heart! what
heart-quaking vibrations of sad and happy remembrances! Reverting for a moment to these, I feel a
mystic importance attached to the minutest circumstances connected with the place, and the time, and
the man (if man he was), that first laid open to me the
paradise of opium-eaters. It was a Sunday afternoon,
wet and cheerless; and a duller spectacle this earth of
ours has not to show than a rainy Sunday in London.
My road homewards lay through Oxford Street; and
near 'the *stately* Pantheon' (as Mr. Wordsworth has
obligingly called it [1]) I saw a druggist's shop.    The
druggist (unconscious minister of celestial pleasures!), as
if in sympathy with the rainy Sunday, looked dull and
stupid, just as any mortal druggist might be expected to
look on a rainy London Sunday; and when I asked for
the tincture of opium, he gave it to me as any other man
might do; and, furthermore, out of my shilling returned
to me what seemed to be real copper halfpence, taken
out of a real wooden drawer. Nevertheless, and notwithstanding all such indications of humanity, he has
ever since figured in my mind as a beatific vision of
an immortal druggist, sent down to earth on a special
mission to myself. And it confirms me in this way of
considering him that, when I next came up to London,
I sought him near the stately Pantheon, and found him
not; and thus to me, who knew not his name (if,
indeed, he had one), he seemed rather to have vanished
from Oxford Street than to have flitted into any other
locality, or (which some abominable man suggested) to
have absconded from the rent. The reader may choose
to think of him as, possibly, no more than a sublunary
druggist; it may be so, but my faith is better. I believe
him to have evanesced.[2] So unwillingly would I con-

[1] ' *Stately* ' :—It is but fair to say that Wordsworth meant to speak
of the *interior*, which could very little be inferred from the mean, un-
distinguished outside, as seen presenting itself endways in Oxford Street.
[2] ' *Evanesced* ' :—This way of going off from the stage of life appears
to have been well known in the seventeenth century, but at that time
to have been considered a peculiar privilege of royalty, and by no

nect any mortal remembrances with that hour, and place, and creature that first brought me acquainted with the celestial drug.

Arrived at my lodgings, it may be supposed that I lost not a moment in taking the quantity prescribed. I was necessarily ignorant of the whole art and mystery of opium-taking; and what I took I took under every disadvantage. But I took it; and in an hour, O heavens! what a revulsion! what a resurrection, from its lowest depths of the inner spirit! what an apocalypse of the world within me. That my pains had vanished was now a trifle in my eyes; this negative effect was swallowed up in the immensity of those positive effects which had opened before me, in the abyss of divine enjoyment thus suddenly revealed. Here was a panacea, a φάρμακον νηπενθές, for all human woes; here was the secret of happiness, about which philosophers had disputed for so many ages, at once discovered; happiness might now be bought for a penny, and carried in the waistcoat-pocket; portable ecstasies might be had corked up in a pint-bottle; and peace of mind could be sent down by the mail.

And, first, one word with respect to its bodily effects; for upon all that has been hitherto written on the subject of opium, whether by travellers in Turkey (who may plead their privilege of lying as an old immemorial right), or by professors of medicine writing *ex cathedra*, I have but one emphatic criticism to pronounce—Nonsense! I remember once, in passing a book-stall, to have caught these words from a page of some satiric author—'By this time I became convinced that the London newspapers spoke truth at least twice a week—viz., on Tuesday and Saturday [1]—and might safely be depended

means open to the use of druggists. For, about the year 1686, a poet of rather ominous name (and who, apparently, did justice to his name) — viz., Mr. FLAT-MAN — in speaking of the death of Charles II., expresses his surprise that any prince should commit so vulgar an act as dying: because, says he,

'Kings should disdain to die, and only *disappear*.'

[1] '*Tuesday and Saturday*':—viz., the two days on which the *Gazette* is (or used to be) published.

upon for—the list of bankrupts.' In like manner, I do by no means deny that some truths have been delivered to the world in regard to opium : thus, it has been repeatedly affirmed by the learned that opium is a tawny brown in colour—and this, take notice, I grant; secondly, that it is rather dear, which also I grant—for, in my time, East India opium has been three guineas a pound, and Turkey eight ; and, thirdly, that, if you eat a good deal of it, most probably you must do what is disagreeable to any man of regular habits—viz., die.[1] These weighty propositions are, all and singular, true ; I cannot gainsay them ; and truth ever was, and will be, commendable. But, in these three theorems, I believe we have exhausted the stock of knowledge as yet accumulated by man on the subject of opium. And therefore, worthy doctors, as there seems to be room for further discoveries, stand aside, and allow me to come forward and lecture on this matter.

First, then, it is not so much affirmed as taken for granted by all who ever mention opium, formally or in cidentally, that it does or can produce intoxication. Now, reader, assure yourself, *meo periculo*, that no quantity of opium ever did, or could, intoxicate. As to the tincture of opium (commonly called laudanum), *that* might certainly intoxicate, if a man could bear to take enough of it ; but why ? Because it contains so much proof spirits of wine, and not because it contains so much opium. But crude opium, I affirm peremptorily, is incapable of producing any state of body at all resembling that which is produced by alcohol ; and not in *degree* only incapable, but even in *kind* ; it is not in the

---

[1] Of this, however, the learned appear latterly to have doubted ; for, in a pirated edition of Buchan's *Domestic Medicine*, which I once saw in the hands of a farmer's wife, who was studying it for the benefit of her health, the doctor was made to caution his readers against taking more than 'twenty-five *ounces*' of laudanum at one dose. The true reading had doubtless been twenty-five *drops* or minims, which in a gross equation is held equivalent to one grain of average opium ; but opium itself—crude opium—varies enormously in purity and strength ; consequently the tincture prepared from it. And most of the medical connoisseurs whom I have known boiled their opium, so as to cleanse it from gross impurities.

quantity of its effects merely, but in the quality, that it differs altogether. The pleasure given by wine is always rapidly mounting, and tending to a crisis, after which as rapidly it declines; that from opium, when once generated, is stationary for eight or ten hours: the first, to borrow a technical distinction from medicine, is a case of acute, the second of chronic, pleasure; the one is a flickering flame, the other a steady and equable glow. But the main distinction lies in this—that whereas wine disorders the mental faculties, opium, on the contrary (if taken in a proper manner), introduces amongst them the most exquisite order, legislation, and harmony. Wine robs a man of his self-possession; opium sustains and reinforces it. Wine unsettles the judgment, and gives a preternatural brightness and a vivid exaltation to the contempts and the admirations, to the loves and the hatreds, of the drinker; opium, on the contrary, communicates serenity and equipoise to all the faculties, active or passive; and, with respect to the temper and moral feelings in general, it gives simply that sort of vital warmth which is approved by the judgment, and which would probably always accompany a bodily constitution of primeval or antediluvian health. Thus, for instance, opium, like wine, gives an expansion to the heart and the benevolent affections; but, then, with this remarkable difference, that, in the sudden development of kind-heartedness which accompanies inebriation, there is always more or less of a maudlin and a transitory character, which exposes it to the contempt of the bystander. Men shake hands, swear eternal friendship, and shed tears—no mortal knows why; and the animal nature is clearly uppermost. But the expansion of the benigner feelings incident to opium is no febrile access, no fugitive paroxysm; it is a healthy restoration to that state which the mind would naturally recover upon the removal of any deep-seated irritation from pain that had disturbed and quarrelled with the impulses of a heart originally just and good. True it is, that even wine up to a certain point, and with certain men, rather tends to exalt and to steady the intellect. I myself, who have never been a great wine-drinker, used to find that half-a-dozen glasses of wine advantageously affected the faculties, brightened and intensified the consciousness, and gave to the mind a feeling of being '*ponderibus librata suis*'; and certainly it is most absurdly said, in popular language, of any man, that he is *disguised* in liquor; for, on the contrary, most men are disguised by sobriety, and exceedingly disguised; and it is when they are drinking that men display themselves in their true complexion of character; which surely is not disguising themselves. But still, wine constantly leads a man to the brink of absurdity and extravagance; and, beyond a certain point, it is sure to volatilise and to disperse the intellectual energies; whereas opium always seems to compose what had been agitated, and to concentrate what had been distracted. In short, to sum up all in one word, a man who is inebriated, or tending to inebriation, is, and feels that he is, in a condition which calls up into supremacy the merely human, too often the brutal, part of his nature; but the opium-eater (I speak of him simply *as* such, and assume that he is in a normal state of health) feels that the diviner part of his nature is paramount—that is, the moral affections are in a state of cloudless serenity; and high over all the great light of the majestic intellect.

This is the doctrine of the true church on the subject of opium: of which church I acknowledge myself to be the Pope (consequently infallible), and self-appointed *legate à latere* to all degrees of latitude and longitude. But then it is to be recollected that I speak from the ground of a large and profound personal experience, whereas most of the unscientific [1] authors who have at

[1] Amongst the great herd of travellers, etc., who show sufficiently by their thoughtlessness that they never held any intercourse with opium, I must caution my readers specially against the brilliant author of *Anastasius*. This gentleman, whose wit would lead one to presume him an opium-eater, has made it impossible to consider him in that character, from the grievous misrepresentation which he has given of its effects at pages 215-217 of Vol. I. Upon consideration, it must appear such to the author himself; for, waiving the errors I have insisted on in the text, which (and others) are adopted in the fullest manner, he will himself admit that an old gentleman, 'with a snow-white beard,' who

all treated of opium, and even of those who have written
professionally on the *materia medica*, make it evident,
by the horror they express of it, that their experimental
knowledge of its action is none at all. I will, however,
candidly acknowledge that I have met with one person
who bore evidence to its intoxicating power, such as
staggered my own incredulity; for he was a surgeon,
and had himself taken opium largely for a most miserable affection (past all hope of cure) seated in one
particular organ. This affection was a subtle inflamma-
tion, not acute, but chronic; and with this he fought for
more (I believe) than twenty years; fought victoriously,
if victory it were, to make life supportable for himself,
and during all that time to maintain in respectability a
wife and a family of children altogether dependent on
him.[1] I happened to say to him, that his enemies

eats ' ample doses of opium,' and is yet able to deliver what is meant
and received as very weighty counsel on the bad effects of that practice,
is but an indifferent evidence that opium either kills people prematurely,
or sends them into a madhouse. But, for my part, I see into this old
gentleman and his motives: the fact is, he was enamoured of ' the little
golden receptacle of the pernicious drug' which Anastasius carried
about him; and no way of obtaining it so safe and so feasible occurred
as that of frightening its owner out of his wits. This commentary
throws a new light upon the case, and greatly improves it as a story;
for the old gentleman's speech, as a lecture on pharmacy, is absurd;
but, considered as a hoax on Anastasius, it reads excellently.

[1] This surgeon it was who first made me aware of the dangerous
variability in opium as to strength under the shifting proportions of its
combination with alien impurities. Naturally, as a man professionally
alive to the danger of creating any artificial need of opium beyond what
the anguish of his malady at any rate demanded, trembling every hour
on behalf of his poor children, lest, by any indiscretion of his own, he
should precipitate the crisis of his disorder, he saw the necessity of
reducing the daily dose to a *minimum*. But to do this he must first
obtain the means of measuring the quantities of opium; not the apparent quantities as determined by weighing, but the *virtual* quantities
after allowing for the alloy or varying amounts of impurity. This, however, was a visionary problem. To allow for it was simply impossible.
The problem, therefore, changed its character. Not to measure the
impurities was the object; for, whilst entangled with the operative and
efficient parts of the opium, they could not be measured. To separate
and eliminate the impure (or inert) parts, this was now the object.
And this was effected finally by a particular mode of boiling the opium.
That done, the residuum became equable in strength; and the daily
doses could be nicely adjusted. About 18 grains formed his daily ration
for many years. This, upon the common hospital equation, expresses
18 times 25 drops of laudanum. But, since 25 is=$\frac{100}{4}$, therefore 18

(as I had heard) charged him with talking nonsense on politics, and that his friends apologised for him, by suggesting that he was constantly in a state of intoxication from opium. Now, the accusation, said I, is not *primâ facie* an absurd one; but the defence *is*. To my surprise, however, he insisted that both his enemies and his friends were in the right. ' I will maintain,' said he, ' that I *do* talk nonsense; and, secondly, I will maintain that I do not talk nonsense upon principle, or with any view to profit, but solely and simply,' said he—' solely and simply—solely and simply ' (repeating it three times over) 'because I am drunk with opium; and that daily.' I replied, that as to the allegation of his enemies, as it seemed to be established upon such respectable testimony, seeing that the three parties concerned all agreed so far, it did not become me to question it; but the defence set up I must demur to. He proceeded to discuss the matter, and to lay down his reasons; but it seemed to me so impolite to pursue an argument which must have presumed a man mistaken in a point belonging to his own profession, that I did not press him, even when his course of argument seemed open to objection; not to mention that a man who talks nonsense, even though ' with no view to profit,' is not altogether the most agreeable respondent in a dispute. I confess, however, that the authority of a surgeon, and one who was reputed a good one, may seem a weighty one to my prejudice; but still I must plead my experience, which was greater than his greatest by more than seven thousand drops a-day; and though it was not possible to suppose a medical man unacquainted with the characteristic symptoms of vinous intoxication, yet it struck me that he might proceed on a logical error of using the

times one quarter of a hundred is=one quarter of 1800, and that, I suppose, is 450. So much this surgeon averaged upon each day for about twenty years. Then suddenly began a fiercer stage of the anguish from his disease. But then, also, the fight was finished, and the victory was won. All duties were fulfilled: his children prosperously launched in life; and death, which to himself was becoming daily more necessary as a relief from torment, now fell injuriously upon nobody.

word intoxication with too careless a latitude, extending it generically to all modes of nervous excitement, instead of restricting it to one special quality of pleasurable elevation, distinguished by well-known symptoms, and connected with tendencies not to be evaded. Two of these tendencies I will mention as diagnostic, or characteristic and inseparable marks of ordinary alcoholic intoxication, but which no excess in the use of opium ever develops. One is the loss of self-command, in relation to all one's acts and purposes, which steals gradually (though with varying degrees of speed) over *all* persons indiscriminately when indulging in wine or distilled liquors beyond a certain limit. The tongue and other organs become unmanageable: the intoxicated man speaks inarticulately; and, with regard to certain words, makes efforts ludicrously earnest, yet oftentimes unavailing, to utter them. The eyes are bewildered, and see double; grasping too little, and too much. The hand aims awry. The legs stumble, and lose their power of *concurrent* action. To this result *all* people tend, though by varying rates of acceleration. Secondly, as another characteristic, it may be noticed that, in alcoholic intoxication, the movement is always along a kind of arch; the drinker rises through continual ascents to a summit or *apex*, from which he descends through corresponding steps of declension. There is a crowning point in the movement upwards, which once attained cannot be renewed: and it is the blind, unconscious, but always unsuccessful effort of the obstinate drinker to restore this supreme altitude of enjoyment which tempts him into excesses that become dangerous. After reaching this *acme* of genial pleasure, it is a mere necessity of the case to sink through corresponding stages of collapse. Some people have maintained, in my hearing, that they had been drunk upon green tea; and a medical student in London, for whose knowledge in his profession I have reason to feel great respect, assured me, the other day, that a patient, in recovering from an illness, had got drunk on a beef-steak. All turns, in fact, upon a rigorous definition of intoxication.

Having dwelt so much on this first and leading error in respect to opium, I shall notice briefly a second and a third; which are, that the elevation of spirits produced by opium is necessarily followed by a proportionate depression, and that the natural and even immediate consequence of opium is torpor and stagnation, animal as well as mental. The first of these errors I shall content myself with simply denying; assuring my reader, that for ten years during which I took opium not regularly, but intermittingly, the day succeeding to that on which I allowed myself this luxury was always a day of unusually good spirits.

With respect to the torpor supposed to follow, or rather (if we were to credit the numerous pictures of Turkish opium-eaters) to accompany, the practice of opium-eating, I deny that also. Certainly, opium is classed under the head of narcotics, and some such effect it may produce in the end; but the primary effects of opium are always, and in the highest degree, to excite and stimulate the system. This first stage of its action always lasted with me, during my novitiate, for upwards of eight hours; so that it must be the fault of the opium-eater himself, if he does not so time his exhibition of the dose, as that the whole weight of its narcotic influence may descend upon his sleep. Turkish opium-eaters, it seems, are absurd enough to sit, like so many equestrian statues, on logs of wood as stupid as themselves. But, that the reader may judge of the degree in which opium is likely to stupefy the faculties of an Englishman, I shall (by way of treating the question illustratively, rather than argumentatively) describe the way in which I myself often passed an opium evening in London during the period between 1804 and 1812. It will be seen, that at least opium did not move me to seek solitude, and much less to seek inactivity, or the torpid state of self-involution ascribed to the Turks. I give this account at the risk of being pronounced a crazy enthusiast or visionary; but I regard that little. I must desire my reader to bear in mind that I was a hard student, and at severe studies for all the rest of my time; and certainly

I had a right occasionally to relaxations as well as other people.

The late Duke of Norfolk [1] used to say, 'Next Monday, wind and weather permitting, I purpose to be drunk'; and in like manner I used to fix beforehand how often within a given time, when, and with what accessory circumstances of festal joy, I would commit a debauch of opium. This was seldom more than once in three weeks; for at that time I could not have ventured to call every day (as afterwards I did), for *a glass of laudanum negus, warm, and without sugar.*' No; once in three weeks sufficed; and the time selected was either a Tuesday or a Saturday night; my reason for which was this:—Tuesday and Saturday were for many years the regular nights of performance at the King's Theatre (or Opera House); and there it was in those times that Grassini sang; and her voice (the richest of *contraltos*) was delightful to me beyond all that I had ever heard. Yes; or have since heard; or ever shall hear. I know not what may be the state of the opera-house now, having never been within its walls for seven or eight years; but at that time it was by much the most pleasant place of resort in London for passing an evening.[2] Half-a-guinea admitted you to the pit, under the troublesome condition, however, of being *en grande tenue*. But to the gallery five shillings admitted you; and that gallery was subject to far less annoyance than the pit of most theatres. The orchestra was distinguished

---

[1] '*The late Duke of Norfolk*':—My authority was the late Sir George Beaumont, an old familiar acquaintance of the duke's. But such expressions are always liable to grievous misapplication. By 'the late' duke Sir George meant that duke once so well known to the nation as the partisan friend of Fox, Burke, Sheridan, etc., at the era of the great French Revolution in 1789-93. Since *his* time, I believe there have been three generations of ducal Howards—who are always interesting to the English nation, first, from the bloody historic traditions surrounding their great house: secondly, from the fact of their being at the head of the British Peerage.

[2] I trust that my reader has not been so inattentive to the windings of my narrative as to fancy me speaking here of the Brown-Brunell and Pyment period. Naturally I had no money disposable at that period for the opera. I am speaking here of years stretching far beyond those boyish scenes—interludes in my Oxford life, or long after Oxford.

by its sweet and melodious grandeur from all English orchestras; the composition of which, I confess, is not acceptable to my ear, from the predominance of the clangorous instruments, and in some instances from the tyranny of the violin. Thrilling was the pleasure with which almost always I heard this angelic Grassini. Shivering with expectation I sat, when the time drew near for her golden epiphany; shivering I rose from my seat, incapable of rest, when that heavenly and harp-like voice sang its own victorious welcome in its prelusive *threttánelo—threttánelo* [1] ($\theta\rho\epsilon\tau\tau\acute{a}\nu\epsilon\lambda\omega$—$\theta\rho\epsilon\tau\tau\acute{a}\nu\epsilon\lambda\omega$). The choruses were divine to hear; and, when Grassini [2] appeared in some interlude, as she often did, and poured forth her passionate soul as Andromache at the tomb of Hector, etc., I question whether any Turk, of all that ever entered the paradise of opium-eaters, can have had half the pleasure I had. But, indeed, I honour the barbarians too much by supposing them capable of any pleasures approaching to the intellectual ones of an Englishman. For music is an intellectual or a sensual pleasure, according to the temperament of him who hears it. And, by-the-bye, with the exception of the fine extravaganza on that subject in *Twelfth Night*, I do not recollect more than one thing said adequately on the subject of music

---

[1] '*Threttánelo—threttánelo*':—The beautiful representative echo by which Aristophanes expresses the sound of the Grecian *phorminx*, or of some other instrument, which conjecturally has been shown most to resemble our modern European harp. In the case of ancient Hebrew instruments used in the temple service, random and idle must be all the guesses through the Greek Septuagint or the Latin Vulgate to identify any one of them. But as to Grecian instruments the case is different; always there is the remote chance of digging up some marble sculpture of orchestral appurtenances and properties.

[2] Yet all things change; this same Grassini, whom once I adored, afterwards, when gorged with English gold, went off to Paris; and when I heard on what terms she lived with a man so unmagnanimous as Napoleon, I came to hate her. Did I complain of any man's hating England, or teaching a woman to hate her benefactress? Not at all; but simply of his adopting at second-hand the malice of a jealous nation, with which originally he could have had no sincere sympathy. Hate us, if you please; but not sycophantishly, by way of paying court to others.

in all literature. It is a passage in the *Religio Medici*[1] of Sir T. Browne, and, though chiefly remarkable for its sublimity, has also a philosophic value, inasmuch as it points to the true theory of musical effects. The mistake of most people is, to suppose that it is by the ear they communicate with music, and therefore that they are purely passive as to its effects. But this is not so; it is by the reaction of the mind upon the notices of the ear (the *matter* coming by the senses, the *form* from the mind) that the pleasure is constructed; and therefore it is that people of equally good ear differ so much in this point from one another. Now opium, by greatly increasing the activity of the mind, generally increases, of necessity, that particular mode of its activity by which we are able to construct out of the raw material of organic sound an elaborate intellectual pleasure. But, says a friend, a succession of musical sounds is to me like a collection of Arabic characters: I can attach no ideas to them. Ideas! my dear friend! there is no occasion for them; all that class of ideas which can be available in such a case has a language of representative feelings. But this is a subject foreign to my present purposes; it is sufficient to say that a chorus, etc., of elaborate harmony displayed before me, as in a piece of arras-work, the whole of my past life—not as if recalled by an act of memory, but as if present and incarnated in the music; no longer painful to dwell upon, but the detail of its incidents removed, or blended in some hazy abstraction, and its passions exalted, spiritualised, and sublimed. All this was to be had for five shillings— that being the price of admission to the gallery; or, if a man preferred the high-bred society of the pit, even this might be had for half-a-guinea; or, in fact, for half-a-crown less, by purchasing beforehand a ticket at the music shops. And over and above the music of the stage and the orchestra, I had all around me, in the intervals of the performance, the music of the Italian

---

[1] I have not the book at this moment to consult; but I think the passage begins, 'And even that tavern music, which makes one man merry, another mad, in me strikes a deep fit of devotion,' etc.

language talked by Italian women—for the gallery was usually crowded with Italians—and I listened with a pleasure such as that which Weld, the traveller, lay and listened, in Canada, to the sweet laughter of Indian women; for the less you understand of a language, the more sensible you are to the melody or harshness of its sounds. For such a purpose, therefore, it was an advantage to me that in those days I was a poor Italian scholar, reading it but little, and not speaking it at all, nor understanding a tenth part of what I heard spoken.

These were my opera pleasures; but another pleasure I had, which, as it could be had only on a Saturday night, occasionally struggled with my love of the opera; for, in those years, Tuesday and Saturday were the regular opera nights. On this subject I am afraid I shall be rather obscure, but, I can assure the reader, not at all more so than Marinus in his *Life of Proclus*, or many other biographers and autobiographers of fair reputation. This pleasure, I have said, was to be had only on a Saturday night. What, then, was Saturday night to me more than any other night? I had no labours that I rested from; no wages to receive; what needed I to care for Saturday night, more than as it was a summons to hear Grassini? True, most logical reader; what thou sayest is, and ever will be, unanswerable. And yet so it was, that, whereas different men throw their feelings into different channels, and most men are apt to show their interest in the concerns of the poor chiefly by sympathy with their distresses and sorrows, I at that time was disposed to express mine by sympathising with their pleasures. The pains of poverty I had lately seen too much of—more than I wished to remember; but the pleasures of the poor, their hopes, their consolations of spirit, and their restings from toil, can never become oppressive to contemplate. Now, Saturday night is the season for the chief regular and periodic return of rest to the poor, and to all that live by bodily labour; in this point the most hostile sects unite, and acknowledge a common link of brotherhood: almost all Christendom rests from its labours. It is a rest introductory to another rest; and divided by a whole day and two nights from the renewal of toil. On this account I feel always, on a Saturday night, as though I also were released from some yoke of bondage, had some wages to receive, and some luxury of repose to enjoy. For the sake, therefore, of witnessing, upon as large a scale as possible, a spectacle with which my sympathy was so entire, I used often, on Saturday nights, after I had taken opium, to wander forth, without much regarding the direction or the distance, to all the markets, and other parts of London, whither the poor resort on a Saturday night, for laying out their wages. Many a family party, consisting of a man, his wife, and sometimes one or two of their children, have I listened to, as they stood consulting on their ways and means, or the strength of their exchequer, or the price of household articles. Gradually I became familiar with their wishes, their difficulties, and their opinions. Sometimes there might be heard murmurs of discontent; but far oftener expressions on the countenance, or uttered in words, of patience, of hope, and of reconciliation to their lot. Generally speaking, the impression left upon my mind was, that the poor are practically more philosophic than the rich; that they show a more ready and cheerful submission to what they consider as irremediable evils or irreparable losses. Whenever I saw occasion, or could do it without appearing to be intrusive, I joined their parties, and gave my opinion upon the matter in discussion, which, if not always judicious, was always received indulgently. If wages were a little higher, or were expected to be so—if the quartern loaf were a little lower, or it was reported that onions and butter were falling, I was glad; yet, if the contrary were true, I drew from opium some means of consolation. For opium (like the bee, that extracts its materials indiscriminately from roses and from the soot[1] of

---

[1] 'Soot':—In the large capacious chimneys of the rustic cottages throughout the Lake district, you can see up the entire cavity from the seat which you occupy, as an honoured visitor, in the chimney corner. There I used often to hear (though not to see) bees. Their

chimneys) can overrule all feelings into a compliance
with the master-key. Some of these rambles led me to
great distances; for an opium-eater is too happy to
observe the motion of time. And sometimes, in my
attempts to steer homewards, upon nautical principles,
by fixing my eye on the pole-star, and seeking ambitiously for a north-west passage, instead of circum-
navigating all the capes and headlands I had doubled
in my outward voyage, I came suddenly upon such
knotty problems of alleys, alleys without soundings,
such enigmatical entries, and such sphinx's riddles of
streets without obvious outlets or thoroughfares, as must
baffle the audacity of porters, and confound the intellects
of hackney coachmen. I could almost have believed,
at times, that I must be the first discoverer of some of
these *terræ incognitæ*, and doubted whether they had
yet been laid down in the modern charts of London.
Positively, in one line of communication to the south
of Holborn, for foot passengers (known, I doubt not, to
many of my London readers), the road lay through a
man's kitchen; and, as it was a small kitchen, you
needed to steer cautiously, or else you might run foul of
the dripping-pan. For all this, however, I paid a heavy
price in distant years, when the human face tyrannised
over my dreams, and the perplexities of my steps in
London came back and haunted my sleep, with the
feeling of perplexities, moral or intellectual, that brought
confusion to the reason, that brought anguish and remorse to the conscience.

Thus I have shown, or tried to show, that opium does
not of necessity produce inactivity or torpor; but that,
on the contrary, it often led me into markets and
theatres. Yet, in candour, I will admit that markets
and theatres are not the appropriate haunts of the
opium-eater, when in the divinest state incident to his
enjoyment. In that state, crowds become an oppression

murmuring was audible, though their bodily forms were too small to
be visible at that altitude. On inquiry, I found that soot (chiefly from
wood and peats) was useful in some stage of their wax or honey
manufacture.

to him; music, even, too sensual and gross. He naturally seeks solitude and silence, as indispensable conditions of those trances, or profoundest reveries, which are the crown and consummation of what opium can do for human nature. I, whose disease it was to meditate too much and to observe too little, and who, upon my first entrance at college, was nearly falling into a deep melancholy, from brooding too much on the sufferings which I had witnessed in London, was sufficiently aware of these tendencies in my own thoughts to do all I could to counteract them. I was, indeed, like a person, who, according to the old Pagan legend, had entered the cave of Trophonius; and the remedies I sought were to force myself into society, and to keep my understanding in continual activity upon subtleties of philosophic speculation. But for these remedies, I should certainly have become hypochondriacally melancholy. In after years, however, when my cheerfulness was more fully re-established, I yielded to my natural inclination for a solitary life. At that time I often fell into such reveries after taking opium; and many a time it has happened to me on a summer night —when I have been seated at an open window, from which I could overlook the sea at a mile below me, and could at the same time command a view of some great town standing on a different radius of my circular prospect, but at nearly the same distance—that from sunset to sunrise, all through the hours of night, I have continued motionless, as if frozen, without consciousness of myself as of an object anywise distinct from the multiform scene which I contemplated from above. Such a scene in all its elements was not unfrequently realised for me on the gentle eminence of Everton. Obliquely to the left lay the many-languaged town of Liverpool; obliquely to the right, the multitudinous sea. The scene itself was somewhat typical of what took place in such a reverie. The town of Liverpool represented the earth, with its sorrows and its graves left behind, yet not out of sight, nor wholly forgotten. The ocean, in everlasting but gentle agitation, yet brooded over by dove-like calm, might not unfitly typify the mind, and the mood which then swayed it. For it seemed to me as if then first I stood at a distance aloof from the uproar of life; as if the tumult, the fever, and the strife, were suspended; a respite were granted from the secret burdens of the heart; some sabbath of repose; some resting from human labours. Here were the hopes which blossom in the paths of life, reconciled with the peace which is in the grave; motions of the intellect as unwearied as the heavens, yet for all anxieties a halcyon calm; tranquillity that seemed no product of inertia, but as if resulting from mighty and equal antagonisms; infinite activities, infinite repose.

O just, subtle, and all-conquering opium! that, to the hearts of rich and poor alike, for the wounds that will never heal, and for the pangs of grief that 'tempt the spirit to rebel,' bringest an assuaging balm;—eloquent opium! that with thy potent rhetoric stealest away the purposes of wrath, pleadest effectually for relenting pity, and through one night's heavenly sleep callest back to the guilty man the visions of his infancy, and hands washed pure from blood;—O just and righteous opium! that to the chancery of dreams summonest, for the triumphs of despairing innocence, false witnesses; and confoundest perjury; and dost reverse the sentences of unrighteous judges;—thou buildest upon the bosom of darkness, out of the fantastic imagery of the brain, cities and temples, beyond the art of Phidias and Praxiteles—beyond the splendours of Babylon and Hekatómpylos;[1] and, 'from the anarchy of dreaming sleep,' callest into sunny light the faces of long-buried beauties, and the blessed household countenances, cleansed from the 'dishonours of the grave.' Thou only givest these gifts to man; and thou hast the keys of Paradise, O just, subtle, and mighty opium!

.    .    .    .    .    .    .

[1] *i.e.* the *hundred-gated* (from ἑκατὸν, *hekaton*, a hundred, and πύλη, *pyle*, a gate). This epithet of hundred-gated was applied to the Egyptian Thebes in contradistinction to the ἑπτάπυλος (*heptápylos*, or *seven-gated*) which designated the Grecian Thebes, within one day's journey of Athens.

Courteous, and I hope indulgent reader, having accompanied me thus far, now let me request you to move onwards for about eight years; that is to say, from 1804 (when I said that my acquaintance with opium began) to 1812. The years of academic life are now over and gone—almost forgotten; the student's cap no longer presses my temples; if my cap exists at all, it presses those of some youthful scholar, I trust, as happy as myself, and as passionate a lover of knowledge. My gown is, by this time, I dare to say, in the same condition with many thousands of excellent books in the Bodleian, —viz., diligently perused by certain studious moths and worms; or departed, however (which is all that I know of its fate), to that great reservoir of *somewhere*, to which all the tea-cups, tea-caddies, tea-pots, tea-kettles, etc., have departed, which occasional resemblances in the present generation of tea-cups, etc., remind me of having once possessed, but of whose departure and final fate I, in common with most gownsmen of either university, could give but an obscure and conjectural history. The persecutions of the chapel bell, sounding its unwelcome summons to matins, interrupts my slumbers no longer; the porter who rang it is dead, and has ceased to disturb anybody; and I, with many others who suffered much from his tintinnabulous propensities, have now agreed to overlook his errors, and have forgiven him. Even with the bell I am now in charity; it rings, I suppose, as formerly, thrice a-day, and cruelly annoys, I doubt not, many worthy gentlemen, and disturbs their peace of mind; but as to me, in this year 1812, I regard its treacherous voice no longer (treacherous, I call it, for, by some refinement of malice, it spoke in as sweet and silvery tones as if it had been inviting one to a party); its tones have no longer, indeed, power to reach me, let the wind sit as favourably as the malice of the bell itself could wish; for I am two hundred and fifty miles away from it, and buried in the depth of mountains.

And what am I doing amongst the mountains? Taking opium. Yes; but what else? Why, reader, in 1812, the year we are now arrived at, as well as for some years previous, I have been chiefly studying German metaphysics, in the writings of Kant, Fichte, Schelling, etc. And how, and in what manner, do I live? in short, what class or description of men do I belong to? I am at this period—viz., in 1812—living in a cottage; and with a single female servant (*honi soit qui mal y pense*), who, amongst my neighbours, passes by the name of my 'housekeeper.' And, as a scholar and a man of learned education, I may presume to class myself as an unworthy member of that indefinite body called *gentlemen*. Partly on the ground I have assigned —partly because, from having no visible calling or business, it is rightly judged that I must be living on my private fortune—I am so classed by my neighbours; and, by the courtesy of modern England, I am usually addressed on letters, etc., *Esquire*, though having, I fear, in the rigorous construction of heralds, antique or antic, dressed like the knaves of spades or diamonds, but slender pretensions to that distinguished honour;—yes, in popular estimation, I am X. Y. Z., Esquire, but not Justice of the Peace, nor Custos Rotulorum. Am I married? Not yet. And I still take opium? On Saturday nights. And, perhaps, have taken it unblushingly ever since 'the rainy Sunday,' and 'the stately Pantheon,' and 'the beatific druggist' of 1804? Even so. And how do I find my health after all this opium-eating? in short, how do I do? Why, pretty well, I thank you, reader. In fact, if I dared to say the real and simple truth (though, in order to satisfy the theories of some medical men, I ought to be ill), I was never better in my life than in the spring of 1812; and I hope sincerely, that in quantity of claret, port, or 'London particular Madeira,' which, in all probability, you, good reader, have taken, and design to take, for every term of eight years during your natural life, may as little disorder your health as mine was disordered by all the opium I had taken (though in quantity such that I might well have bathed and swum in it) for the eight years between 1804 and 1812. Hence you may see again the danger of taking any medical advice from

*Anastasius ;*[1] in divinity, for anything I know, he may be a
safe counsellor, but not in medicine. No ; it is far better
to consult Dr Buchan, as I did ; for I never forgot that
worthy man's excellent suggestion, and I was 'particularly careful not to take above five-and-twenty ounces of
laudanum.' To this moderation and temperate use of
the article I may ascribe it, I suppose, that as yet at
least (that is, in 1812) I am ignorant and unsuspicious
of the avenging terrors which opium has in store for
those who abuse its long-suffering. At the same time,
as yet I had been only a *dilettante* eater of opium ; even
eight years' practice, with the single precaution of allowing sufficient intervals between every indulgence, has not
been sufficient to make opium necessary to me as an
article of daily diet. But now comes a different era.
Move on, then, if you please, reader, to 1813. In the
summer of the year we have just quitted, I had suffered
much in bodily health from distress of mind connected
with a melancholy event. This event, being nowise
related to the subject now before me, further than
through the bodily illness which it produced, I need not
more particularly notice. Whether this illness of 1812
had any share in that of 1813, I know not ; but so it
was, that, in the latter year, I was attacked by a most
appalling irritation of the stomach, in all respects the
same as that which had caused me so much suffering in
youth, and accompanied by a revival of all the old
dreams. Now, then, it was—viz., in the year 1813—
that I became a regular and confirmed (no longer an
intermitting) opium-eater. And here I find myself in a
perplexing dilemma. Either, on the one hand, I must
exhaust the reader's patience by such a detail of my
malady, and of my struggles with it, as might suffice to

---

[1] '*Anastasius*' :—The reader of this generation will marvel at these
repeated references to *Anastasius :* it is now an almost forgotten book,
so vast has been the deluge of novel-writing talent, really original and
powerful, which has overflowed our literature during the lapse of
thirty-five years from the publication of these Confessions. *Anastasius*
was written by the famous and opulent Mr. Hope, and was in 1821 a
book both of high reputation and of great influence amongst the leading
circles of society.

establish the fact of my inability to wrestle any longer with irritation and constant suffering; or, on the other hand, by passing lightly over this critical part of my story, I must forego the benefit of a stronger impression left on the mind of the reader, and must lay myself open to the misconstruction of having slipped by the easy and gradual steps of self-indulging persons, from the first to the final stage of opium eating (a misconstruction to which there will be lurking predisposition in most readers, from my previous acknowledgments. This is the dilemma, the first horn of which is not to be thought of. It remains, tnen, that I *postulate* so much as is necessary for my purpose. And let me take as full credit for this as if I had demonstrated it, good reader, at the expense of your patience and my own. Be not so ungenerous as to let me suffer in your good opinion through my own forbearance and regard for your comfort. No; believe all that I ask of you—viz., that I could resist no longer—believe it liberally, and as an act of grace, or else in mere prudence; for, if not, then in my next edition I will make you believe and tremble; and *à force d'ennuyer*, by mere dint of pandiculation, vulgarly called yawning, I will terrify all readers of mine from ever again questioning any postulate that I shall think fit to make.

This, then, let me repeat: I postulate that, at the time I began to take opium daily, I could not have done otherwise. Whether, indeed, afterwards I might not have succeeded in breaking off the habit, even when it seemed to me that all efforts would be unavailing, and whether many of the innumerable efforts which I *did* make might not have been carried much further, and my gradual re-conquests of lost ground might not have been followed up much more energetically—these are questions which I must decline. Perhaps I might make out a case of palliation; but (shall I speak ingenuously?) I confess it, as a besetting infirmity of mine, that I am too much of an Eudæmonist; I hanker too much after a state of happiness, both for myself and others; I cannot face misery, whether my own or not, with an eye of sufficient firmness, and am little capable of encountering present pain for the sake of any reversionary benefit. On some other matters, I can agree with the gentlemen of The Porch [1] at Manchester in affecting the Stoic philosophy; but not in this. Here I take the liberty of an Eclectic philosopher, and I look out for some courteous and considerate sect that will condescend more to the infirm condition of an opium-eater; that are pleasant men and courteous, such as Chaucer describes, to hear confession or to give absolution, and will show some conscience in the penances they inflict, or the efforts of abstinence they exact from poor sinners like myself. An inhuman moralist I can no more endure, in my nervous state, than opium that has not been boiled. At any rate, he who summons me to send out a large freight of self-denial and mortification upon any cruising voyage of moral improvement, must make it clear to my understanding that the concern is a hopeful one. At my time of life (six-and-thirty years of age [2]), it cannot be supposed that I have much energy to spare; in fact, I find it all little enough for the intellectual labours I have on my hands; and, therefore, let no man expect to frighten me, by a few hard words, into embarking any part of it upon desperate adventures of morality.

Desperate or not, however, the issue of the struggle in 1813 was what I have mentioned; and from this date the reader is to consider me as a regular and confirmed opium-eater, of whom to ask whether on any particular day he had or had not taken opium, would be to ask whether his lungs had performed respiration, or the heart fulfilled its functions. Now, then, reader, you understand what I am; and you are by this time aware, that no old gentleman, 'with a snow-white beard,' will

---

[1] A handsome news-room, of which I was very courteously made free, in passing through Manchester, by several gentlemen of that place, is called either *The Porch* or *The Portico*, which in Greek is the *Stoa;* from which I, a stranger in Manchester, inferred that the subscribers meant to profess themselves Stoics, or followers of Zeno. But I have been since assured that this is a mistake.

[2] This was written at the time of original publication.

have any chance of persuading me (like Anastasius) to surrender 'the little golden receptacle of the pernicious drug.' No; I give notice to all, whether moralists or surgeons, that, whatever be their pretensions and skill in their respective lines of practice, they must not hope for any countenance from me, if they think to begin by any savage proposition for a Lent or Ramadan of abstinence from opium. This being fully understood between us, we shall in future sail before the wind; now, then, reader, from the year 1813, where all this time we have been sitting down and loitering, rise up, if you please, walk forward about three years more; draw up the curtain, and you shall see me in a new character.

If any man, poor or rich, were to say that he would tell us what had been the happiest day in his life, and the why and the wherefore, I suppose that we should all cry out, Hear him! hear him! As to the happiest day, that must be very difficult for any wise man to assign; because any event that could occupy so distinguished a place in a man's retrospect of life, or be entitled to have shed a special, separate, and supreme felicity on any one day, ought to be of such an enduring character, as that (accidents apart) it should have continued to shed the same felicity, or one not distinguishably less, on very many years together. To the happiest *lustrum*, however, or even to the happiest *year*, a man may perhaps allowably point without discountenance from wisdom. This year, in *my* case, reader, was the one which we have now reached; though it stood, I confess, as a parenthesis between years of a gloomier character. It was a year of brilliant water (to speak after the manner of jewellers), set, as it were, and insulated, in the gloomy umbrage of opium. Strange as it may sound, I had a little before this time descended suddenly, and without any considerable effort, from three hundred and twenty grains of opium (that is, eight[1] thousand drops of laudanum)

---

[1] I here reckon twenty-five drops of laudanum as equivalent to one grain of opium, which, I believe, is the common estimate. However, as both may be considered variable quantities (the crude opium varying much in strength, and the tincture still more), I suppose that no

per day, to forty grains, or one-eighth part.    Instantaneously, and as if by magic, the cloud of profoundest
melancholy which rested upon my brain, like some black
vapours that I have seen roll away from the summit of a
mountain, drew off in one week ; passed away with its
murky banners as simultaneously as a ship that has been
stranded, and is floated off by a spring-tide,

> ' That moveth altogether, if it move at all.'

Now, then, I was again happy : I now took only one
thousand drops of laudanum per day—and what was
that ?    A latter spring had come to close up the season
of youth.    My brain performed its functions as healthily
as ever before.    I read Kant again ; and again I understood him, or fancied that I did.    Again my feelings of
pleasure expanded themselves to all around me ; and, if
any man from Oxford or Cambridge, or from neither,
had been announced to me in my unpretending cottage,
I should have welcomed him with as sumptuous a reception as so poor a man could offer.    Whatever else might
be wanting to a wise man's happiness, of laudanum I
would have given him as much as he wished, and in a
silver-gilt, if not golden, cup.    And, by the way, now
that I speak of giving laudanum away, I remember about
this time a little incident, which I mention because,
trifling as it was, the reader will soon meet it again
in my dreams, which it influenced more fearfully than
could be imagined.    One day a Malay knocked at my
door.    What business a Malay could have to transact
amongst the recesses of English mountains, is not my
business to conjecture ; but possibly he was on his road
to a seaport—viz., Whitehaven, Workington, etc.—about
forty miles distant.[1]

infinitesimal accuracy can be had in such a calculation.  Tea-spoons
vary as much in size as opium in strength.  Small ones hold about
one hundred drops ; so that eight thousand drops, which obviously
read into eighty hundred drops, fill a *small* tea-spoon eighty times.
But large modern tea-spoons hold very much more.  Some even
approach in their capacity to dessert-spoons.  The reader sees how
much I kept within Dr. Buchan's indulgent allowance.

[1] Between the seafaring populations on the coast of Lancashire, and
the corresponding populations on the coast of Cumberland (such as

The servant who opened the door to him was a young girl, born and bred amongst the mountains, who had never seen an Asiatic dress of any sort: his turban, therefore, confounded her not a little; and as it turned out that *his* knowledge of English was exactly commensurate with *hers* of Malay, there seemed to be an impassable gulf fixed between all communication of ideas, if either party had happened to possess any. In this dilemma, the girl, recollecting the reputed learning of her master (and, doubtless, giving me credit for a knowledge of all the languages of the earth, besides, perhaps, a few of the lunar ones), came and gave me to understand that there was a sort of demon below, whom she clearly imagined that my art could exorcise from the house. The group which presented itself, arranged as it was by accident, though not very elaborate, took hold of my fancy and my eye more powerfully than any of the statuesque attitudes or groups exhibited in the ballets at the opera-house, though so ostentatiously complex. In a cottage kitchen, but not looking so much like *that* as a rustic hall of entrance, being pannelled on the wall with dark wood, that from age and rubbing resembled oak, stood the Malay, his turban and loose trousers of dingy white relieved upon the dark pannelling; he had placed himself nearer to the girl than she seemed to relish, though her native spirit of mountain intrepidity contended with the feeling of simple awe which her countenance expressed, as she gazed upon the tiger-cat before her. A more striking picture there could not be

Ravenglass, Whitehaven, Workington, Maryport, etc.), there was a slender current of interchange constantly going on, and especially in the days of pressgangs—in part by sea, but in part also by land. By the way, I may mention, as an interesting fact which I discovered from an almanack and itinerary, dated about the middle of Queen Elizabeth's reign (say 1579), that the official route in *her* days for queen's messengers to the north of Ireland, and of course for travellers generally, was not (as now) through Grasmere, and thence by St. John's Vale, Threlkeld (for the short cut by Shoulthwaite Moss was then unknown), Keswick, Cockermouth, and Whitehaven. Up to St. Oswald's Church, Gresmere (so it was then spelled, in deference to its Danish original), the route lay as at present. Thence it turned round the lake to the left, crossed Hammerscar, up *Little* Langdale, across Wrynose to Egremont, and from Egremont to Whitehaven.

imagined, than the beautiful English face of the girl,[1] and its exquisite bloom, together with her erect and independent attitude, contrasted with the sallow and bilious skin of the Malay, veneered with mahogany tints by climate and marine air, his small, fierce, restless eyes, thin lips, slavish gestures and adorations. Half-hidden by the ferocious-looking Malay, was a little child from a neighbouring cottage, who had crept in after him, and was now in the act of reverting its head and gazing upwards at the turban and the fiery eyes beneath it, whilst with one hand he caught at the dress of the lovely girl for protection.

My knowledge of the Oriental tongues is not remarkably extensive, being, indeed, confined to two words— the Arabic word for barley, and the Turkish for opium (*madjoon*), which I have learned from *Anastasius*. And, as I had neither a Malay dictionary, nor even Adelung's *Mithridates*, which might have helped me to a few words, I addressed him in some lines from the *Iliad*; considering that, of such languages as I possessed, the Greek, in point of longitude, came geographically nearest to an Oriental one. He worshipped me in a devout manner, and replied in what I suppose to have been Malay. In this way I saved my reputation as a linguist with my neighbours; for the Malay had no means of betraying the secret. He lay down upon the floor for about an hour, and then pursued his journey. On his departure,

---

[1] This girl, Barbara Lewthwaite, was already at that time a person of some poetic distinction, being (unconsciously to herself) the chief speaker in a little pastoral poem of Wordsworth's. That she was really beautiful, and not merely so described by me for the sake of improving the picturesque effect, the reader will judge from this line in the poem, written perhaps ten years earlier, when Barbara might be six years old :—

' 'Twas little Barbara Lewthwaite, a child of beauty rare !'

This, coming from William Wordsworth, both a fastidious judge and a truth-speaker of the severest literality, argues some real pretensions to beauty, or real at that time. But if is notorious that, in the anthologies of earth through all her  zones, one flower beyond every other is liable to change, which flower is the countenance of woman. Whether in his fine stanzas upon ' Mutability,' where the most pathetic instances of this earthly doom are solemnly arrayed, Spenser has dwelt sufficiently upon this, the saddest of all, I do not remember.

I presented him, *inter alia*, with a piece of opium.  To him, as a native of the East, I could have no doubt that opium was not less familiar than his daily bread; and the expression of his face convinced me that it was. Nevertheless, I was struck with some little consternation when I saw him suddenly raise his hand to his mouth, and bolt the whole, divided into three pieces, at one mouthful.  The quantity was enough to kill some half dozen dragoons, together with their horses, supposing neither bipeds nor quadrupeds to be regularly trained opium-eaters.  I felt some alarm for the poor creature; but what could be done?  I had given him the opium in pure compassion for his solitary life, since, if he had travelled on foot from London, it must be nearly three weeks since he could have exchanged a thought with any human being.  Ought I to have violated the laws of hospitality by having him seized and drenched with an emetic, thus frightening him into a notion that we were going to sacrifice him to some English idol?  No: there was clearly no help for it.  The mischief, if any, was done.  He took his leave, and for some days I felt anxious; but, as I never heard of any Malay, or of any man in a turban, being found dead in any part of the very slenderly peopled road between Grasmere and Whitehaven, I became satisfied that he was familiar with opium,[1] and that I must doubtless have done him the service I designed, by giving one night of respite from the pains of wandering.

This incident I have digressed to mention, because this Malay (partly from the picturesque exhibition he assisted to frame, partly from the anxiety I connected with his image for some days) fastened afterwards upon my fancy, and through *that* upon my dreams, bringing with him other Malays worse than himself, that ran

---

[1] This, however, is not a necessary conclusion; the varieties of effect produced by opium on different constitutions are infinite.  A London magistrate (Hariott's *Struggles through Life*, vol. iii. p. 391, third edition) has recorded that, on the first occasion of his trying laudanum for the gout, he took FORTY drops; the next night SIXTY, and on the fifth night EIGHTY, without any effect whatever; and this at an advanced age.

'a-muck'[1] at me, and led me into a world of nocturnal troubles. But to quit this episode, and to return to my intercalary year of happiness. I have said already that, on a subject so important to us all as happiness, we should listen with pleasure to any man's experience or experiments, even though he were but a ploughboy, who cannot be supposed to have ploughed very deep in such an intractable soil as that of human pains and pleasures, or to have conducted his researches upon any very enlightened principles. But I, who have taken happiness, both in a solid and a liquid shape, both boiled and unboiled, both East Indian and Turkish—who have conducted my experiments upon this interesting subject with a sort of galvanic battery, and have, for the general benefit of the world, inoculated myself, as it were, with the poison of eight thousand drops of laudanum per day (and for the same reason as a French surgeon inoculated himself lately with a cancer, an English one, twenty years ago, with plague, and a third,[2] who was also English, with hydrophobia), I, it will be admitted, must surely now know what happiness is, if anybody does. And therefore I will here lay down an analysis of happiness ; and, as the most interesting mode of communicating it, I will give it, not didactically, but wrapped up and involved in a picture of one evening, as I spent every evening during the intercalary year, when laudanum, though taken daily, was to me no more than the elixir of pleasure.

Let there be a cottage, standing in a valley,[3] eighteen

---

[1] See the common accounts, in any eastern traveller or voyager, of the frantic excesses committed by Malays who have taken opium, or are reduced to desperation by ill luck at gambling.

[2] He was a surgeon at Brighton.

[3] The cottage and the valley concerned in this description were not imaginary : the valley was the lovely one, *in those days*, of Grasmere ; and the cottage was occupied for more than twenty years by myself, as immediate successor, in the year 1809, to Wordsworth. Looking to the limitation here laid down—viz., *in those days*—the reader will inquire in what way *Time* can have affected the beauty of Grasmere. Do the Westmoreland valleys turn grey-headed? O reader ! this is a painful memento of some of us ! Thirty years ago, a gang of Vandals (nameless, I thank heaven, to me), for the sake of building a mail-coach road that never would be wanted, carried, at a cost of £3000 to

miles from any town; no spacious valley, but about two miles long by three-quarters-of-a-mile in average width, —the benefit of which provision is, that all the families resident within its circuit will compose, as it were, one larger household, personally familiar to your eye, and more or less interesting to your affections. Let the mountains be real mountains, between three and four thousand feet high, and the cottage a real cottage, not (as a witty author has it) 'a cottage with a double coach-house'; let it be, in fact (for I must abide by the actual scene), a white cottage, embowered with flowering shrubs, so chosen as to unfold a succession of flowers upon the walls and clustering around the windows, through all the months of spring, summer, and autumn; beginning, in fact, with May roses, and ending with jasmine. Let it, however, *not* be spring, nor summer, nor autumn; but winter, in its sternest shape. This is a most important point in the science of happiness. And I am surprised to see people overlook it, as if it were actually matter of congratulation that winter is going, or, if coming, is not likely to be a severe one. On the contrary, I put up a petition, annually, for as much snow, hail, frost, or storm of one kind or other, as the skies can possibly afford. Surely everybody is aware of the divine pleasures which attend a winter fireside—candles at four o'clock, warm hearth-rugs, tea, a fair tea-maker, shutters closed, curtains flowing in ample draperies on the

---

the defrauded parish, a horrid causeway of sheer granite masonry, for three-quarters-of-a-mile, right through the loveliest succession of secret forest dells and shy recesses of the lake, margined by unrivalled ferns, amongst which was the *Osmunda regalis*. This sequestered angle of Grasmere is described by Wordsworth, as it unveiled itself on a September morning, in the exquisite poems on the ' Naming of Places.' From this also—viz., this spot of ground, and this magnificent crest (the Osmunda)—was suggested that unique line—the finest independent line through all the records of verse,

' Or lady of the lake,
Sole-sitting by the shores of old romance.'

Rightly, therefore, did I introduce this limitation. The Grasmere before and after this outrage were two different vales.

floor, whilst the wind and rain are raging audibly without,

> ' And at the doors and windows seem to call,
> As heaven and earth they would together mell;
> Yet the least entrance find they none at aii;
> Whence sweeter grows our rest secure in massy hall.
> *Castle of Indolence.*

All these are items in the description of a winter evening which must surely be familiar to everybody born in a high latitude. And it is evident that most of these delicacies cannot be ripened, without weather stormy or inclement in some way or other. I am not '*particular*' whether it be snow, or black frost, or wind so strong that (as Mr. Anti-slavery Clarkson says) 'you may lean your back against it like a post.' I can put up even with rain, provided that it rains cats and dogs, or, as sailors say, 'great guns and marlinespikes'; but something of the sort I must have; and if I have it not, I think myself in a manner ill-used: for why am I called on to pay so heavily in winter for coals, candles, etc., if I am not to have the article good of its kind? No: a Canadian winter for my money, or a Russian one, where every man is but a co-proprietor with the north wind in the fee-simple of his own ears. Indeed, so great an epicure am I in this matter that I cannot relish a winter night fully, if it be much past St. Thomas's Day, and have degenerated into disgusting tendencies towards vernal indications: in fact, it must be divided by a thick wall of dark nights from all return of light and sunshine. Start, therefore, at the first week of November: thence to the end of January, Christmas Eve being the meridian line, you may compute the period when happiness is in season, which in my judgment, enters the room with the tea-tray. For tea, though ridiculed by those who are naturally coarse in their nervous sensibilities, or are become so from wine-drinking, and are not susceptible of influence from so refined a stimulant, will always be the favourite beverage of the intellectual; and, for my part, I would have joined Dr. Johnson in a *bellum internecinum* against Jonas Hanway, or any other impious person who should have presumed to disparage it. But here, to save myself the trouble of too much verbal description, I will introduce a painter, and give him directions for the rest of the picture. Painters do not like white cottages, unless a good deal weather-stained; but, as the reader now understands that it is a winter night, his services will not be required except for the *inside* of the house.

Paint me, then, a room seventeen feet by twelve, and not more than seven and a half feet high. This, reader, is somewhat ambitiously styled, in my family, the drawing-room; but, being contrived 'a double debt to pay,' it is also, and more justly, termed the library; for it happens that books are the only article of property in which I am richer than my neighbours. Of these I have about five thousand, collected gradually since my eighteenth year. Therefore, painter, put as many as you can into this room. Make it populous with books; and, furthermore, paint me a good fire; and furniture plain and modest, befitting the unpretending cottage of a scholar. And near the fire paint me a tea-table; and (as it is clear that no creature can come to see one on such a stormy night) place only two cups and saucers on the tea-tray; and, if you know how to paint such a thing, symbolically or otherwise, paint me an eternal tea-pot—eternal *a parte ante*, and *a parte post;* for I usually drink tea from eight o'clock at night to four in the morning. And, as it is very unpleasant to make tea, or to pour it out for one's-self, paint me a lovely young woman sitting at the table. Paint her arms like Aurora's, and her smiles like Hebe's; but no, dear M——! not even in jest let me insinuate that thy power to illuminate my cottage rests upon a tenure so perishable as mere personal beauty; or that the witchcraft of angelic smiles lies within the empire of any earthly pencil. Pass, then, my good painter, to something more within its power; and the next article brought forward should naturally be myself—a picture of the Opium-eater, with his 'little golden receptacle of the pernicious drug' lying beside him on the table. As to the opium, I have no objection to see a picture of *that;* you may paint it, if you choose; but I apprise you that no 'little' receptacle would, even in 1816, answer *my* purpose, who was at a distance from the 'stately Pantheon' and all druggists (mortal or otherwise). No: you may as well paint the real receptacle, which was not of gold, but of glass, and as much like a sublunary wine-decanter as possible. In fact, one day, by a series of happily-conceived experiments, I discovered that it *was* a decanter. Into this you may put a quart of ruby-coloured laudanum; that, and a book of German metaphysics placed by its side, will sufficiently attest my being in the neighbourhood; but, as to myself, there I demur. I admit that, naturally, I ought to occupy the foreground of the picture; that, being the hero of the piece, or (if you choose) the criminal at the bar, my body should be had into court. This seems reasonable; but why should I confess on this point to a painter? or why confess it at all? If the public (into whose private ear I am confidentially whispering my Confessions, and not into any painter's) should chance to have framed some agreeable picture for itself of the Opium-eater's exterior—should have ascribed to him, romantically, an elegant person or a handsome face—why should I barbarously tear from it so pleasing a delusion?—pleasing both to the public and to me. No: paint me, if at all, according to your own fancy; and since a painter's fancy should teem with beautiful creations, I cannot fail, in that way, to be a gainer. And now, reader, we have run through all the ten categories of my condition, as it stood about 1816-17, up to the middle of which latter year I judge myself to have been a happy man; and the elements of that happiness I have endeavoured to place before you, in the above sketch of the interior of a scholar's library, in a cottage among the mountains, on a stormy winter evening, rain driving vindictively and with malice aforethought against the windows, and darkness such that you cannot see your own hand when held up against the sky.

But now farewell, a long farewell, to happiness, winter or summer! farewell to smiles and laughter! farewell to peace of mind, to tranquil dreams, and to the blessed consolations of sleep! For more than three years and a-half I am summoned away from these. Here opens upon me an Iliad of woes: for I now enter upon

## THE PAINS OF OPIUM

'As when some great painter dips
His pencil in the gloom of earthquake and eclipse.'
SHELLEY'S *Revolt of Islam.*

Reader, who have thus far accompanied me, I must request your attention, before we go farther, to a few explanatory notes.

1. You are already aware, I hope—else you must have a low opinion of my logic—that the opium miseries, which are now on the point of pressing forward to the front of this narrative, connect themselves with my early hardships in London (and therefore more remotely with those in Wales) by natural links of affiliation—that is, the early series of sufferings was the parent of the later. Otherwise, these Confessions would break up into two disconnected sections—first, a record of boyish calamities; secondly, a record (totally independent) of sufferings consequent upon excesses in opium. And the two sections would have no link whatever to connect them, except the slight one of having both happened to the same person. But a little attention will show the strictness of the inter-connection. The boyish sufferings, whether in Wales or London, pressing upon an organ peculiarly weak in my bodily system—viz., the stomach—caused that subsequent distress and irritability of the stomach which drove me to the use of opium as the sole remedy potent enough to control it. Here already there is exposed a sufficient *casual* connection between the two several sections of my experience. The opium would probably never have been promoted into the dignity of a daily and a life-long resource, had it not proved itself to be the one sole agent equal to the task of tranquillising the miseries left behind by the youthful privations. Thus far the *nexus,*

as between cause and effect, is sufficiently established between the one experience and the other—between the boyish records and the records of mature life. There needed no other *nexus* to justify the unity of the entire Confessions. But, though not wanted, nevertheless it happens that there *is* another and a distinct link connecting the two separate records. The main phenomenon by which opium expressed itself permanently, and the sole phenomenon that was communicable, lay in the dreams (and in the peculiar dream-scenery) which followed the opium excesses. But naturally these dreams, and this dream-scenery, drew their outlines and materials—their great lights and shadows—from those profound revelations which had been ploughed so deeply into the heart, from those *encaustic* records which in the mighty furnaces of London life had been burnt into the undying memory by the fierce action of misery. And thus in reality the early experiences of erring childhood not only led to the secondary experiences of opium, but also determined the particular form and pressure of the chief phenomena in those secondary experiences. Here is the briefest possible abstract of the total case:—The final object of the whole record lay in the dreams. For the sake of those the entire narrative arose. But what caused the dreams? Opium used in unexampled excess. But what caused this excess in the use of opium? Simply the early sufferings; these, and these only, through the derangements which they left behind in the animal economy. On this mode of viewing the case, moving regressively from the end to the beginning, it will be seen that there is one uninterrupted bond of unity running through the entire succession of experiences—first and last: the dreams were an inheritance from the opium; the opium was an inheritance from the boyish follies.

2. You will think, perhaps, that I am too confidential and communicative of my own private history. It may be so. But my way of writing is rather to think aloud, and follow my own humours, than much to inquire who is listening to me; for, if once I stop to

consider what is proper to be said, I shall soon come to doubt whether any part at all is proper. The fact is, I imagine myself writing at a distance of twenty—thirty —fifty years ahead of this present moment, either for the satisfaction of the few who may then retain any interest in myself, or of the many (a number that is sure to be continually growing) who will take an inextinguishable interest in the mysterious powers of opium. For opium *is* mysterious; mysterious to the extent, at times, of apparent self-contradiction; and *so* mysterious, that my own long experience in its use—sometimes even in its abuse—did but mislead me into conclusions ever more and more remote from what I now suppose to be the truth. Fifty-and-two years' experience of opium, as a magical resource under *all* modes of bodily suffering, I may now claim to have had—allowing only for some periods of four and six months, during which, by unexampled efforts of self-conquest, I had accomplished a determined abstinence from opium.[1] These parantheses

1 With what final result, I have much difficulty in saying. Invariably, after such victories, I returned, upon deliberate choice (after weighing all the consequences on this side and on that), to the daily use of opium. But with silent changes, many and great (worked apparently by these reiterated struggles), in the opium-eating habits. Amongst other changes was this, that the quantity required gradually fell by an enormous proportion. According to the modern slang phrase, I had in the meridian stage of my opium career used '*fabulous*' quantities. Stating the quantities—not in solid opium, but in the tincture (known to everybody as *laudanum*)—my daily ration was eight thousand drops. If you write down that amount in the ordinary way as 8000, you see at a glance that you may read it into eight quantities of a thousand, or into eight hundred quantities of ten, or lastly, into eighty quantities of one hundred. Now, a single quantity of one hundred will about fill a very old-fashioned obsolete tea-spoon, of that order which you find still lingering amongst the respectable poor. Eighty such quantities, therefore, would have filled eighty of such antediluvian spoons—that is, it would have been the common hospital dose for three hundred and twenty adult patients. But the ordinary tea-spoon of this present nineteenth century is nearly as capacious as the dessert-spoon of our ancestors. Which I have heard accounted for thus:—Throughout the eighteenth century, when first tea became known to the working population, the tea-drinkers were almost exclusively women; men, even in educated classes, very often persisting (down to the French Revolution) in treating such a beverage as an idle and effeminate indulgence. This obstinate twist in masculine habits it was that secretly controlled the manufacture of tea-spoons. Up to Waterloo, tea-spoons were adjusted chiefly to the calibre of female

being subtracted, as also, and secondly, some off-and-on
fits of tentative and intermitting dalliance with opium in
the opening of my career—these deductions allowed for,
I may describe myself as experimentally acquainted with
opium for something more than half-a-century. What,
then, is my final report upon its good and evil results?
In particular, upon these two capital tendencies of
habitual opium-eating under the popular misconceptions; viz., its supposed necessity of continually clamour-
ing for increasing quantities; secondly, its supposed
corresponding declension in power and efficacy. Upon
these ugly scandals, what is my most deliberate award?
At the age of forty, the reader is aware that, under our
ancestral proverb, every man is a fool or a physician.
Apparently our excellent ancestors, aiming undeniably
at alliteration, spelled *physician* with an *f*. And why
not? A man's physic might be undeniable, although
his spelling should be open to some slight improvements. But I presume that the proverb meant to exact
from any man only so much medical skill as should
undertake the responsibility of his own individual health.
It is my duty, it seems, thus far to be a physician—to
guarantee, so far as human foresight *can* guarantee, my
own corporeal sanity. And this, trying the case by
ordinary practical tests, I have accomplished. And I
add solemnly, that without opium most certainly I could
not have accomplished such a result. Thirty-five years
ago, beyond all doubt, I should have been in my grave.
And as to the two popular dilemmas—that either you
must renounce opium, or else indefinitely augment the
daily ration; and, secondly, that, even submitting to
such a postulate, you must content yourself, under any
scale of doses, with an effect continually decaying, in
fact, that you must ultimately descend into the despairing condition of the martyr to dram-drinking—at this

mouths. Since then, greatly to the benefit of the national health, the
grosser and browner sex have universally fallen into the effeminate
habit of tea-drinking; and the capacity of tea-spoons has naturally
conformed to the new order of cormorant mouths that have alighted
by myriads upon the tea-trays of these later generations.

point, I make a resolute stand, in blank denial of the whole doctrine. Originally, when first entering upon my opium career, I did so with great anxiety: and before my eyes floated for ever the analogies—dim, or *not* dim, according to my spirits at the moment—of the poor, perishing brandy-drinker, often on the brink of *delirium tremens!* Opium I pursued under a harsh necessity, as an unknown, shadowy power, leading I knew not whither, and a power that might suddenly change countenance upon this unknown road. Habitually I lived under such an impression of awe as we have all felt from stories of fawns, or seeming fawns, that have run before some mounted hunter for many a league, until they have tempted him far into the mazes of a boundless forest, and at that point, where all regress had become lost and impossible, either suddenly vanished, leaving the man utterly bewildered, or assumed some more fearful shape. A part of the evil which I feared actually unfolded itself; but all was due to my own ignorance, to neglect of cautionary measures, or to gross mismanagement of my health in points where I well knew the risks, but grievously underrated their urgency and pressure. I was temperate: that solitary advantage I had; but I sank under the lulling seductions of opium into total sedentariness, and *that* whilst holding firmly the belief, that powerful exercise was omnipotent against all modes of debility or obscure nervous irritations. The account of my depression, and almost of my helplessness, in the next memorandum (No. 3), is faithful as a description to the real case. But, in ascribing that case to opium, as any transcendent and overmastering agency, I was thoroughly wrong. Twenty days of exercise, twenty times twenty miles of walking, at the ordinary pace of three and a-half miles an hour, or perhaps half that amount, would have sent me up as buoyantly as a balloon into regions of natural and healthy excitement, where dejection is an impossible phenomenon. O heavens! how man abuses or neglects his natural resources! Yes, the thoughtful reader is disposed to say; but very possibly distinguishing between such *natural* resources and opium as a resource that is *not* natural, but highly artificial, or even absolutely unnatural. I think otherwise: upon the basis of my really vast, perhaps unequalled, experience (let me add of my *tentative* experience, varying its trials in every conceivable mode, so as to meet the question at issue under every angle), I advance these three following propositions, all of them unsuspected by the popular mind, and the last of them (as cannot much longer fail to be discovered) bearing a national value—I mean, as meeting our English hereditary complaint :—

I. With respect to the morbid growth upon the opium-eater of his peculiar habit, when once rooted in the system, and throwing out *tentacula* like a cancer, it is out of my power to deliver any such oracular judgment upon the case—*i.e.*, upon the apparent danger of such a course, and by what stages it might be expected to travel towards its final consummation—as naturally I should wish to do. Being an oracle, it is my wish to behave myself like an oracle, and not to evade any decent man's questions in the way that Apollo too often did at Delphi. But, in this particular instance before me, the accident of my own individual seamanship in presence of this storm interfered with the natural evolution of the problem in its extreme form of danger. I had become too uneasy under the consciousness of that intensely artificial condition into which I had imperceptibly lapsed through unprecedented quantities of opium ; the shadows of eclipse were too dark and lurid not to rouse and alarm me into a spasmodic effort for reconquering the ground which I had lost. Such an effort I made : every step by which I had gone astray did I patiently unthread. And thus I fought off the natural and spontaneous catastrophe, whatever *that* might be, which mighty Nature would else have let loose for redressing the wrongs offered to herself. But what followed? In six or eight months more, upon fresh movements arising of insupportable nervous irritation, I fleeted back into the same opium lull. To and fro, up and down, did I tilt upon those mountainous seas, for year after year. 'See-saw,[1] like Margery Daw, that sold her bed and lay on straw.' Even so did I, led astray, perhaps, by the classical example of Miss Daw, see-saw for year after year, out and in, of manœuvres the most intricate, dances the most elaborate, receding or approaching, round my great central sun of opium. Sometimes I ran perilously close into my perihelion; sometimes I became frightened, and wheeled off into a vast cometary aphelion, where for six months 'opium' was a word unknown. How nature stood all these see-sawings is quite a mystery to me : I must have led her a sad life in those days. Nervous irritation forced me, at times, upon frightful excesses ; but terror from anomalous symptoms sooner or later forced me back. This terror was strengthened by the vague hypotheses current at that period about spontaneous combustion. Might I not myself take leave of the literary world in that fashion ? According to the popular fancy, there were two modes of this spontaneity; and really very little to choose between them. Upon one variety of this explosion, a man blew up in the dark, without match or candle near him, leaving nothing behind him but some bones, of no use to anybody, and which were supposed to be *his* only because nobody else ever applied for them. It was fancied that some volcanic agency—an unknown deposition—accumulated from some vast redundancy of brandy, furnished the self-exploding principle. But this startled the faith of most people ; and a more plausible scheme suggested itself, which depended upon the concurrence of a lucifer-match. Without an incendiary, a man could not take fire. We sometimes see the hands of inveterate dram-drinkers throw off an atmosphere of intoxicating vapours, strong enough to lay flies into a state of sleep or *coma ;* and on the same principle, it was supposed that the breath might be so loaded with spirituous

1 '*See-saw*,' etc. :—O dear reader, surely you don't want an oracle to tell you that this is a good old nursery lyric, which through four centuries has stood the criticism — stood the anger against Daw's enemies—stood the pity for Daw herself, so infamously reduced to straw—of children through eighty generations, reckoning five years to each nursery succession.

particles, as to catch fire from a match applied to a pipe when held between the lips. If so, then what should hinder the 'devouring element' (as newspapers call fire) from spreading through the throat to the cavity of the chest: in which case, not being insured, the man would naturally become a total loss. Opium, however, it will occur to the reader, is not alcohol. That is true. But it might, for anything that was known experimentally, be ultimately worse. Coleridge, the only person known to the public as having dallied systematically and for many years with opium, could not be looked to for any candid report of its history and progress; besides that, Coleridge was under a permanent craze of having nearly accomplished his own liberation from opium; and thus he had come to have an *extra* reason for self-delusion. Finding myself, therefore, walking on a solitary path of bad repute, leading *whither* no man's experience could tell me, I became proportionably cautious; and if nature had any plot for making an example of me, I was resolved to baulk her. Thus it was that I never followed out the seductions of opium to their final extremity. But, nevertheless, in evading that extremity, I stumbled upon as great a discovery as if I had *not* evaded it. After the first or second self-conquest in this conflict—although finding it impossible to persist through more than a few months in the abstinence from opium — I remarked, however, that the domineering tyranny of its exactions was at length steadily declining. Quantities noticeably less had now become sufficient: and after the fourth of these victories, won with continually decreasing efforts, I found that not only had the daily dose (upon relapsing) suffered a self-limitation to an enormous extent, but also that, upon any attempt obstinately to renew the old doses, there arose a new symptom—viz., an irritation on the surface of the skin— which soon became insupportable, and tended to distraction. In about four years, without any further efforts, my daily ration had fallen *spontaneously* from a varying quantity of eight, ten, or twelve thousand drops of laudanum to about three hundred. I describe the drug as *laudanum*, because another change ran along collaterally with this supreme change—viz., that the solid opium began to require a length of time, continually increasing, to expand its effects sensibly, oftentimes not less than four hours; whereas the tincture manifested its presence instantaneously.

Thus, then, I had reached a position from which authoritatively it might be pronounced, as a result of long, anxious, and vigilant experience, that, on the assumption of earnest (even though intermitting) efforts towards recurrent abstinences on the part of the opium-eater, the practice of indulging to the very greatest excess in this narcotic tends to a natural (almost an inevitable) euthanasy. Many years ago, when briefly touching on this subject, I announced (as a fact even *then* made known to me) that no instance of abstinence, though it were but of three days' continuance, ever perishes. Ten grains, deducted from a daily ration of five hundred, will tell through a series of many weeks, and will be found again modifying the final result, even at the close of the year's reckoning. At this day, after a half-century of oscillating experience, and after no efforts or trying acts of self-denial beyond those severe ones attached to the several processes (five or six in all) of reconquering my freedom from the yoke of opium, I find myself pretty nearly at the same station which I occupied at that vast distance of time. It is recorded of Lord Nelson that, even after the Nile and Copenhagen, he still paid the penalty, on the first days of resuming his naval life, which is generally exacted by nature from the youngest little middy or the rawest griffin — viz., sea-sickness. And this happens to a considerable proportion of sailors : they do not recover their sea-legs till some days after getting afloat. The very same thing happens to veteran opium-eaters, when first, after long intermissions, resuming too abruptly their ancient familiarities with opium. It is a fact, which I mention as indicating the enormous revolutions passed through, that, within these five years, I have turned pale, and felt warnings, pointing towards such an uneasiness, after taking not more than twenty grains of opium. At present and for some years, I have been habitually content with five or six grains daily, instead of three hundred and twenty to four hundred grains. Let me wind up this retrospect with saying, that the powers of opium, as an anodyne, but still more as a tranquilliser of nervous and anomalous sensations, have not in the smallest degree decayed; and that, if it has casually unveiled its early power of exacting slight penalties from any trivial inattention to accurate proportions, it has more than commensurately renewed its ancient privilege of lulling irritation and of supporting preternatural calls for exertion.

My first proposition, therefore, amounts to this—that the process of weaning one's-self from the deep bondage of opium, by many people viewed with despairing eyes, is not only a possible achievement, and one which grows easier in every stage of its progress, but is favoured and promoted by nature in secret ways that could not, without some experience, have been suspected. This, however, is but a sorry commendation of any resource making great pretensions, that, by a process confessedly trying to human firmness, it can ultimately be thrown aside. Certainly little would be gained by the negative service of cancelling a drawback upon any agency what-ever, until it were shown that this drawback has availed to disturb and neutralise great positive blessings lying within the gift of that agency. What are the advantages connected with opium that can merit any such name as blessings?

II. Briefly let me say, in the *second* proposition, that if the reader had, in any South American forest, seen growing rankly some great febrifuge (such as the Jesuits' bark), he would probably have noticed it with slight regard. To understand its value, he must first have suffered from intermittent fever. Bark might strike him as an unnatural stimulant; but, when he came to see that tertian or quartan fever was also an unnatural pressure upon human energies, he would begin to guess that two counter unnaturals may terminate in one most natural and salubrious result. Nervous irritation is the secret desolator of human life; and for this there is probably no adequate controlling power but that of opium, taken daily, under steady regulation.

III. But even more momentous is the burden of my *third* proposition. Are you aware, reader, what it is that constitutes the scourge (physically speaking) of Great Britain and Ireland? All readers, who direct any part of their attention to medical subjects, must know that it is pulmonary consumption. If you walk through a forest at certain seasons, you will see what is called a *blaze* of white paint upon a certain *élite* of the trees marked out by the forester as ripe for the axe. Such a blaze, if the shadowy world could reveal its futurities, would be seen everywhere distributing its secret badges of cognisance amongst our youthful men and women. Of those that, in the expression of Pericles, constitute the vernal section of our population, what a multitudinous crowd would be seen to wear upon their foreheads the same sad ghastly blaze, or some equivalent symbol of dedication to an early grave. How appalling in its amount is this annual slaughter amongst those that should by birthright be specially the children of hope, and levied impartially from *every* rank of society! Is the income-tax or the poor-rate, faithful as each is to its regulating tide-tables, paid by *any* class with as much punctuality as this premature *florilegium*, this gathering and rendering up of blighted blossoms, by *all* classes? Then comes the startling question—that pierces the breaking hearts of so many thousand afflicted relatives —Is there no remedy? Is there no palliation of the evil? Waste not a thought upon the idle question whether he that speaks is armed with this form or that form of authorisation and sanction! Think within yourself how infinite would be the scorn of any poor sorrow-stricken mother, if she—standing over the coffin of her daughter—could believe or could imagine that any vestige of ceremonial scruples, or of fool-born superstitions, or the terror of a word, or old traditional prejudice, had been allowed to neutralise one chance in a thousand for her daughter—had by possibility (but, as I could tell

her, had sometimes to a certainty) stepped between
patients and deliverance from the grave, sure and perfect! 'What matter,' she would cry out, indignantly,
'who it is that says the thing, so long as the thing itself
is true?' It is the potent and faithful *word* that is
wanted, in perfect slight of the organ through which it is
uttered. Let me premise this notorious fact, that all
consumption, though latent in the constitution, and
indicated often to the eye in bodily conformation, does
not therefore manifest itself as a disease, until some form
of 'cold,' or bronchitis, some familiar affection of the
chest or of the lungs, arises to furnish a starting-point
for the morbid development.[1] Now the one fatal
blunder lies in suffering that development to occur;
and the one counter-working secret for pre-arrestment
of this evil lies in steadily, by whatever means, keeping
up and promoting the insensible perspiration. In that
one simple art of controlling a constant function of the
animal economy, lies a magician's talisman for defeating
the forces leagued against the great organs of respiration.
Pulmonary affections, if not *previously* suffered to develop
themselves, cannot live under the hourly counter-working
of this magical force. Consequently, the one question
in arrear is, what potent drug is that which possesses
this power, a power like that of 'Amram's son,' for
evoking salubrious streams, welling forth benignly from
systems else parched and arid as rocks in the wilderness?
There is none that I know of answering the need but
opium. The powers of that great agent I first learned
dimly to guess at from a remark made to me by a lady

---

[1] Here is a parallel case, equally fatal where it occurs, but happily
moving within a far narrower circle. About fifty years ago, Sir
Everard Home, a surgeon of the highest class, mentioned as a dreadful
caution, that, within his own experience, many an indolent tumour in
the face, not unfrequently the most trifling pimple, which for thirty or
more years had caused no uneasiness whatever, suddenly might chance
to receive the slightest possible wound from a razor in the act of
shaving. What followed? Once disturbed, the trivial excrescence
became an open cancer. Is the parallel catastrophe in the pulmonary
system, when pushed forward into development, at all less likely to
hide its importance from uninstructed eyes? Yet, on the other hand,
it is a thousand times more likely to happen.

in London; then, and for some time previously, she
had been hospitably entertaining Coleridge, whom,
indeed, she tended with the anxiety of a daughter.
Consequently, she was familiarly acquainted with his
opium habits; and on my asking, in reply to some
remark of hers, how she could be so sure as her words
implied, that Coleridge was just then likely to be in-
capacitated for writing (or, indeed, for any literary
*exertion*), she said, 'Oh, I know it well by the glistening of his cheeks.' Coleridge's face, as is well known to
his acquaintances, exposed a large surface of cheek;
too large for the intellectual expression of his features
generally, had not the final effect been redeemed by
what Wordsworth styled his 'godlike forehead.' The
result was, that no possible face so broadly betrayed and
published any effects whatever, especially these lustrous
effects from excesses in opium. For some years I failed
to consider reflectively, or else, reflecting, I failed to
decipher, this resplendent acreage of cheek. But at last,
either *proprio marte*, or prompted by some medical hint,
I came to understand that the glistening face, glorious
from afar like the old Pagan face of the demigod
Æsculapius, simply reported the gathering accumula-
tions of insensible perspiration. In the very hour, a
memorable hour, of making that discovery, I made
another. My own history, medically speaking, involved
a mystery. At the commencement of my opium career,
I had myself been pronounced repeatedly a martyr-elect
to pulmonary consumption. And although, in the
common decencies of humanity, this opinion upon my
prospects had always been accompanied with some
formal words of encouragement—as, for instance, that
constitutions, after all, varied by endless differences;
that nobody could fix limits to the powers of medicine,
or, in default of medicine, to the healing resources of
nature herself: yet, without something like a miracle
in my favour, I was instructed to regard myself as a
condemned subject. That was the upshot of these
agreeable communications; alarming enough; and they
were rendered more so by these three facts:—first, that

the opinions were pronounced by the highest authorities in Christendom—viz., the physicians at Clifton and the Bristol Hotwells, who saw more of pulmonary disorders in one twelvemonth than the rest of the profession through all Europe in a century; for the disease, it must be remembered, was almost peculiar as a national scourge to Britain, interlinked with the local accidents of the climate and its restless changes; so that only in England could it be studied; and even there only in perfection at these Bristolian adjacencies—the reason being this, all opulent patients resorted to the Devonshire watering-places, where the balmy temperature of the air and prevailing winds allowed the myrtle and other greenhouse shrubs to stand out-of-doors all winter through; and naturally on the road to Devonshire all patients alike touched at Clifton. There I was myself continually resident. Many, therefore, and of supreme authority, were the prophets of evil that announced to me my doom. Secondly, they were countenanced by the ugly fact that I out of eight children was the one who most closely inherited the bodily conformation of a father who had died of consumption at the early age of thirty-nine. Thirdly, I offered at the first glance, to a medical eye, every symptom of *phthisis* broadly and conspicuously developed. The hectic colours on the face, the nocturnal perspirations, the growing embarrassment of the respiration, and other expressions of gathering feebleness under any attempts at taking exercise—all these symptoms were steadily accumulating between the age of twenty-two and twenty-four. What was it that first arrested them? Simply the use, continually becoming more regular, of opium. Nobody recommended this drug to me; on the contrary, under that ignorant horror which everywhere invested opium, I saw too clearly that any avowed use of it would expose me to a rabid persecution.[1] Under the sincere and

---

[1] *'Rabid persecution'* :—I do not mean that, in the circumstances of my individual position, any opening could have arisen to an opposition more than verbal; since it would have been easy for me at all times to withdraw myself by hundreds of leagues from controversies

unaffected hope of saving me from destruction, I should have been hunted into the grave within six months. I kept my own counsel; said nothing; awakened no suspicions; persevered more and more determinately in the use of opium; and finally effected so absolute a conquest over all pulmonary symptoms, as could not have failed to fix upon me the astonishment of Clifton, had not the sense of wonder been broken by the lingering time consumed in the several stages of the malady, and still more effectually by my own personal withdrawal from Clifton and its neighbourhoods.

Finally, arose what will inevitably turn out a more decisive chapter in such a record. I had always fixed my eyes and my expectations upon a revolution in the social history of opium, which could not (as I assured myself) by accident or by art be materially deferred. The great social machinery of life-insurance, supposing no other agency to be brought into play, how would *that* affect the great medicinal interests of opium? I knew that insurance offices, and the ablest actuaries of such offices, were not less ignorant upon the real merits of the opium question, and (which was worse) not less profoundly *prejudiced*, or less fanatical in their prejudices, than the rest of society. But, then, there were interests, growing continually, which would very soon force them into relaxing these prejudices. It would be alleged, at first, that opium-eating increased the risk of a life-insurance. Waiving the question whether it really *did* increase that risk, in any case that increase of risk, like other risks, could be valued, and *must* be valued. New habits were arising in society: that I well knew. And the old machineries for insuring life interests, under these or any other shifting conditions, would be obliged to adapt themselves to changing circum-

upon the case. But the reasons for concealment were not the less urgent. For it would have been painful to find myself reduced to the dilemma of either practising habitual and complex dissimulation, or, on the other hand, of throwing myself headlong into that fiery vortex of hotheaded ignorance upon the very name of opium, which to this hour (though with less of rancorous bigotry) makes it hazardous to avow any daily use of so potent a drug.

stances. If the old offices should be weak enough to persist in their misdirected obstinacy, new ones would arise. Meantime the history of this question moved through the following aspects :—Sixteen and seventeen years ago, the offices all looked with horror upon opium-eaters. Thus far, all men must have disapproved the principles of their policy. Habitual brandy-drinkers met with no repulse. And yet alcohol leads into daily dangers—for instance, that of *delirium tremens*. But no man ever heard of opium leading into *delirium tremens*. In the one case, there are well-ascertained and notorious dangers besetting the path ; but, in the other, supposing any corresponding dangers to exist, they have yet to be discovered. However, the offices would not look at us who came forward avowing ourselves to be opium-eaters. Myself in particular they regarded, I believe, as the abomination of desolation. And fourteen offices in succession, within a few months, repulsed me as a candidate for insurance on that solitary ground of having owned myself to be an opium-eater. The insurance was of very little consequence to myself, though involving some interest to others. And I contented myself with saying, ' Ten years hence, gentlemen, you will have come to understand your own interests better.' In less than *seven* years I received a letter from Mr. Tait, surgeon to the Police Force in Edinburgh, reporting a direct investigation officially pursued by him under private instructions received from two or more insurance offices. I knew, at the beginning of these seven years, or had strong reasons for believing, that the habit of opium-eating was spreading extensively, and through classes of society widely disconnected. This diffusion would, beyond a doubt, as one of its earliest consequences, coerce the insurance offices into a strict revision of their old blind policy. Accordingly it had already done so ; and the earliest fruits of this revolution were now before me in the proof-sheets so obligingly transmitted by Mr. Tait. His object, as I understood it, in sending these proofs to myself, was simply to collect such additional notices, suggestions, or sceptical queries, as might reasonably be anticipated from any reflective opium experience so extensive as my own. Most unhappily, this gentleman, during the course of our brief correspondence, was suddenly attacked by typhus fever; and, after a short illness, to my own exceeding regret, he died. On all accounts I had reason for sorrow. Knowing him only through his very interesting correspondence with myself, I had learned to form high expectations from Mr. Tait's philosophic spirit and his determined hostility to traditional cant. He had recorded, in the communications made to myself, with great minuteness and anxiety for rigour of accuracy, the cases of more than ninety patients. And he had shown himself inexorably deaf to all attempts at confounding evils specially belonging to opium as a stimulant, as a narcotic, or as a poison, with those which belong to opium merely as a cause of constipation or other ordinary irregularities in the animal economy. Most people of sedentary habits, but amongst such people notoriously those who think much, need some slight means of stimulating the watchwork of the animal system into action. Neglect of such means will of course derange the health. But in such derangements there is no special impeachment of opium: many thousands of agents terminate in the same or more obstinate derangements, unless vigilantly counteracted. The paramount mission of Mr. Tait, under his instructions from insurance offices, as I interpreted his own account of this mission, was, to report firmly and decisively upon the tendencies of opium in relation to the lengthening or shortening of life. At that point where his proof-sheets were interrupted by the fatal attack of fever, he had not entirely finished his record of cases; so that his final judgment or summing up had not commenced. It was, however, evident to me in what channel this final judgment would have flowed. To a certainty, he would have authorised his clients (the insurance offices) to dismiss all anxiety as to the life-abridging tendencies of opium. But he would have pointed their jealousy in another direction—viz., this, that in some proportion of cases there may always be a reasonable ground for suspecting, not the opium as

separately in itself any cause of mischief, but the opium
as a conjectural indication of some secret distress or
irritation that had fastened upon the system, and had
in that way sought relief; cases, in short, which the use
of opium had not caused, but which, on the contrary,
had caused the use of opium ;—opium having been
called in to redress or to relieve the affection. In all
such circumstances, the insurance office is entitled to
call for a frank disclosure of the ailment; but not, as
hitherto, entitled to assume the opium as itself an
ailment. It may very easily have happened, that simply
the genial restoration derived from opium, its power of
qualifying a man suddenly to face (that is, upon an
hour's warning to face) some twelve hours' unusual
exertion, qualifying him both as to spirits and as to
strength; or again, simply the general purpose of seeking relief from ennui, or *tædium vitæ*—any one of these
motives may satisfactorily account for the applicant's
having resorted to opium. He might reply to the office
in Professor Wilson's word,[1] 'Gentlemen, I am a
*Hedonist;* and, if you *must* know why I take opium,
that's the reason why.' But still, upon every admission
from a candidate that he took opium, it would be a
prudent question and a just question on the part of the
office, to ask '*why*'; and in what circumstances the
practice had originated. If in any local uneasiness,
then would arise a natural right on the part of the office
to press for a surgical examination. But, apart from
such special cases, it was evident that this acute and
experienced surgeon saw no reason whatever in the simple
practice of opium-eating for hesitating upon a life-insurance proposal, or for exacting a higher rate of premium.

Here I pause. The reader will infer, from what I
have now said, that all passages, written at an earlier
period under cloudy and uncorrected views of the evil
agencies presumable in opium, stand retracted ; although,
shrinking from the labour of altering an error diffused so

---

[1] From the Greek word for *voluptuous pleasure*—viz., *Hedone*
('Ηδονή)—Professor Wilson coined the English word *Hedonist*, which
he sometimes applied in playful reproach to myself and others.

widely under my own early misconceptions of the truth, I have suffered them to remain as they were. My general views upon the powers and natural tendencies of opium were all supported and strengthened by this fortunate advantage of a professional correspondence. My special doctrine I now repeat at this point of valediction, and in a rememberable form. Lord Bacon said once, too boldly and hazardously, that he who discovers the secret of making myrrh soluble by human blood has discovered the secret of immortal life. I propose a more modest form of magic—that he who discovers the secret of stimulating and keeping up unintermittingly the insensible perspiration, has discovered the secret of intercepting pulmonary consumption. In my medical character, I here take leave of the reader, and fall back into the current of my regular narrative.

   .     .     .     .     .     .

3. My studies have now been long interrupted. I cannot read to myself with any pleasure, hardly with a moment's endurance. Yet I sometimes read aloud for the pleasure of others; because reading is an accomplishment of mine, and, in the slang use of the word *accomplishment* as a superficial and ornamental attainment, almost the only one I possess; and formerly, if I had any vanity at all connected with any endowment or attainment of mine, it was with this; for I had observed that no accomplishment is more rare. Actors are the worst readers of all. John Kemble is not effective as a reader, though he has the great advantage of mature scholarship; and his sister, the immortal Siddons, with all her superiority to him in voice, reads even less effectively. She reads nothing well but dramatic works. In the *Paradise Lost*, which I heard her attempt at Barley Wood, her failure was distressing; almost as distressing as the sycophantic applause of the surrounding company—all lost, of course, in nearly speechless admiration. Yet I am sensible that this contemptuous feeling for the circle of admirers is scarcely justified. What *should* the poor creatures have done? Already, in the mere attempt to win their suffrages, in placing

herself once again upon trial, there was a condescension on the part of Mrs. Siddons, after which free judgment became impossible. I felt a wish to address Mrs. Siddons thus—You that have read to royalty at Windsor, nay, have even been desired to *sit down* at Windsor whilst reading, ever afterwards are a privileged person, liable to no accent of truth. Our feelings, as not free to take any natural expression, can be of no value. Suffer us to be silent, if only for the dignity of human nature. And do yourself be silent, if only for the dignity of that once unequalled voice. Neither Coleridge nor Southey is a good reader of verse. Southey is admirable almost in all things, but not in this. Both he and Coleridge read as if crying, or at least wailing lugubriously. People in general either read poetry without any passion at all, or else overstep the modesty of nature. Of late, if I have felt moved by anything in books, it has been by the grand lamentations of *Samson Agonistes*, or the great harmonies of the Satanic speeches in *Paradise Regained*, when read aloud by myself. We are far from towns; but a young lady sometimes comes and drinks tea with us; at her request and M——'s, I now and then read Wordsworth's poems to them. (Wordsworth, by-the-bye, is the only poet I ever met who could read his own verses; often, indeed, he reads admirably.)

For nearly two years I believe that I read nothing and studied nothing. Analytic studies are continuous studies, and not to be pursued by fits and starts, or fragmentary efforts. All these were become insupportable to me; I shrank from them with a sense of powerless and infantine feebleness that gave me an anguish the greater from remembering the time when I grappled with them to my own hourly delight; and for this further reason, because I had devoted the labour of my whole life, had dedicated my intellect, blossoms and fruits, to the slow and elaborate toil of constructing one single work, to which I had presumed to give the title of an unfinished work of Spinosa's—viz., *De Emendatione Humani Intellectûs*. This was now lying locked up as by frost, like any Spanish bridge or aqueduct begun upon too great a scale for the resources of the architect, and, instead of surviving me, as a monument of wishes at least, and aspirations, and long labours, dedicated to the exaltation of human nature in that way in which God had best fitted me to promote so great an object, it was likely to stand a memorial to my children of hopes defeated, of baffled efforts, of materials uselessly accumulated, of foundations laid that were never to support a superstructure, of the grief and the ruin of the architect. In this state of imbecility, I had, for amusement, turned my attention to political economy; my understanding, which formerly had been as active and restless as a panther, could not, I suppose (so long as I lived at all), sink into utter lethargy; and political economy offers this advantage to a person in my state, that, though it is eminently an organic science (no part, that is to say, but what acts on the whole, as the whole again reacts on and through each part), yet still the several parts may be detached and contemplated singly. Great as was the prostration of my powers at this time, yet I could not forget my knowledge; and my understanding had been for too many years intimate with severe thinkers, with logic, and the great masters of knowledge, not to be aware of a great call made by political economy at this crisis for a new law and a transcendent legislator. Suddenly, in 1818, a friend in Edinburgh sent me down Mr. Ricardo's book; and, recurring to my own prophetic anticipation of some coming legislator for this science, I said, before I had finished the first chapter, 'Thou art the man!' Wonder and curiosity were emotions that had long been dead in me. Yet I wondered once more—wondered at myself that could once again be stimulated to the effort of reading; and much more I wondered at the book. Had this profound work been really written during the tumultuous hurry of the nineteenth century? Could it be that an Englishman, and he not in academic bowers, but oppressed by mercantile and senatorial cares, had accomplished what all the universities of Europe, and a century of thought, had failed even to advance by one hair's-breadth? Previous writers had been crushed and overlaid by the enormous weights of facts, details, and exceptions; Mr. Ricardo had deduced, *a priori*, from the understanding itself, laws which first shot arrowy light into the dark chaos of materials, and had thus constructed what hitherto was but a collection of tentative discussions into a science of regular proportions, now first standing upon an eternal basis.

Thus did one simple work of a profound understanding avail to give me a pleasure and an activity which I had not known for years; it roused me even to write, or, at least, to dictate what M—— wrote for me. It seemed to me that some important truths had escaped even 'the inevitable eye' of Mr. Ricardo; and, as these were, for the most part, of such a nature that I could express or illustrate them briefly and elegantly by algebraic symbols, the whole would hardly have reached the bulk of a pamphlet. With M—— for my amanuensis, even at this time, incapable as I was of all general exertion, I drew up, therefore, my *Prolegomena to all Future Systems of Political Economy*.

This exertion, however, was but a momentary flash, as the sequel showed. Arrangements were made at a provincial press, about eighteen miles distant, for printing it. An additional compositor was retained for some days, on this account. The work was even twice advertised; and I was, in a manner, pledged to the fulfilment of my intention. But I had a preface to write, and a dedication, which I wished to make impressive, to Mr. Ricardo. I found myself quite unable to accomplish all this. The arrangements were countermanded, the compositor dismissed, and my *Prolegomena* rested peacefully by the side of its elder and more dignified brother.

In thus describing and illustrating my intellectual torpor, I use terms that apply, more or less, to every part of the years during which I was under the Circean spells of opium. But for misery and suffering, I might, indeed, be said to have existed in a dormant state. I seldom could prevail on myself to write a letter; an answer of a few words, to any that I received, was the utmost that I could accomplish; and often *that* not until the letter had lain for weeks, or even months, on my writing-table. Without the aid of M——, my whole domestic economy, whatever became of political economy, must have gone into irretrievable confusion. I shall not afterwards allude to this part of the case; it is one, however, which the opium-eater will find, in the end, most oppressive and tormenting, from the sense of incapacity and feebleness, from the direct embarrassments incident to the neglect or procrastination of each day's appropriate labours, and from the remorse which must often exasperate the stings of these evils to a conscientious mind. The opium-eater loses none of his moral sensibilities or aspirations; he wishes and longs as earnestly as ever to realise what he believes possible, and feels to be exacted by duty; but his intellectual apprehension of what is possible infinitely outruns his power, not of execution only, but even of proposing or willing. He lies under a world's weight of incubus and nightmare; he lies in sight of all that he would fain perform, just as a man forcibly confined to his bed by the mortal languor of paralysis, who is compelled to witness injury or outrage offered to some object of his tenderest love:—he would lay down his life if he might but rise and walk; but he is powerless as an infant, and cannot so much as make an effort to move.

But from this I now pass to what is the main subject of these latter Confessions—to the history and journal of what took place in my dreams; for these were the immediate and proximate cause of shadowy terrors that settled and brooded over my whole waking life.

The first notice I had of any important change going on in this part of my physical economy, was from the re-awaking of a state of eye oftentimes incident to childhood. I know not whether my reader is aware that many children have a power of painting, as it were, upon the darkness all sorts of phantoms; in some that power is simply a mechanic affection of the eye; others have a voluntary or semi-voluntary power to dismiss or summon such phantoms; or, as a child once said to me, when I questioned him on this matter, 'I can tell them to go, and they go; but sometimes they come when I don't tell them to come.' He had by one-half as unlimited a command over apparitions as a Roman centurion over his soldiers. In the middle of 1817 this faculty became increasingly distressing to me: at night, when I lay awake in bed, vast processions moved along continually in mournful pomp; friezes of never-ending stories, that to my feelings were as sad and solemn as stories drawn from times before Œdipus or Priam, before Tyre, before Memphis. And, concurrently with this, a corresponding change took place in my dreams; a theatre seemed suddenly opened and lighted up within my brain, which presented nightly spectacles of more than earthly splendour. And the four following facts may be mentioned, as noticeable at this time :—

1. That, as the creative state of the eye increased, a sympathy seemed to arise between the waking and the dreaming states of the brain in one point—that whatsoever I happened to call up and to trace by a voluntary act upon the darkness was very apt to transfer itself to my dreams; and at length I feared to exercise this faculty; for, as Midas turned all things to gold that yet baffled his hopes and defrauded his human desires, so whatsoever things capable of being visually represented I did but think of in the darkness, immediately shaped themselves into phantoms for the eye; and, by a process apparently no less inevitable, when thus once traced in faint and visionary colours, like writings in sympathetic ink, they were drawn out by the fierce chemistry of my dreams, into insufferable splendour that fretted my heart.

2. This and all other changes in my dreams were accompanied by deep-seated anxiety and funereal melancholy, such as are wholly incommunicable by words. I seemed every night to descend—not metaphorically, but literally to descend—into chasms and sunless abysses, depths below depths, from which it seemed hopeless that I could ever re-ascend. Nor did I, by waking, feel that I *had* re-ascended. Why should I dwell upon this? For indeed the state of gloom which attended these

gorgeous spectacles, amounting at last to utter darkness, as of some suicidal despondency, cannot be approached by words.

3. The sense of space, and in the end the sense of time, were both powerfully affected. Buildings, landscapes, etc., were exhibited in proportions so vast as the bodily eye is not fitted to receive. Space swelled, and was amplified to an extent of unutterable and self-repeating infinity. This disturbed me very much less than the vast expansion of time. Sometimes I seemed to have lived for seventy or a hundred years in one night; nay, sometimes had feelings representative of a duration far beyond the limits of any human experience.

4. The minutest incidents of childhood, or forgotten scenes of later years, were often revived. I could not be said to recollect them; for, if I had been told of them when waking, I should not have been able to acknowledge them as parts of my past experience. But placed as they were before me, in dreams like intuitions, and clothed in all their evanescent circumstances and accompanying feelings, I *recognised* them instantaneously. I was once told by a near relative of mine, that having in her childhood fallen into a river, and being on the very verge of death but for the assistance which reached her at the last critical moment, she saw in a moment her whole life, clothed in its forgotten incidents, arrayed before her as in a mirror, not successively, but simultaneously; and she had a faculty developed as suddenly for comprehending the whole and every part.[1] This,

---

[1] The heroine of this remarkable case was a girl of about nine years old; and there can be little doubt that she looked down as far within the *crater* of death—that awful volcano—as any human being ever *can* have done that has lived to draw back and to report her experience. Not less than ninety years did she survive this memorable escape; and I may describe her as in all respects a woman of remarkable and interesting qualities. She enjoyed throughout her long life, as the reader will readily infer, serene and cloudless health; had a masculine understanding; reverenced truth not less than did the Evangelists; and led a life of saintly devotion, such as might have glorified ' *Hilarion or Paul.*'—(The words in italic are Ariosto's.)—I mention these traits as characterising her in a memorable extent, that the reader may not suppose himself relying upon a dealer in exaggerations, upon a credulous enthusiast, or upon a careless wielder of language. Forty-

from some opium experiences, I can believe; I have, indeed, seen the same thing asserted twice in modern books, and accompanied by a remark which probably is true—viz., that the dread book of account, which the Scriptures speak of, is, in fact, the mind itself of each individual. Of this, at least, I feel assured, that there is no such thing as ultimate *forgetting;* traces once impressed upon the memory are indestructible; a thousand accidents may and will interpose a veil between our present consciousness and the secret inscriptions on the mind. Accidents of the same sort will also rend away this veil. But alike, whether veiled or unveiled, the inscription remains for ever; just as the stars seem to withdraw before the common light of day, whereas, in fact, we all know that it is the light which is drawn over them as a veil; and that they are waiting to be revealed,

five years had intervened between the first time and the last time of her telling me this anecdote, and not one iota had shifted its ground amongst the incidents, nor had any the most trivial of the circumstantiations suffered change. The scene of the accident was the least of valleys, what the Greeks of old would have called an ἄγκος, and we English should properly call a dell. Human tenant it had none : even at noonday it was a solitude ; and would oftentimes have been a silent solitude but for the brawling of a brook—not broad, but occasionally deep—which ran along the base of the little hills. Into this brook, probably into one of its dangerous pools, the child fell : and, according to the ordinary chances she could have had but a slender prospect indeed of any deliverance ; for, although a dwelling-house was close by, it was shut out from view by the undulations of the ground. How long the child lay in the water was probably never inquired earnestly until the answer had become irrecoverable ; for a servant, to whose care the child was then confided, had a natural interest in suppressing the whole case. From the child's own account, it should seem that *asphyxia* must have announced its commencement. A process of struggle and deadly suffocation was passed through half consciously. This process terminated by a sudden blow apparently *on* or *in* the brain, after which there was no pain or conflict ; but in an instant succeeded a dazzling rush of light ; immediately after which came the solemn apocalypse of the entire past life. Meantime, the child's disappearance in the water had happily been witnessed by a farmer who rented some fields in this little solitude, and by a rare accident was riding through them at the moment. Not being very well mounted, he was retarded by the hedges and other fences in making his way down to the water ; some time was thus lost ; but once at the spot, he leaped in, booted and spurred, and succeeded in delivering one that must have been as nearly counted amongst the populations of the grave as perhaps the laws of the shadowy world can suffer to return.

whenever the obscuring daylight itself shall have withdrawn.

Having noticed these four facts as memorably distinguishing my dreams from those of health, I shall now cite a few illustrative cases; and shall then cite such others as I remember, in any order that may give them most effect as pictures to the reader.

I had been in youth, and ever since, for occasional amusement, a great reader of Livy, whom I confess that I prefer, both for style and matter, to any other of the Roman historians; and I had often felt as solemn and appalling sounds, emphatically representative of Roman majesty, the two words so often occurring in Livy, *Consul Romanus;* especially when the consul is introduced in his military character. I mean to say, that the words king, sultan, regent, etc., or any other titles of those who embody in their own persons the collective majesty of a great people, had less power over my reverential feelings. I had also, though no great reader of history, made myself critically familiar with one period of English history—viz., the period of the Parliamentary War— having been attracted by the moral grandeur of some who figured in that day, and by the interesting memoirs which survive those unquiet times. Both these parts of my lighter reading, having furnished me often with matter of reflection, now furnished me with matter for my dreams. Often I used to see, after painting upon the blank darkness a sort of rehearsal whilst waking, a crowd of ladies, and perhaps a festival and dances. And I heard it said, or I said to myself, 'These are English ladies from the unhappy times of Charles I. These are the wives and daughters of those who met in peace, and sat at the same tables, and were allied by marriage or by blood; and yet, after a certain day in August 1642,[1]

---

[1] I think (but at the moment have no means of verifying my conjecture) that this day was the 24th of August. On or about that day Charles raised the royal standard at Nottingham; which, ominously enough (considering the strength of such superstitions in the seventeenth century, and, amongst the generations of that century, more especially in this particular generation of the Parliamentary War), was blown down during the succeeding night. Let me remark, in passing, that

never smiled upon each other again, nor met but in the field of battle; and at Marston Moor, at Newbury, or at Naseby, cut asunder all ties of love by the cruel sabre, and washed away in blood the memory of ancient friendship.' The ladies danced, and looked as lovely as at the court of George IV. Yet even in my dream I knew that they had been in the grave for nearly two centuries. This pageant would suddenly dissolve; and, at a clapping of hands, would be heard the heart-shaking sound of *Consul Romanus*; and immediately came 'sweeping by' in gorgeous paludaments, Paullus or Marius, girt around by a company of centurions, with the crimson tunic[1] hoisted on a spear, and followed by the *alalagmos*[2] of the Roman legions.

Many years ago, when I was looking over Piranesi's *Antiquities of Rome*, Coleridge, then standing by, described to me a set of plates from that artist, called his *Dreams*, and which record the scenery of his own visions during the delirium of a fever. Some of these (I describe only from memory of Coleridge's account) represented vast Gothic halls; on the floor of which stood mighty engines and machinery, wheels, cables, catapults, etc., expressive of enormous power put forth, or resistance overcome. Creeping along the sides of the walls, you perceived a staircase; and upon this, groping his way upwards, was Piranesi himself. Follow the stairs a little farther, and you perceive them reaching an abrupt termination, without any balustrade, and allowing no step onwards to him who should reach the extremity, except into the depths below. Whatever is to become of poor Piranesi, at least you suppose that his labours must now in some way terminate. But raise your eyes, and behold a second flight of stairs still higher, on which again Piranesi is perceived, by this time standing on the very

no falsehood can virtually be greater or more malicious than that which imputes to Archbishop Laud a special or exceptional faith in such mute warnings.

[1] '*The crimson tunic*':—The signal which announced a day of battle.

[2] '*Alalagmos*':—A word expressing collectively the gathering of the Roman war-cries—*Alála, Alála!*

brink of the abyss. Once again elevate your eye, and a still more aërial flight is descried; and there, again, is the delirious Piranesi, busy on his aspiring labours : and so on, until the unfinished stairs and the hopeless Piranesi both are lost in the upper gloom of the hall. With the same power of endless growth and self-reproduction did my architecture proceed in dreams. In the early stage of the malady, the splendours of my dreams were indeed chiefly architectural; and I beheld such pomp of cities and palaces as never yet was beheld by the waking eye, unless in the clouds. From a great modern poet[1] I cite the part of a passage which describes, as an appearance actually beheld in the clouds, what in many of its circumstances I saw frequently in sleep :—

> ' The appearance, instantaneously disclosed,
> Was of a mighty city—boldly say
> A wilderness of building, sinking far
> And self-withdrawn into a wondrous depth,
> Far sinking into splendour without end !
> Fabric it seem'd of diamond and of gold,
> With alabaster domes and silver spires,
> And blazing terrace upon terrace, high
> Uplifted ; here, serene pavilions bright,
> In avenues disposed ; there towers begirt
> With battlements that on their restless fronts
> Bore stars—illumination of all gems !
> By earthly nature had the effect been wrought
> Upon the dark materials of the storm
> Now pacified ; on them, and on the coves,
> And mountain-steeps and summits, whereunto
> The vapours had receded—taking there
> Their station under a cerulean sky.'

---

[1] '*From a great modern poet*' :—What poet? It was Wordsworth; and why did I not formerly name him? This throws a light backwards upon the strange history of Wordsworth's reputation. The year in which I wrote and published these Confessions was 1821 ; and at that time the name of Wordsworth, though beginning to emerge from the dark cloud of scorn and contumely which had hitherto overshadowed it, was yet most imperfectly established. Not until ten years later was his greatness cheerfully and generally acknowledged. I, therefore, as the very earliest (without one exception) of all who came forward, in the beginning of his career, to honour and welcome him, shrank with disgust from making any sentence of mine the occasion for an explosion of vulgar malice against him. But the grandeur of the passage here cited inevitably spoke for itself; and he that would have been most scornful on hearing the name of the poet coupled with this epithet of ' great ' could not but find his malice intercepted, and himself cheated into cordial admiration, by the splendour of the verses.

The sublime circumstance—'that on their *restless* fronts bore stars'—might have been copied from my own architectural dreams, so often did it occur. We hear it reported of Dryden, and in later times of Fuseli, that they ate raw meat for the sake of obtaining splendid dreams: how much better, for such a purpose, to have eaten opium, which yet I do not remember that any poet is recorded to have done, except the dramatist Shadwell; and in ancient days, Homer is, I think, rightly reputed to have known the virtues of opium as a φάρμακον νηπενθές—*i.e.*, as an anodyne.

To my architecture succeeded dreams of lakes and silvery expanses of water: these haunted me so much, that I feared lest some dropsical state or tendency of the brain might thus be making itself (to use a metaphysical word) *objective*;[1] and that the sentient organ might be projecting itself as its own object. For two months I suffered greatly in my head—a part of my bodily structure which had hitherto been so clear from all touch or taint of weakness (physically, I mean), that I used to say of it, as the last Lord Orford said of his stomach, that it seemed likely to survive the rest of my person. Till now, I had never felt a headache even, or any the slightest pain, except rheumatic pains caused by my own folly.

The waters gradually changed their character—from translucent lakes, shining like mirrors, they became seas and oceans. And now came a tremendous change, which, unfolding itself slowly like a scroll, through many months, promised an abiding torment; and, in fact, it never left me, though recurring more or less intermittingly. Hitherto the human face had often mixed in my dreams, but not despotically, nor with any special power of tormenting. But now that affection, which I have called the tyranny of the human face, began to unfold itself. Perhaps some part of my London life

---

[1] '*Objective*':—This word, so nearly unintelligible in 1821, so intensely scholastic, and, consequently, when surrounded by familiar and vernacular words, so apparently pedantic, yet, on the other hand, so indispensable to accurate thinking, and to *wide* thinking, has since 1821 become too common to need any apology.

(the searching for Ann amongst fluctuating crowds) might be answerable for this. Be that as it may, now it was that upon the rocking waters of the ocean the human face began to reveal itself; the sea appeared paved with innumerable faces, upturned to the heavens; faces, imploring, wrathful, despairing; faces that surged upwards by thousands, by myriads, by generations: infinite was my agitation; my mind tossed, as it seemed, upon the billowy ocean, and weltered upon the weltering waves.

*May* 1818.—The Malay has been a fearful enemy for months. Every night, through his means, I have been transported into Asiatic scenery. I know not whether others share in my feelings on this point; but I have often thought that if I were compelled to forego England, and to live in China, among Chinese manners and modes of life and scenery, I should go mad. The causes of my horror lie deep, and some of them must be common to others. Southern Asia, in general, is the seat of awful images and associations. As the cradle of the human race, if on no other ground, it would have a dim, reverential feeling connected with it. But there are other reasons. No man can pretend that the wild, barbarous, and capricious superstitions of Africa, or of savage tribes elsewhere, affect him in the way that he is affected by the ancient, monumental, cruel, and elaborate religions of Hindostan. The mere antiquity of Asiatic things, of their institutions, histories, above all, of their mythologies, &c., is so impressive, that to me the vast age of the race and name overpowers the sense of youth in the individual. A young Chinese seems to me an antediluvian man renewed. Even Englishmen, though not bred in any knowledge of such institutions, cannot but shudder at the mystic sublimity of *castes* that have flowed apart, and refused to mix, through such immemorial tracts of time; nor can any man fail to be awed by the sanctity of the Ganges, or by the very name of the Euphrates. It contributes much to these feelings that South-eastern Asia is, and has been for thousands of years, the part of the earth most swarming with human life, the great *officina gentium*. Man is a weed in those regions. The vast empires, also, into which the enormous population of Asia has always been cast give a further sublimity to the feelings associated with all oriental names or images. In China, over and above what it has in common with the rest of Southern Asia, I am terrified by the modes of life, by the manners, by the barrier of utter abhorrence placed between myself and *them*, by counter-sympathies deeper than I can analyse. I could sooner live with lunatics, with vermin, with crocodiles or snakes. All this, and much more than I can say, the reader must enter into before he can comprehend the unimaginable horror which these dreams of oriental imagery and mythological tortures impressed upon me. Under the connecting feeling of tropical heat and vertical sunlights, I brought together all creatures, birds, beasts, reptiles, all trees and plants, usages and appearances, that are found in all tropical regions, and assembled them together in China or Hindostan. From kindred feelings, I soon brought Egypt and her gods under the same law. I was stared at, hooted at, grinned at, chattered at, by monkeys, by paroquets, by cockatoos. I ran into pagodas, and was fixed for centuries at the summit, or in secret rooms; I was the idol; I was the priest; I was worshipped; I was sacrificed. I fled from the wrath of Brama through all the forests of Asia; Vishnu hated me; Seeva lay in wait for me. I came suddenly upon Isis and Osiris: I had done a deed, they said, which the ibis and the crocodile trembled at. Thousands of years I lived and was buried in stone coffins, with mummies and sphinxes, in narrow chambers at the heart of eternal pyramids. I was kissed, with cancerous kisses by crocodiles, and was laid, confounded with all unutterable abortions, amongst reeds and Nilotic mud.

Some slight abstraction I thus attempt of my oriental dreams, which filled me always with such amazement at the monstrous scenery, that horror seemed absorbed for a while in sheer astonishment. Sooner or later came a reflux of feeling that swallowed up the astonishment, and left me, not so much in terror, as in hatred and abomi-

nation of what I saw. Over every form, and threat, and
punishment, and dim sightless incarceration, brooded a
killing sense of eternity and infinity. Into these dreams
only it was, with one or two slight exceptions, that any
circumstances of physical horror entered. All before
had been moral and spiritual terrors. But here the
main agents were ugly birds, or snakes, or crocodiles,
especially the last. The cursed crocodile became to me
the object of more horror than all the rest. I was compelled to live with him ; and (as was always the case in
my dreams) for centuries. Sometimes I escaped, and
found myself in Chinese houses. All the feet of the
tables, sofas, &c., soon became instinct with life : the
abominable head of the crocodile, and his leering eyes,
looked out at me, multiplied into ten thousand repetitions ; and I stood loathing and fascinated. So often did
this hideous reptile haunt my dreams, that many times
the very same dream was broken up in the very same
way : I heard gentle voices speaking to me (I hear everything when I am sleeping), and instantly I awoke ; it
was broad noon, and my children were standing, hand in
hand, at my bedside, come to show me their coloured
shoes, or new frocks, or to let me see them dressed for
going out. No experience was so awful to me, and at
the same time so pathetic, as this abrupt translation from
the darkness of the infinite to the gaudy summer air of
highest noon, and from the unutterable abortions of
miscreated gigantic vermin to the sight of infancy, and
innocent *human* natures.

*June* 1819.—I have had occasion to remark, at various
periods of my life, that the deaths of those whom we
love, and, indeed, the contemplation of death generally,
is (*cæteris paribus*) more affecting in summer than in any
other season of the year. And the reasons are these
three, I think : first, that the visible heavens in summer
appear far higher, more distant, and (if such a solecism
may be excused) more infinite ; the clouds by which
chiefly the eye expounds the distance of the blue pavilion
stretched over our heads are in summer more voluminous, more massed, and are accumulated in far grander

and more towering piles; secondly, the light and the
appearances of the declining and the setting sun are
much more fitted to be types and characters of the infinite; and, thirdly (which is the main reason), the exu-
berant and riotous prodigality of life naturally forces the
mind more powerfully upon the antagonist thought of
death, and the wintery sterility of the grave. For it may
be observed generally, that wherever two thoughts stand
related to each other by a law of antagonism, and exist,
as it were, by mutual repulsion, they are apt to suggest
each other. On these accounts it is that I find it impossible to banish the thought of death when I am
walking alone in the endless days of summer; and any
particular death, if not actually more affecting, at least
haunts my mind more obstinately and besiegingly, in
that season. Perhaps this cause, and a slight incident
which I omit, might have been the immediate occasions
of the following dream, to which, however, a predisposition must always have existed in my mind; but, having
been once roused, it never left me, and split into a thousand fantastic variations, which often suddenly re-com-
bined; locked back into startling unity, and restored the
original dream.

I thought that it was a Sunday morning in May; that
it was Easter Sunday, and as yet very early in the morning. I was standing, as it seemed to me, at the door of
my own cottage. Right before me lay the very scene
which could really be commanded from that situation,
but exalted, as was usual, and solemnised by the power
of dreams. There were the same mountains, and the
same lovely valley at their feet; but the mountains were
raised to more than Alpine height, and there was inter-
space far larger between them of savannahs and forest
lawns; the hedges were rich with white roses; and no
living creature was to be seen, excepting that in the
green churchyard there were cattle tranquilly reposing
upon the verdant graves, and particularly round about
the grave of a child whom I had once tenderly loved,
just as I had really beheld them, a little before sunrise,
in the same summer when that child died. I gazed upon

the well-known scene, and I said to myself, 'It yet wants much of sunrise; and it is Easter Sunday; and that is the day on which they celebrate the first-fruits of Resurrection. I will walk abroad; old griefs shall be forgotten to-day: for the air is cool and still, and the hills are high, and stretch away to heaven; and the churchyard is as verdant as the forest lawns, and the forest lawns are as quiet as the churchyard; and with the dew I can wash the fever from my forehead; and then I shall be unhappy no longer.' I turned, as if to open my garden gate, and immediately I saw upon the left a scene far different; but which yet the power of dreams had reconciled into harmony. The scene was an oriental one; and there also it was Easter Sunday, and very early in the morning. And at a vast distance were visible, as a stain upon the horizon, the domes and cupolas of a great city—an image or faint abstraction, caught perhaps in childhood from some picture of Jerusalem. And not a bow-shot from me, upon a stone, shaded by Judean palms, there sat a woman; and I looked, and it was—Ann! She fixed her eyes upon me earnestly; and I said to her at length, 'So, then, I have found you at last.' I waited; but she answered me not a word. Her face was the same as when I saw it last; the same, and yet, again, how different! Seventeen years ago, when the lamp-light of mighty London fell upon her face, as for the last time I kissed her lips (lips, Ann, that to me were not polluted!), her eyes were streaming with tears. The tears were now no longer seen. Sometimes she seemed altered; yet again sometimes *not* altered; and hardly older. Her looks were tranquil, but with unusual solemnity of expression, and I now gazed upon her with some awe. Suddenly her countenance grew dim; and, turning to the mountains, I perceived vapours rolling between us; in a moment all had vanished; thick darkness came on; and in the twinkling of an eye I was far away from mountains, and by lamp-light in London, walking again with Ann—just as we had walked, when both children, eighteen years before, along the endless terraces of Oxford Street.

Then suddenly would come a dream of far different character—a tumultuous dream—commencing with a music such as now I often heard in sleep—music of preparation and of awakening suspense. The undulations of fast-gathering tumults were like the opening of the Coronation Anthem; and, like *that*, gave the feeling of a multitudinous movement, of infinite cavalcades filing off, and the tread of innumerable armies. The morning was come of a mighty day—a day of crisis and of ultimate hope for human nature, then suffering mysterious eclipse, and labouring in some dread extremity. Somewhere, but I knew not where—somehow, but I knew not how—by some beings, but I knew not by whom—a battle, a strife, an agony, was travelling through all its stages—was evolving itself, like the catastrophe of some mighty drama, with which my sympathy was the more insupportable, from deepening confusion as to its local scene, its cause, its nature, and its undecipherable issue. I (as is usual in dreams where, of necessity, we make ourselves central to every movement) had the power, and yet had not the power, to decide it. I had the power, if I could raise myself to will it; and yet again had not the power, for the weight of twenty Atlantics was upon me, or the oppression of inexpiable guilt. ' Deeper than ever plummet sounded,' I lay inactive. Then, like a chorus, the passion deepened. Some greater interest was at stake, some mightier cause, than ever yet the sword had pleaded, or trumpet had proclaimed. Then came sudden alarms; hurryings to and fro; trepidations of innumerable fugitives, I knew not whether from the good cause or the bad; darkness and lights; tempest and human faces; and at last, with the sense that all was lost, female forms, and the features that were worth all the world to me; and but a moment allowed—and clasped hands, with heart-breaking partings, and then—everlasting farewells! and, with a sigh such as the caves of hell sighed when the incestuous mother uttered the abhorred name of Death, the sound was reverberated—everlasting farewells! and again, and yet again reverberated—everlasting farewells!

And I awoke in struggles, and cried aloud, ' I will sleep no more ! '

Now, at last, I had become awestruck at the approach of sleep, under the condition of visions so afflicting, and so intensely life-like as those which persecuted my phantom-haunted brain. More and more also I felt violent palpitations in some internal region, such as are commonly, but erroneously, called palpitations of the heart—being, as I suppose, referable exclusively to derangements in the stomach. These were evidently increasing rapidly in frequency and in strength. Naturally, therefore, on considering how important my life had become to others besides myself, I became alarmed ; and I paused seasonably ; but with a difficulty that is past all description. Either way it seemed as though death had, in military language, ' thrown himself astride of my path.' Nothing short of mortal anguish, in a physical sense, it seemed, to wean myself from opium ; yet, on the other hand, death through overwhelming nervous terrors—death by brain fever or by lunacy— seemed too certainly to besiege the alternative course. Fortunately I had still so much of firmness left as to face that choice, which, with most of instant suffering, showed in the far distance a possibility of final escape.

This possibility was realised : I *did* accomplish my escape. And the issue of that particular stage in my opium experiences (for such it was—simply a provisional stage, that paved the way subsequently for many milder stages, to which gradually my constitutional system accommodated itself) was, pretty nearly in the following words, communicated to my readers in the earliest edition of these Confessions :—

I triumphed. But infer not, reader, from this word ' *triumphed*,' a condition of joy or exultation. Think of me as of one, even when four months had passed, still agitated, writhing, throbbing, palpitating, shattered ; and much, perhaps, in the situation of him who has been racked, as I collect the torments of that state from the affecting account of them left by a most innocent sufferer[1] (in the time of James i.).   Meantime, I derived no benefit from any medicine whatever, except ammoniated tincture of valerian.   The moral of the narrative is addressed to the opium-eater; and therefore, of necessity, limited in its application.   If he is taught to fear and tremble, enough has been effected.   But he may say that the issue of my case is at least a proof that opium, after an eighteen years' use, and an eight years' abuse of its powers, may still be renounced; and that he may chance to bring to the task greater energy than I did, or that, with a stronger constitution, he may obtain the same results with less.   This may be true; I would not presume to measure the efforts of other men by my own.   Heartily I wish him more resolution; heartily I wish him an equal success.   Nevertheless, I had motives external to myself which he may unfortunately want; and these supplied me with conscientious supports, such as merely selfish interests might fail in supplying to a mind debilitated by opium.

Lord Bacon conjectures that it may be as painful to be born as to die.[2]   That seems probable; and, during the whole period of diminishing the opium, I had the torments of a man passing out of one mode of existence into another, and liable to the mixed or the alternate pains of birth and death.   The issue was not death, but a sort of physical regeneration; and I may add, that ever since, at intervals, I have had a restoration of more than youthful spirits.

One memorial of my former condition nevertheless remains: my dreams are not calm; the dread swell and

---

[1] William Lithgow.   His book (Travels, etc.) is tedious and not well written; but the account of his own sufferings on the rack at Malaga, and subsequently, is overpoweringly affecting.   Less circumstantial, but the same in tendency, is the report of the results from torture published in 1830 by Juan Van Halen.

[2] In all former editions, I had ascribed this sentiment to Jeremy Taylor.   On a close search, however, wishing to verify the quotation, it appeared that I had been mistaken.   Something very like it occurs more than once in the bishop's voluminous writings: but the exact passage moving in my mind had evidently been this which follows, from Lord Bacon's *Essay on Death*:—' It is as natural to die as to be born; and to a little infant perhaps the one is as painful as the other.'

agitation of the storm have not wholly subsided; the legions that encamped in them are drawing off, but not departed; my sleep is still tumultuous; and, like the gates of Paradise to our first parents when looking back from afar, it is still (in the tremendous line of Milton)—

'With dreadful faces thronged and fiery arms.'

# THE DAUGHTER OF LEBANON

DAMASCUS, first-born of cities, *Om el Denia*,[1] mother of generations, that wast before Abraham, that wast before the Pyramids! what sounds are those that, from a postern gate, looking eastwards over secret paths that wind away to the far distant desert, break the solemn silence of an oriental night? Whose voice is that which calls upon the spearmen, keeping watch for ever in the turret surmounting the gate, to receive him back into his Syrian home? Thou knowest him, Damascus, and hast known him in seasons of trouble as one learned in the afflictions of man; wise alike to take counsel for the suffering spirit or for the suffering body. The voice that breaks upon the night is the voice of a great evangelist —one of the four; and he is also a great physician This do the watchmen at the gate thankfully acknowledge, and joyfully they give him entrance. His sandals are white with dust; for he has been roaming for weeks beyond the desert, under the guidance of Arabs, on missions of hopeful benignity to Palmyra;[2] and in spirit he is weary of all things, except faithfulness to God, and burning love to man.

Eastern cities are asleep betimes; and sounds few or none fretted the quiet of all around him, as the evangelist paced onward to the market-place; but there another scene awaited him. On the right hand, in an upper chamber, with lattices widely expanded, sat a festal

[1] *'Om el Denia'*:—Mother of the World is the Arabic title of Damascus. That it was before Abraham—*i.e.*, already an old establishment much more than a thousand years before the siege of Troy, and than two thousand years before our Christian era—may be inferred from Gen. xv. 2; and by the general consent of all eastern races, Damascus is accredited as taking precedence in age of all cities to the west of the Indus.

[2] Palmyra had not yet reached its meridian splendour of Grecian development, as afterwards near the age of Aurelian, but it was already a noble city.

company of youths, revelling under a noonday blaze of light, from cressets and from bright tripods that burned fragrant woods—all joining in choral songs, all crowned with odorous wreaths from Daphne and the banks of the Orontes. Them the evangelist heeded not; but far away upon the left, close upon a sheltered nook, lighted up by a solitary vase of iron fretwork filled with cedar boughs, and hoisted high upon a spear, behold there sat a woman of loveliness so transcendent, that, when suddenly revealed, as now, out of deepest darkness, she appalled men as a mockery, or a birth of the air. Was she born of woman? Was it perhaps the angel—so the evangelist argued with himself—that met him in the desert after sunset, and strengthened him by secret talk? The evangelist went up, and touched her forehead; and when he found that she was indeed human, and guessed, from the station which she had chosen, that she waited for some one amongst this dissolute crew as her companion, he groaned heavily in spirit, and said, half to himself, but half to her, 'Wert thou, poor ruined flower, adorned so divinely at thy birth—glorified in such excess that not Solomon in all his pomp—no, nor even the lilies of the field—can approach thy gifts—only that thou shouldest grieve the holy spirit of God?' The woman trembled exceedingly, and said, 'Rabbi, what should I do? For behold! all men forsake me.' The evangelist mused a little, and then secretly to himself he said, 'Now will I search this woman's heart—whether in very truth it inclineth itself to God, and hath strayed only before fiery compulsion.' Turning therefore to the woman, the Prophet[1] said, 'Listen: I am the messenger

---

[1] '*The Prophet*':—Though a Prophet was not *therefore* and in virtue of that character an Evangelist, yet every Evangelist was necessarily in the scriptural sense a Prophet. For let it be remembered that a Prophet did not mean a *Pre*dicter, or *Fore*shower of events, except derivatively and inferentially. What *was* a Prophet in the uniform scriptural sense? He was a man, who drew aside the curtain from the secret counsels of Heaven. He declared, or made public, the previously hidden truths of God: and because future events might chance to involve divine truth, therefore a revealer of future events might happen so far to be a Prophet. Yet still small was that part of a Prophet's functions which concerned the foreshowing of events; and not necessarily *any* part.

of Him whom thou hast not known; of Him that made
Lebanon and the cedars of Lebanon; that made the
sea, and the heavens, and the host of the stars; that
made the light; that made the darkness; that blew the
spirit of life into the nostrils of man. His messenger I
am: and from Him all power is given me to bind and
to loose, to build and to pull down. Ask, therefore,
whatsoever thou wilt—great or small—and through me
thou shalt receive it from God. But, my child, ask not
amiss. For God is able out of thy own evil asking to
weave snares for thy footing. And oftentimes to the
lambs whom He loves, He gives by seeming' to refuse;
gives in some better sense, or' (and his voice swelled
into the power of anthems) 'in some far happier world.
Now, therefore, my daughter, be wise on thy own behalf;
and say what it is that I shall ask for thee from God.'
But the Daughter of Lebanon needed not his caution;
for immediately dropping on one knee to God's ambassador, whilst the full radiance from the cedar torch fell
upon the glory of a penitential eye, she raised her
clasped hands in supplication, and said, in answer to
the evangelist asking for a second time what gift he
should call down upon her from Heaven, 'Lord, that
thou wouldest put me back into my father's house.'
And the evangelist, because he was human, dropped
a tear as he stooped to kiss her forehead, saying,
'Daughter, thy prayer is heard in heaven; and I tell
thee that the daylight shall not come and go for thirty
times, not for the thirtieth time shall the sun drop
behind Lebanon, before I will put thee back into thy
father's house.'

Thus the lovely lady came into the guardianship of
the evangelist. She sought not to varnish her history,
or to palliate her own transgressions. In so far as she
had offended at all, her case was that of millions in
every generation. Her father was a prince in Lebanon,
proud, unforgiving, austere. The wrongs done to his
daughter by her dishonourable lover, because done
under favour of opportunities created by her confidence in his integrity, her father persisted in resenting

as wrongs done by this injured daughter herself; and, refusing to her all protection, drove her, whilst yet confessedly innocent, into criminal compliances under sudden necessities of seeking daily bread from her own uninstructed efforts. Great was the wrong she suffered both from father and lover; great was the retribution. She lost a churlish father and a wicked lover; she gained an apostolic guardian. She lost a princely station in Lebanon; she gained an early heritage in heaven. For this heritage is hers within thirty days, if she will not defeat it herself. And, whilst the stealthy motion of time travelled towards this thirtieth day, behold! a burning fever desolated Damascus, which also laid its arrest upon the Daughter of Lebanon, yet gently, and so that hardly for an hour did it withdraw her from the heavenly teachings of the evangelist. And thus daily the doubt was strengthened — would the holy apostle suddenly touch her with his hand, and say, 'Woman, be thou whole!' or would he present her on the thirtieth day as a pure bride to Christ? But perfect freedom belongs to Christian service, and she only must make the election.

Up rose the sun on the thirtieth morning in all his pomp, but suddenly was darkened by driving storms. Not until noon was the heavenly orb again revealed; then the glorious light was again unmasked, and again the Syrian valleys rejoiced. This was the hour already appointed for the baptism of the new Christian daughter. Heaven and earth shed gratulation on the happy festival; and, when all was finished, under an awning raised above the level roof of her dwelling-house, the regenerate daughter of Lebanon, looking over the rose-gardens of Damascus, with amplest prospect of her native hills, lay in blissful trance, making proclamation, by her white baptismal robes, of recovered innocence and of reconciliation with God. And, when the sun was declining to the west, the evangelist, who had sat from noon by the bedside of his spiritual daughter, rose solemnly, and said, 'Lady of Lebanon, the day is already come, and the hour is coming, in which my covenant must be fulfilled with thee. Wilt thou, therefore, being now wiser in thy thoughts, suffer God, thy new Father, to give by seeming to refuse; to give in some better sense, or in some far happier world?' But the Daughter of Lebanon sorrowed at these words; she yearned after her native hills; not for themselves, but because there it was that she had left that sweet twin-born sister with whom from infant days hand-in-hand she had wandered amongst the everlasting cedars. And again the evangelist sat down by her bedside; whilst she by intervals communed with him, and by intervals slept gently under the oppression of her fever. But, as evening drew nearer, and it wanted now but a brief space to the going down of the sun, once again, and with deeper solemnity, the evangelist rose to his feet, and said, 'O daughter! this is the thirtieth day, and the sun is drawing near to his rest; brief, therefore, is the time within which I must fulfil the word that God spoke to thee by me.' Then, because light clouds of delirium were playing about her brain, he raised his pastoral staff, and pointing it to her temples, rebuked the clouds, and bade that no more they should trouble her vision, or stand between her and the forests of Lebanon. And the delirious clouds parted asunder, breaking away to the right and to the left. But upon the forests of Lebanon there hung a mighty mass of overshadowing vapours, bequeathed by the morning's storm. And a second time the evangelist raised his pastoral staff, and, pointing it to the gloomy vapours, rebuked them, and bade that no more they should stand between his daughter and her father's house, and immediately the dark vapours broke away from Lebanon to the right and to the left; and the farewell radiance of the sun lighted up all the paths that ran between the everlasting cedars and her father's palace. But vainly the lady of Lebanon searched every path with her eyes for memorials of her sister. And the evangelist, pitying her sorrow, turned away her eyes to the clear blue sky, which the departing vapours had exposed. And he showed her the peace that was there. And then he said, 'O daughter! this also is but a mask.' And immediately for the third time he raised his pastoral staff, and, pointing it to the fair blue sky, he rebuked it, and bade that no more it should stand between her and the vision of God. Immediately the blue sky parted to the right and to the left, laying bare the infinite revelations that can be made visible only to dying eyes. And the Daughter of Lebanon said to the evangelist, 'O father! what armies are these that I see mustering within the infinite chasm?' And the evangelist replied, 'These are the armies of Christ, and they are mustering to receive some dear human blossom, some first-fruits of Christian faith, that shall rise this night to Christ from Damascus.' Suddenly, as thus the child of Lebanon gazed upon the mighty vision, she saw bending forward from the heavenly host, as if in gratulation to herself, the one countenance for which she hungered and thirsted. The twin sister, that should have waited for her in Lebanon, had died of grief, and was waiting for her in Paradise. Immediately in rapture she soared upwards from her couch; immediately in weakness she fell back; and being caught by the evangelist, she flung her arms around his neck; whilst he breathed into her ear his final whisper, 'Wilt thou now suffer that God should give by seeming to refuse?'—'Oh yes—yes—yes,' was the fervent answer from the Daughter of Lebanon. Immediately the evangelist gave the signal to the heavens, and the heavens gave the signal to the sun; and in one minute after the Daughter of Lebanon had fallen back a marble corpse amongst her white baptismal robes; the solar orb dropped behind Lebanon; and the evangelist, with eyes glorified by mortal and immortal tears, rendered thanks to God that had thus accomplished the word which he spoke through himself to the Magdalen of Lebanon—that not for the thirtieth time should the sun go down behind her native hills, before he had put her back into her Father's house.

# APPENDIX

## De Quincey.—Page 79.

This family, which split (or, as a grammatical purist lately said to me in a tone of expostulation, *splat*) into three national divisions — English, French, and American — originally was Norwegian : and in the year of our Christian era *one thousand*, spoke (I believe) the most undeniable Norse. Throughout the eleventh century the heads of this family (in common with all the ruffians and martial vagabonds of Europe that had Venetian sequins enough disposable for such a trip) held themselves in readiness to join any *likely* leader ; and did join William the Norman. Very few indeed, or probably none, of his brigands were Frenchmen, or native Neustrians ; Normans being notoriously a name not derived *from* any French province, but imported *into* that province by trans-Baltic, and in a smaller proportion by cis-Baltic, aliens. This Norwegian family, having assumed a territorial denomination from the district or village of Quincy, in the province now called Normandy, transplanted themselves to England : where, and subsequently by marriage in Scotland, they ascended to the highest rank in both kingdoms, and held the highest offices open to a subject. A late distinguished writer, Mr. Moir of Musselburgh, the ‘Delta’ of *Blackwood's Magazine*, took the trouble (which must have been considerable) of tracing their aspiring movements in Scotland, through a period when Normans transferred themselves from England to Scotland in considerable numbers, and with great advantages. This elaborate paper, published many years ago in *Blackwood's Magazine*, first made known the leading facts of their career in Scotland. Meantime in England they continued to flourish through nine or ten generations ; took a distinguished part in one, at least, of the Crusades ; and a still more perilous share in the Barons Wars under Henry III. No family drank more deeply or more frequently from the cup of treason ; which in those days was not always a very grave offence in people who, having much territorial influence, had also much money. But, happening to drink once too often, or taking too long a ‘pull’ at the cup, the Earls of Winchester suddenly came to grief. Amongst the

romances of astronomy there is one, I believe, which has
endeavoured to account for the little asteroids of our system
by supposing them fragments of some great planet that had,
under internal convulsion or external collision, at some
period suddenly exploded. In our own planet Tellus such
a county as York, under a similar catastrophe, would make
a very pretty little asteroid. And with some miniature
resemblance to such a case, sometimes benefiting by the
indulgence of the crown, sometimes by legal devices,
sometimes by aid of matrimonial alliances, numerous
descendants, confessedly innocent, from the guilty earl
projected themselves by successive efforts, patiently watching their opportunities, from the smoking ruins of the great
feudal house : stealthily through two generations creeping
out of their lurking holes; timidly, when the great shadows
from the threatening throne had passed over, re-assuming
the family name. Concurrently with these *personal* fragments projected from the ancient house, flew off random
splinters and fragments from the great planetary disk of
the Winchester estates, little asteroids that formed ample
inheritances for the wants of this or that provincial squire,
of this or that tame villatic squireen.[1]

The kingly old oak, that had been the leader of the forest,
was thus suddenly (in the technical language of woodcraft),
cut down into a 'pollard.' This mutilation for ever prevented it from aspiring cloudwards by means of some
mighty stem, such as grows upon Norwegian hills, fit to
be the mast of 'some great ammiral.' Nevertheless, we
see daily amongst the realities of nature that a tree, after
passing through such a process of degradation, yet manifests
the great arrears of vindictive life lurking within it by
throwing out a huge radiation of slender boughs and
miniature shoots, small but many, so that we are forced
exactly to invert the fine words of Lucan, saying no longer
*trunco, non frondibus, efficit umbram*, but, on the contrary,
*non trunco sed frondibus efficit umbram*. This great
cabbage-head of this ancient human tree threw a broad
massy umbrage over more villages than one; sometimes
yielding representatives moody and mutinous, sometimes
vivacious and inventive, sometimes dull and lethargic, until

---

[1] This last variety of the rustic *regulus* is of Hibernian origin, and,
as regards the name, was unknown to us in England until Miss
Edgeworth had extended the horizon of our social experience. Yet,
without the name, I presume that the *thing* must have been known
occasionally even in England.

at last, one fine morning, on rubbing their eyes, they found themselves actually in the sixteenth century abreast of Henry VIII. and his fiery children. Ah, what a century was that! Sculptured as only Froude can sculpture those that fight across the chasms of eternity, grouped as only Froude can group the mighty factions, acting or suffering, arraigning before chanceries of man, or protesting before chanceries of God—what vast arrays of marble gladiators fighting for truth, real or imagined, throng the arenas in each generation of that and the succeeding century. And how ennobling a distinction of modern humanity, that in Pagan antiquity no truth as yet existed, none had been revealed, none emblazoned, on behalf of which man *could* have fought! As Lord Bacon remarks—though strangely, indeed, publishing in the very terms of this remark his own blindness to the causes and consequences—religious wars were unknown to antiquity. Personal interests, and those only, did or could furnish a subject of conflict. But throughout the sixteenth century, whether in England, in France, or in Germany, it was a spiritual interest, shadowy and aerial, which embattled armies against armies. Simply the nobility of this interest it was, simply the grandeur of a cause moving by springs transcendent to all vulgar and mercenary collisions of prince with prince, or family with family, that arrayed man against man, not upon petty combinations of personal intrigue, but upon questions of everlasting concern—this majestic principle of the strife it was that constituted for the noblest minds its secret magnetism. Early in the seventeenth century, when it seemed likely that the interests of a particular family would be entangled with the principles at issue, multitudes became anxious to evade the strife by retiring to the asylum of forests. Amongst these was one branch of the De Quinceys. Enamoured of democracy, this family, laying aside the aristocratic *De* attached to their name, settled in New England, where they subsequently rose, through long public services, to the highest moral rank—as measured by all possible expressions of public esteem that are consistent with the simplicities of the great republic. Mr. Josiah Quincy, as head of this distinguished family, is appealed to as one who takes rank by age and large political experience with the founders of the American Union. Another branch of the same family had at a much earlier period settled in France. Finally, the squires and squireens—*i.e.*, those who benefited in any degree by those 'asteroids' which I have explained as exploded from the ruins of the Winchester estates—naturally remained in England. The last of them who enjoyed any relics whatever of that ancient territorial domain was an elder kinsman of my father. I never had the honour of seeing him; in fact, it was impossible that I *should* have such an honour, since he died during the American War, which war had closed, although it had not paid its bills, some time before my birth. He enacted the part of squireen, I have been told, creditably enough in a village belonging either to the county of Leicester, Nottingham, or Rutland. Sir Andrew Aguecheek observes as one of his sentimental remembrances, that he also at one period of his life had been 'adored': 'I was adored once,' says the knight, seeming to acknowledge that he was not adored then. But the squireen was 'adored' in a limited way to the last. This fading representative of a crusading house declined gradually into the oracle of the bar at the Red Lion, and was adored by two persons at the least (not counting himself)—viz., the landlord, and occasionally the waiter. Mortgages had eaten up the last vestiges of the old territorial wrecks; and with his death a new era commenced for this historical family, which now (as if expressly to irritate its ambition) finds itself distributed amongst three mighty nations—France, America, and England—and precisely those three that are usually regarded as the leaders of civilisation.[1]

### BARBARA LEWTHWAITE.—Page 203.

Already Barbara Lewthwaite had contributed to the composition of two impressive pictures: first, in her infancy, with her pet lamb, under the evening shadows of the mighty Fairfield; secondly, in her girlhood, with the turbaned Malay and the little cottage child. But subsequently, when a young woman, she entered unconsciously into the composition of another picture, even more rememberable, suggesting great names, connected with the greatest of

[1] The omission of the *De*, as an addition looking better at a tournament than as an indorsement on a bill of exchange, began, as to many hundreds of English names, full three hundred years ago. Many English families have disused this affix simply from indolence. As to the terminal variations, *cy*, *cie*, *cey*, those belong, as natural and inevitable exponents of a transitional condition, to the unsettled spelling that characterises the early stages of literature in all countries alike.

themes; the names being those of Plato, and, in this instance at least, of a mightier than Plato—viz., William Wordsworth; and the theme concerned being that problem which, measured by its interest to man, by its dependencies, by the infinite jewel staked upon the verdict, we should all confess to be the most solemn and heart-shaking that is hung out by golden chains from the heaven of heavens to human investigation—viz., Is the spirit of man numbered amongst things naturally perishable? The doctrine of our own Dodwell (a most orthodox man) was that naturally and *per se* it was perishable, but that by supernatural endowment it was made immortal. Apparently the ancient oracles of the Hebrew literature had all and everywhere assumed the soul's natural mortality. The single passage in Job that *seemed* to look in the counter direction has long since received an interpretation painfully alien from such a meaning; not to mention that the same objection would apply to this passage, if read into a Christian sense, as applies to the ridiculous interpolation in Josephus describing Christ's personal appearance—viz., Once suppose it genuine, and why were there not myriads of other passages in the same key? Imagine, for a moment, the writer so penetrated with premature Christian views, by what inexplicable rigour of abstinence had he forborne to meet ten thousand calls, at other turns of his work, for similar utterances of Christian sentiment? It must not be supposed that the objections to this Christian interpretation of Job rest solely with German scholars. Coleridge, one of the most devout and evangelical amongst modern theologians, took the same view, and has expressed it with decision. But Job is of slight importance in comparison with Moses. Now Warburton, in his well-known argument, held not only that Moses *did* (as a fact) assume the mortality of the soul, but that, as a necessity, he did so, since upon this assumption rests the weightiest argument for his own divine mission. That Moses could dispense with a support which Warburton fancied all other legislators had needed and postulated argued, in the bishop's opinion, a vicarious support—a secret and divine support. This extreme view will be rejected, perhaps, by most people. But, in the meantime, the very existence of such a sect as the Sadducees proves sufficiently that no positive affirmation of the soul's immortality could have been accredited amongst the Hebrew nation as a Mosaic doctrine. The rise of a counter sect, the Pharisees, occurred in later days, clearly under a principle of 'development' applied to old traditions current among the Jews. It was not alleged as a Mosaic doctrine, but as something deducible from traditions countenanced by Moses. From Hebrew literature, therefore, no help is to be looked for on this great question. Pagan literature first of all furnishes any response upon it favourable to human yearnings. But, unhappily, the main argument upon which the sophist in the *Phædo* relies is a pure scholastic conundrum, baseless and puerile. The homogeneity of human consciousness, upon which is made to rest its indestructibility, is not established or made probable by any plausible logic. If we should figure to ourselves some mighty angel mounting guard upon human interests twenty-three centuries ago, this tutelary spirit would have smiled derisively upon the advent and the departure of Plato. At length, once again, after many centuries, was heard the clarion of immortality—not as of any preternatural gift, but as a natural prerogative of the human spirit. This time the angel would have paused and hearkened. The auguries for immortality which Wordsworth drew from indications running along the line of daily human experience were two.

The first was involved in the exquisite little poem of *We are Seven*. That authentic voice, said Wordsworth, which affirmed life as a necessity inalienable from man's consciousness was a revelation through the lips of childhood. Life in its torrent fulness—that is, life in its earliest stage—affirmed itself ; whereas the voice which whispered doubts was an adventitious and secondary voice consequent upon an earthly experience. The child in this little poem is unable to admit the thought of death, though, in compliance with custom, she uses the word :—

> ' " The first that *died* was little Jane ;
>    In bed she moaning lay,
> Till God released her from her pain ;
>    And then she went away.' "

The graves of her brother and sister she is so far from regarding as any argument of their having died that she supposes the stranger simply to doubt her statement, and she reiterates her assertion of their graves as lying in the churchyard, in order to prove that they were *living* :—

> ' " Their graves are green, they may be seen,"
>    The little maid replied,
> " Twelve steps or more from my mother's door,
>    And they are side by side.

> And often after sunset, sir,
>     When it is light and fair,
> I take my little porringer,
>     And eat my supper there.
> My stockings there I often knit,
>     My kerchief there I hem :
> And there upon their graves I sit—
>     I sit, and sing to them." '

The other argument was developed in the sublime *Ode upon the Intimations of Immortality*, etc. Man in his infancy stood *nearest* (so much was matter of fact) to the unseen world of the Infinite. What voices he heard most frequently, murmuring through the cells of his infantine brain, were echoes of the great realities which, as a new-born infant, he had just quitted. Hanging upon his mother's breast, he heard dim prolongations of a music which belonged to a life ever more and more receding into a distance buried in clouds and vapours. Man's orient, in which lie the fountains of the dawn, must be sought for in that Eden of infancy which first received him as a traveller emerging from a world now daily becoming more distant. And it is a great argument of the divine splendour investing man's natural home that the heavenly lights which burned in his morning grow fainter and fainter as he ' travels further from the East.'

The little Carnarvonshire child in *We are Seven*, who is represented as repelling the idea of death under an absolute inability to receive it, had completed her eighth year. But this might be an ambitious exaggeration, such as aspiring female children are generally disposed to practise. It is more probable that she might be in the currency of her eighth year. Naturally we must not exact from Wordsworth any pedantic rigour of accuracy in such a case ; but assuredly we have a right to presume that his principle, if tenable at all, must apply to all children below the age of *five*. However I will say *four*. In that case the following anecdote seems to impeach the philosophic truth of this doctrine. I give the memorandum as it was drawn up by myself at the time :—

My second child, but eldest daughter, little M——, is between two and three weeks less than two years old ; and from the day of her birth she has been uniformly attended by Barbara Lewthwaite. We are now in the first days of June ; but, about three weeks since, consequently in the earlier half of May, some one of our neighbours gave to

M—— a little bird. I am no great ornithologist. 'Perhaps only a tenth-rate one,' says some too flattering reader. Oh dear, no, nothing near it : I fear, no more than a 510th rater. Consequently, I cannot ornithologically describe or classify the bird. But I believe that it belonged to the family of finches—either a goldfinch, bullfinch, or at least something ending in *inch*. The present was less splendid than at first it seemed. For the bird was wounded, though not in a way that made the wound apparent ; and too sensibly as the evening wore away it drooped. None of us knew what medical treatment to suggest ; and all that occurred was to place it with free access to birdseed and water. At length sunset arrived, which was the signal for M——'s departure to bed. She came therefore as usual to me, threw her arms round my neck, and went through her ordinary routine of prayers : viz., first, the Lord's Prayer, and finally the four following lines (a Roman Catholic bequest to the children of Northern England) :—

> ' Holy[1] Jesus, meek and mild,
> Look on me, a little child :
> Pity my simplicity ;
> Grant that I may come to thee.'

M——, as she was moving off to bed, whispered to me that I was to ' mend ' the bird with ' yoddonum.' Having always seen *me* taking laudanum, and for the purpose (as she was told) of growing better in health, reasonably it struck her that the little bird would improve under the same regimen. For her satisfaction, I placed a little diluted laudanum near to the bird ; and she then departed to bed, though with uneasy looks reverting to her sick little pet. Occupied with some point of study, it happened that I sat up through the whole night : and long before seven o'clock in the morning she had summoned Barbara to dress her, and soon I heard the impatient little foot descending the stairs to my study. I had such a Jesuitical *bulletin* ready, by way of a report upon the bird's health, as might not seem absolutely despairing, though not too dangerously sanguine. And, as the morning was one of heavenly splendour, I proposed that we should improve the bird's chances by taking it out-of-doors

---

[1] ' *Holy Jesus*' :—This was a very judicious correction introduced by Wordsworth. Originally the traditional line had stood—' Gentle Jesus, meek and mild.' But Wordsworth, offended by the idle iteration of one idea in the words, gentle, meek, mild, corrected the text into *Holy*.

into the little orchard at the foot of Fairfield—our loftiest
Grasmere mountain. Thither moved at once Barbara
Lewthwaite, little M——, myself, and the poor languishing
bird. By that time in May, in any far southern county,
perhaps the birds would be ceasing to sing ; but not so with
us dilatory people in Westmoreland. Suddenly, as we all
stood around the little perch on which the bird rested, one
thrilling song, louder than the rest, arose from a neighbouring hedge. Immediately the bird's eye, previously dull,
kindled into momentary fire; the bird rose on its perch,
struggled for an instant, seemed to be expanding its wings,
made one aspiring movement upwards, in doing so fell back,
and in another moment was dead. Too certainly and
apparently all these transitions symbolically interpreted
themselves, and to all of us alike : the proof of which was
that man, woman, and child spontaneously shed tears : a
weakness, perhaps, but more natural under the regular
processional evolution of the scenical stages than when
simply read as a narrative : for too evident it was, to one
and all of us, without needing to communicate by words,
*what* vision had revealed itself to all alike—to the child
under two years old, not less than to the adults : too
evident it was that, on this magnificent May morning,
there had been exhibited, as on the stage of a theatre—
there had passed before the eyes of us all—passed, and
was finished—the everlasting mystery of death ! It seemed
to me that little M——, by her sudden burst of tears, must
have read this saddest of truths—must have felt that the
bird's fate was sealed—not less clearly than Barbara or
myself.

# PENGUIN POPULAR CLASSICS

*Published or forthcoming*

# PENGUIN POPULAR CLASSICS

# PENGUIN POPULAR CLASSICS

*Published or forthcoming*

# PENGUIN POPULAR CLASSICS

*Published or forthcoming*

| | |
|---|---|
| **Charles and Mary Lamb** | Tales from Shakespeare |
| **D. H. Lawrence** | The Rainbow |
| | Sons and Lovers |
| | Women in Love |
| **Edward Lear** | Book of Nonsense |
| **Gaston Leroux** | The Phantom of the Opera |
| **Jack London** | White Fang *and* The Call of the Wild |
| **Captain Marryat** | The Children of the New Forest |
| **Herman Melville** | Moby Dick |
| **John Milton** | Paradise Lost |
| **Edith Nesbit** | Five Children and It |
| | The Railway Children |
| **Francis Turner Palgrave** | The Golden Treasury |
| **Edgar Allan Poe** | Selected Tales |
| **Sir Walter Scott** | Ivanhoe |
| | Rob Roy |
| | Waverley |
| **Saki** | The Best of Saki |
| **Anna Sewell** | Black Beauty |
| **William Shakespeare** | Antony and Cleopatra |
| | As You Like It |
| | Hamlet |
| | Henry V |
| | Julius Caesar |
| | King Lear |
| | Macbeth |
| | The Merchant of Venice |
| | A Midsummer Night's Dream |
| | Othello |
| | Romeo and Juliet |
| | The Tempest |
| | Twelfth Night |

# PENGUIN POPULAR CLASSICS

*Published or forthcoming*

| | |
|---|---|
| **Mary Shelley** | Frankenstein |
| **Johanna Spyri** | Heidi |
| **Robert Louis Stevenson** | The Black Arrow |
| | A Child's Garden of Verses |
| | Dr Jekyll and Mr Hyde |
| | Kidnapped |
| | Treasure Island |
| **Bram Stoker** | Dracula |
| **Jonathan Swift** | Gulliver's Travels |
| **W. M. Thackeray** | Vanity Fair |
| **Anthony Trollope** | Barchester Towers |
| | Doctor Thorne |
| | Framley Parsonage |
| | The Small House at Allington |
| | The Warden |
| **Mark Twain** | The Adventures of Huckleberry Finn |
| | The Adventures of Tom Sawyer |
| | The Prince and the Pauper |
| **Jules Verne** | Around the World in Eighty Days |
| | Journey to the Centre of the Earth |
| | Twenty Thousand Leagues under the Sea |
| **Edith Wharton** | The Age of Innocence |
| | Ethan Frome |
| **Oscar Wilde** | De Profundis |
| | The Happy Prince and Other Stories |
| | The Importance of Being Earnest |
| | Lord Arthur Savile's Crime |
| | The Picture of Dorian Gray |
| | A Woman of No Importance |
| **Virginia Woolf** | Mrs Dalloway |
| | To the Lighthouse |
| **J. D. Wyss** | The Swiss Family Robinson |